GARRY WILLS

WHY PRIESTS?

A Failed Tradition

PENGUIN BOOKS

PENGUIN BOOKS
Published by the Penguin Group
Penguin Group (USA) LLC
375 Hudson Street
New York, New York 10014

USA | Canada | UK | Ireland | Australia | New Zealand | India | South Africa | China
penguin.com
A Penguin Random House Company

First published in the United States of America by Viking Penguin,
a member of Penguin Group (USA) Inc., 2013
Published in Penguin Books 2014

THE LIBRARY OF CONGRESS HAS CATALOGED THE HARDCOVER EDITION AS FOLLOWS:
Wills, Garry, 1934–
Why priests? : a failed tradition / Garry Wills.
pages cm
Includes bibliographical references and index.
ISBN 978-0-670-02487-2 (hc.)
ISBN 978-0-14-312439-9 (pbk.)
1. Transubstantiation.   2. Lord's Supper—Catholic Church.   3. Lord's Supper—
Real presence.   4. Catholic Church—Doctrines.   5. Lord's Supper—Biblical
teaching.   6. Priests.   7. Lord's Supper—Miracles.   I. Title.
BX2220.W57 2013
262'.14—dc23
2012037034

Printed in the United States of America
1 3 5 7 9 10 8 6 4 2

Set in Adobe Jenson Pro
Designed by Francesca Belanger

Praise for Garry Wills and
the *New York Times* Bestseller *Why Priests?*

"Wills draws on his expertise in classical languages and his wide reading in ecclesiastical history to argue that the Catholic/Orthodox priesthood has been one long mistake."   —*The Washington Post*

"Using his linguistic skills and his impressive command of both secondary literature and patristic sources, Wills raises doubts aplenty about 'the Melchizedek myth,' and the priestly claims for Jesus in the 'idiosyncratic' Epistle to the Hebrews. . . . His final chapter is a model of elegant simplicity, a contrast (intended or not) to the flummery often associated with his own church. . . . 'There is one God, and Jesus is one of his prophets,' Wills concludes, 'and I am one of his millions of followers.' For those millions, scattered across time and space, that's an affirmation worthy of celebration."
                                  —*The New York Times Book Review*

"Wills sets out to persuade his fellow Catholics that the priesthood is both unnecessary and un-Christian. . . . Wills is not attempting to break with the Church or to dismantle it. Rather, he wants to assure the faithful that they can get by without priests. 'If we need fellowship in belief,' he writes, 'we have each other.'"   —*The New Yorker*

"American Catholicism's most formidable lay scholar."
                                               —*Los Angeles Times*

"How . . . did priests become dominant and then essential in Catholic Christianity? And why, Wills asks, in this provocative [and] historically rich . . . book, does the Vatican continue to sustain such falsehoods? . . . Wills's demolition of the many myths surrounding the origins of priestly status and function is in itself crucially informative and enlightening."
                                               —*The New Republic*

"Pulitzer Prize winner Wills, a venerable voice on church history, thought, and practice, provides a stunning critique of the Roman Catholic priesthood."   —*Kirkus Reviews* (starred review)

"Wills brings to bear the skills that have justly brought him renown as America's greatest public intellectual: encyclopedic erudition, concise prose, and a polyglot's gift for ancient languages."   —*Chicago Tribune*

"Fascinating . . . Wills's small volume is like a long, rich conversation with a learned friend and is, Wills writes, a devotional exercise not a scholarly one. His is a kind of devotion, though, that engages the heart and mind, to the ultimate benefit of both."   —Jon Meacham, author of *American Gospel*

"Faithful to the heart of tradition, yet entirely original, Garry Wills's meditation cuts through cant, piety, and political exploitation to bring Jesus alive in all his urgent significance."

—James Carroll, author of *Constantine's Sword*

"Do we really need Catholic priests? Wills, Pulitzer Prize winner and author of *Why I Am a Catholic*, dares to pose this controversial question. . . . One cannot help but be impressed with this brilliant work written by a scholar whose love for the Church compels him to make it better."

—*Publishers Weekly*

"Clearly a thought-provoker destined to inspire debate."   —*Library Journal*

"Wills's position is . . . original and insightful . . . [and] his task is a worthy one, namely to bring the institution of the priesthood under the gaze of historical and theological scrutiny. . . . Through his erudite scholarship and his compelling argumentation Wills has made an important contribution to this field of study and, in the process, has written a book that is thoroughly absorbing and engaging."   —*The Irish Times*

"[Wills] combin[es] historical and literary analysis with journalistic observations on the present Catholic Church. . . . *Why Priests?* should be required of all seminarians."   —*National Catholic Reporter*

PENGUIN BOOKS

WHY PRIESTS?

Garry Wills has written many acclaimed and bestselling books, including *What Jesus Meant*, *What the Gospels Meant*, and *Why I Am a Catholic*. His books have received many awards, including the Pulitzer Prize. A professor of history emeritus at Northwestern University, Wills is a frequent contributor to *The New York Review of Books* and other publications. He lives in Evanston, Illinois.

To the Memory of Henri de Lubac, S.J.

Contents

Key to Brief Citations

ABD *The Anchor Bible Dictionary,* five volumes (Doubleday, 1992).

C *Catechism of the Catholic Church,* revised edition (Liguori Press, 1994).

K Craig R. Koester, *Hebrews* (Doubleday, 2001).

NJ *The New Jerome Biblical Commentary* (Prentice Hall, 1990).

S Ceslas Spicq, *L'épître aux Hébreux,* second edition, two volumes (J. Gabalda, 1952–1953).

ST Thomas Aquinas, *Summa Theologiae,* revised edition, five volumes (Biblioteca de Autores Cristianos, 1965).

WHY PRIESTS?

Introduction

I have nothing against priests. In fact, I tried for a time to be one. I spent over five years in a Jesuit seminary for that purpose. Those who inspired me to do that were some of the most benign influences on my life. One of the greatest men I ever met was my novice master, Joseph Fisher, S.J., to whom I dedicated one of my books. Another priest who has served as a guiding light to me is Daniel Berrigan, S.J., to whom I dedicated another book. I have been privileged to know scholar-priests I admired—Walter Ong, S.J., Raymond Brown, S.S. (I dedicated a book to him, too), and John O'Malley S.J. And this book is itself dedicated to a priest. I admire from a distance brilliant priests of the past—John Henry Newman, Gerard Manley Hopkins, S.J., the Curé d'Ars, and others. I even revere the fictional priests who have moved me—in Bernanos's *Diary of a Country Priest*, Greene's *The Power and the Glory*, Powers's *Morte d'Urban*, Endo's *Silence*, Guareschi's *Don Camillo*. The Irish side of my family—the Collinses and Meehans and Driscolls—had a number of priests in it. I found good friends in the priests who served the campus churches I have attended for the last fifty years. It should be clear, then, that I respect, and am often fond of, the many priests in my life.

Why, then, having been such a fan of many priests of all sorts, close to me and far, do I now ask why we need priests at all? It is not a personal issue but an historical one. Why did the priesthood come into a religion that began without it and, indeed, opposed it? Would it have been better off without this incursion? What other deflections from the original path came from this new element in the mix? Why was it felt that priests were required, after an initial period when they were not? Without the priesthood, would there have been belief in an apostolic succession, the real presence in the

Eucharist, the sacrificial interpretation of the Mass, or the ransom theory of redemption?

This book will argue that there would not have been. Without the priesthood, all of these would have a flimsy base to stand on—and the priesthood itself has a dubious basis. This does not mean, as some would instantly protest, that Christianity itself must then have a weak foundation. On the contrary, it stood without the priesthood at the outset, and it can stand stronger without it now.

Some think that the dwindling number of priests can be remedied by the addition of women priests, or married priests, or openly gay priests. In fact, the real solution is: no priests. It should not be difficult to imagine a Christianity without priests. Read carefully through the entire New Testament and you will not find an individual human priest mentioned in the Christian communities (only Jewish priests in service to the Temple). Only one book of the New Testament, the Letter to Hebrews, mentions an individual priest, and he is unique—Jesus. He has no followers in that office, according to the Letter.

It is not surprising, then, that some Protestant communities are able to be good Christians without having any priests. Some priests of my youth mocked them for that reason. They said a Protestant ceremony was just a town meeting, without the sacramental consecration and consumption of the body and blood of Jesus. When I told one of my pastors that I had admired the sermon of a visiting priest, he said I should not be looking to have my ears tickled, like some Protestant, but should concentrate on the mystery of the Eucharist. Without the Eucharist, he was implying, we would have no religion at all.

We Catholics were taught not only that we must have priests but that they must be the right kind of priests. Eastern Orthodox priests, and Anglican ones, and Lutheran ones do not count, because they were not ordained by successors to Saint Peter, the first bishop of Rome. As recently as 1998, Cardinal Ratzinger (the present pope) instructed Anglican/Episcopalian priests that any sacraments they administered were "void."[1] Catholic children, given these teachings, did not at first know that there is no historical evidence for Peter being bishop anywhere—least of all at Rome, where the office of bishop did not exist in the first century CE—or that the linear "apostolic succession" is a chain of historical fabrications.[2] What we were supposed to accept is that all priesthoods are invalid ones except the Roman Catholic. Even if we grant the Roman myths, and say that the Catholic priesthood is valid, how is it Christian to make that priesthood a means for excluding all Christians but Roman Catholics?

I shall be arguing here that priesthood, despite the many worthy men who have filled that office, keeps Catholics at a remove from other Christians—and at a remove from the Jesus of the Gospels, who was a biting critic of the priests of his day. To make this argument, I must consider the claim that has set priests apart from all other human beings, their unique power to change bread and wine into the body and blood of Christ. On this claim the entire sacramental structure of the medieval church was built up. The priesthood stands or falls with that claim. I mean to examine it here—dispassionately, thoroughly, historically. The outcome of this debate will determine the future (if any) of the priesthood.

NOTES

1. Leo XIII declared Anglican orders invalid in his 1896 encyclical *Apostolicae Curae*. In 1998, Cardinal Ratzinger, the head of the Congregation for the Doctrine of the Faith, appended to John Paul II's *motu proprio Ad Tuendam Fidem* an instruction saying that *Apostolicae Curae* is still binding.
2. Raymond E. Brown et al., *Peter in the New Testament* (Augsburg Publishing House, 1973), pp. 8, 19–20, 167–68.

I

Priest Power: The Eucharist

ONE

A Priestless Movement

I thought at first of calling this chapter "A Priestless Christianity." But no such thing as Christianity existed in Gospel days—only a Jesus movement within the Jewish community.[1] In fact, there was no "church" in the first generation of Jesus' followers—just "gatherings" (ekklēsiae, which meant "house gatherings"), where the followers first met.[2] Followers of Jesus were called "Housefellows," Oikeioi (Gal 6.10, Eph 2.19). In these gatherings, there were no priests, though there were many "charisms"— activities inspired by the Holy Spirit. There were at least sixteen of them (1 Cor 12.4–11, 27–31, Rom 12.6–8, Eph 4.11). Some of these actors in the early gatherings are no longer recognized as regular church ministries— like prophets or miracle workers (1 Cor 12.9–10, 28). Some roles continue as rare or irregular activities in certain Christian gatherings—speakers in tongues, exorcists, healers (1 Cor 12.9–10, 28, Rom 12.8). Isn't it odd that—with so many of Jesus' early followers inspired by the Spirit to serve their brothers and sisters—none of these ministries was that of a priest?

The principal activity of the Jesus movement was a communal meal, in which memories of Jesus were shared—memories that would in time accumulate into the Gospels. Since there was no New Testament yet, the community prayed, prophesied (elaborating on the words of the Jewish prophets), sang hymns of their own composition, and baptized newcomers into their company (even early baptisms were effected at the meal).[3] Nothing is said in the first century of a "consecration" that changed food into anything other than a sign of shared fellowship.

One of the charisms that lapsed after the Jesus generation was that of apostle—which means "emissary" (from apo-stello, "I send off"). The house gathering(s) in one town would send off a representative to other houses in the town or to other towns altogether. Reception of such emissaries in a house helps explain the emphasis on hospitality (*philoxenia*, Rom 12.13, Hb 13.2). Paul, for example, did not belong to one gathering, but shuttled about from many gatherings to other ones. The word's meaning was explained when Jesus began to send his followers off (*apo-stellein*, Mk 6.7) to heal, cast out devils, and carry the revelation. Despite these spiritual powers granted to apostles, the term used of them was secular and diplomatic in origin. It meant "ambassador."

> The basic definition [of apostle] given by Origen is simple: "Everyone who is sent by someone is an apostle of the one who sent him." The concept involves legal and administrative aspects, and is basic to all types of representatives, envoys, and ambassadors . . . Chronologically, in the earliest use of the term in the New Testament, *apostolos* is an administrative designation for envoys, delegates, and representatives. Their title and function are given in 2 Corinthians 8.23 as "envoys of the churches" (*apostoloi ekklēsiōn*), that is, envoys appointed and sent out by the churches to represent them.[4]

Thus Paul was an apostle because he belonged to no one gathering, but was an emissary sent to all Gentile followers of Jesus, some of them his converts: however, many of them—like most of those listed at Romans 16.1–15— were believers before he met them. He refers to several of his co-workers as apostles, including a married couple, Andronicus and Junia, as people who were "sent" between communities (Rom 16.7).

People now may think of apostles as confined to The Twelve (with Paul added as a thirteenth). But the term originally had a wider meaning than that. The Twelve's extraordinary status is indicated by the fact that they are referred to as apostles when Jesus sends them off to others (Mk 3.14–16, Mt 10.2, Lk 6.13), but are often referred to simply as The Twelve, where their number is clearly a symbol of the End Time, as judges of the Twelve Tribes. This eschatological role for The Twelve is given several expressions:

> You are men who were there with me while I underwent my testings. So I grant you a share in the reign that my Father granted me, that you may eat and drink at table with me in my reign, and you may sit on thrones to judge the Twelve Tribes of Israel. (Lk 22.28–30)

> I tell you solemnly that in the New World, when the Son of Man is seated on his throne of splendor, you who have been with me will be seated on twelve thrones, to judge the Twelve Tribes of Israel. (Mt 19.28)

> In the Spirit he swept me off to a large towering mountain, and revealed to me the holy city of Jerusalem descending from God's heaven. It shone with God's splendor, its brightness was that of a rare jewel, like glowing jasper. It had a large high wall with twelve gates, where twelve angels were posted, bearing the names of the Twelve Tribes of Israel— three gates to the east, three to the north, three to the south, and three to the west. The city wall rested on twelve stones of foundation, inscribed with the names of The Twelve Apostles of the Lamb. (Rev 21.10–14)

Since there were no "Christians" in the Gospels, how did believers in Jesus identify themselves to one another or to outsiders? They were most often called, or called themselves, Followers (*Akolouthontes*—seventy-nine times in the Gospels). Or they were called Learners (*Mathētai*, normally translated as "disciples"—nineteen times in the Gospels).[5] In accord with the designation Followers, the Acts of the Apostles calls what they follow The Path (*Hē Hodos*).[6] In accord with the designation Learners, Jesus is addressed by them as Teacher—*Didaskale* (twenty-nine times in the Gospels) or Rabbi (eleven times in the Gospels). All the followers of Jesus are, therefore, Followers or Learners, and none is put above another. Even The

Twelve are not rulers of their fellow Followers/Learners—they are to judge the Twelve Tribes, but only in the End Time.

If Followers and Learners are the titles of adherents to Jesus in the Gospels, Paul has another range of references for his fellow believers— most commonly The Brothers (*Adelphoi*) and The Sisters (*Adelphai*), but also The Housefellows (*Oikeioi*), The Called (*Klētoi*), The Holy (*Hagioi* or *Hēgiasmenoi*), or Those-in-Messiah (*Hoi en Christō [i]*).[7] As one would surmise from these designations, the communities Paul addresses were radically egalitarian and charismatic, not authoritarian or hierarchical. Paul addresses entire gatherings, not a leader (or leaders) in them. When Jesus left the earth, he did not turn his Followers/Learners over to human guidance. Instead he sent them a Champion (*Paraklētos*, literally one "summoned to one's side" to strengthen one; Jn 14.16, 26, 15.26, 16.7).

Thus community functions (not offices) are direct gifts (*charismata*) of the Spirit, making the early community charismatic in the root original sense, entirely guided by the Spirit, not by hierarchical rule or appointment to offices. Paul mentions eleven such *charismata* in his First Letter to Corinthians:

> There are diverse charisms, but from the same Spirit. There are distinct ways of serving, but of the same Lord. There are distinct ways of acting, but the same God is at work in all acts of all the actors. The Spirit makes itself known in a particular person for the general good. One man, through the Spirit, has the gift of wise speech, while another, by the power of the same Spirit, can put the deepest knowledge into words. Another's fidelity is from the same Spirit. Another has the gift of healing and it is still one Spirit. Another can work miracles, another can prophesy, another can read spiritual impulses, another can speak different languages, another can interpret the languages. At work in all these things is the single and shared Spirit, distributing them as seems best individually. (12.4–11)

> You are the body of Christ, each individually a part of it, from which God has provided for the gathering—first, apostles; second, prophets;

third, teachers; then miracle-working, then healing gifts, help-providing, guidance-offering, kinds of speaking in tongues. Are all people apostles, all prophets, all teachers, all miracle workers, all with the gift of healing, all speaking in tongues, all interpreters of tongues? Strive for higher gifts than these. (12.27–31)

At Romans 12.7–8 he mentions four other *charismata*—for the supporter (*parakalōn*), the servant (*diakonos*), the almsgiver (*metadidous*), and the representative (*proistamenos*). At Ephesians 4.11 he adds another charism, that of the shepherd (*poimēn*).[8] That makes sixteen actions prompted by the Spirit, none of them an office, each distinguished from the rest. Nowhere is the word "priest" (*hiereus*) used in describing the services rendered by those receiving *charismata*.

The egalitarian spirit of the early communities came from Christ himself, who said that none of his Followers should try to be above another.

And they came to Capernaum, and inside the house he asked them, "What were you discussing along the road?" But they fell silent, because they had been discussing along the way who was greater. And after being seated he called The Twelve and says to them, "If anyone wishes to be first, he will be last of all and the servant of all." And taking a child he placed it in their midst, and hugging it, he told them, "The one who would welcome such a child in my name welcomes me. And whoever welcomes me, welcomes not only me but the one who sent me." (Mk 9.33–37)

Luke's Gospel (14.7–11) makes the same point this way:

When he noticed how the guests were trying to secure the places of honor, he told them a model story: "When you are asked by someone to be a wedding-guest, do not sit down in the place of honor. It may be that some person more distinguished than yourself has been invited; and the host will come and say to you, 'Give this man your seat,' and then you will move with embarrassment to take the lowliest seat. Rather, when invited, take on arrival the lowliest seat. Then you will be splendid before every one of your fellow guests, should your host come and say to you, 'Friend, rise higher up.' For everyone who boosts himself up will be lowered down, and everyone who lowers himself will be boosted up."

Jesus is telling his Followers not to be like the Sadducees and Pharisees who seek the "first places":

Everything they do is done to impress people. They enlarge their tefillins and lengthen their tassels. They like the most important place at meals, and the chairs of honor in their synagogues, and to be cheered on the street, and to be called by people "Rabbi." You, however, must not be addressed as "Rabbi," since you have only one Teacher, and you are brothers to each other. Do not address any man on earth as father, since you have only one Father, and he is in heaven. And you must not be addressed as leaders, since you have only one Leader, the Messiah. The greater among you will be your servant. For whoever boosts himself up will be lowered, and whoever lowers himself down will be boosted up. (Mt 23.5–12)

What could be more against this teaching than popes who adopt the title "Holy Father"?

A purely charismatic movement is hard to sustain. I found that out when reporting on radical communes in the 1960s and early 1970s. They all began with opposition to "the cult of personality," and with promises that all chores would be equally shared. But soon it turned out that certain people were more interested in making out schedules, buying groceries, and maintaining the property. Thus the post-Gospel literature of the Jesus movement introduces people in administrative roles—Servants, Elders, Overseers. These are not charisms bestowed by the Spirit, but offices to which people are appointed by their fellow human beings—and once more the priesthood is missing from the list.

Servants (*diakonoi*, usually translated "deacons"). This is a term Paul uses to describe himself (1 Cor 3.5) and his co-worker Timothy (1 Thess 3.2).[9]

He calls a woman, Phoebe, a *diakonos* (Rom 16.1). He greets the servants and overseers in Philippi (Phil 1.1). It is not surprising that the role of the servant would later be more prominent in the Deutero-Pauline "pastoral" epistles (1 Tim 3.8, 12, 4.6, Titus 1.9). Though Luke does not use the word *diakonoi*, it is generally agreed that the seven men chosen to handle food distribution for the community in Acts were "deacons" (Ac 6.2–5).

Elders (*presbyteroi*). Paul and Barnabas preached from town to town, and "they [the two emissaries] also appointed Elders for them [the inhabitants] in each town" (Ac 14.23). Acts 11.30 shows that Elders were, among other things, liaisons for congregations to keep in contact with each other. Peter, in the first letter attributed to him (5.1), calls himself a "fellow Elder" (*sympresbyteros*) of other Elders.

Overseers (*episkopoi*, usually translated as "bishops"). In Philippians 1.1, Paul and Timothy greet, in this order, (1) God's people, (2) the Overseers, (3) the Servants, at Philippi. This is Paul's only use of *episkopoi*. It occurs elsewhere only in three places. In Acts, Paul is made to say to the Elders of Ephesus: "Keep watch, then, over yourselves and over the whole flock, of which the Holy Spirit has appointed you Overseers, to shepherd the church of God" (20.28).[10] So Paul and Luke use the term in the plural, even for one congregation. Only in two places in the late pastorals is it used in the singular, and there it occurs in combination with Elders (*presbyteroi*) or a board of Elders (*presbyterion*, 1 Tim 4.14), and the office has a "complete lack of theological legitimation."[11] The qualifications for an *episkopos* are entirely moral, and they are not only appointed by their fellows but monitored by them, and can be removed by them.

> If one aspires to the overseership, it is a worthy role he has in mind. For the overseer must be beyond criticism—the husband of one wife, sober, disciplined, presentable, approachable, able to teach, not bibulous or quarrelsome, but mild, pacific, not in thrall to money; a good manager of his home, commanding his children's respect, along with all virtues. If, after all, a man does not know how to manage his own home, how will he take care of God's gathering? He should not be recently baptized lest, inflated with self-importance, he should succumb to the devil's

sentence. He should have, too, a good reputation elsewhere, so as not to fall into disgrace and the devil's snare. (1 Tim 3.1–7)

The other use of *episkopos* in the singular also stresses "approachability," showing that the office is a diplomatic one, making for good relations between communities (which explains the reference in 1 Timothy to a good reputation outside the congregation).

Of course an overseer, as the householder [*oikonomos*] of God, must be beyond criticism, not stubborn, not quick-tempered, not a drinker or a fighter, not concentrating on money; but approachable, benevolent, disciplined, fair, religious, and self-denying. He should adhere to sound teaching, so he may strengthen others by his healing discourse, and refute adversaries. (Titus 1.7–9)

These pastoral letters are moving toward the single-overseer system— the so-called monarchical episcopacy—that first appears full-blown in the letters of Ignatius of Antioch (dated by John Meier to 108–117 CE). He notes that even the single overseer of his time has to preside in conjunction with *presbyteroi* and *diakonoi*.[12] Indeed, Ignatius refers to himself as a *diakonos* as well as an overseer.[13] Despite the emphasis of Ignatius on his own authority as an overseer, it is clear that he had lost control of the church in Antioch even before his arrest by the imperial authorities.[14]

It will be seen, then, that there is a wide variety of charisms, functions, and tasks referred to in the New Testament. If the priesthood existed then, would it not have been included in this exhaustive list, or at least referred to? But in fact Jesus nowhere refers to his Followers or Learners as priests. Paul never calls himself—or Timothy, or any of his other co-workers—a priest. He never gives anyone that status, either as a charism or an appointment. The Peter of the first Pseudo-Petrine letter does not call himself a priest, much less a bishop, but only a "fellow Elder" (*sympresbyteros*) of the other Elders in the Diaspora (1 Pet 5.1). His only reference to a priesthood (*hierateuma*) is that of the whole people as "living stones built up into a spiritual structure," *lithoi zontes oikodomeisthe oikos pneumatikos* (1 Pet 2.5, 9).

Not only is there no mention of a single priest among the Followers and Learners in the New Testament, there is no mention of the acts we now associate with the priesthood—no hearing of confessions, no giving the last rites, no marrying, no confirmation, no presiding at the Mass, no consecrating of the Eucharist. Baptism has never been the exclusive rite of priests. When rival factions in Corinth were engaged in different baptisms, Paul stood above the fray by pointing out that he did not normally baptize:

I thank God that I baptized none of you, except Crispus and Gaius. So no one can say you were baptized in my name. True, I did baptize the household of Stephanas; I am not aware of anyone else I baptized. Christ did not send me to baptize, but to carry the revelation. (1 Cor 1.14–17)

As for the Eucharist, we have a detailed description of troubles at the agape meal in Corinth, and there is no one in charge there. Paul does not lament the lack of a priest at the meal. He complains that people are eating in separate groups, with separate and widely differing foods.

First of all, I hear that when you assemble as a gathering, you divide into factions. I partly believe this, since divisions are necessary to make clear who among you is of sound doctrine. Nonetheless, in your gathering it is not the Lord's Supper you eat. Each prefers to eat what he has brought, so that while one lacks food, another has too much to drink. Have you no homes for your own eating and drinking, that you insult the gathering and humiliate the poor? . . . Accordingly, should one eat the food or drink the cup unworthily, he is guilty of the death of the Lord's body and blood. Let a man examine himself, and only then eat of the food and drink of the cup. Otherwise he who eats and drinks is eating and drinking a verdict on himself, since he does not understand what the body is. (1 Cor 11.18–22, 27–29)

In future years those last two sentences would be interpreted as saying that the unworthy participant in the Mass would be desecrating the real presence of the Lord in the consecrated bread and wine. But there is no mention of consecrating the bread and wine in this passage. In fact, people are eating and drinking a variety of different foods and beverages, according to class and wealth—and that is their offense. How is that desecrating the body and blood of Jesus? Because the body of Jesus is the people of his Followers, and breaking into factions at the meal is rending that body. As Paul says, "Now you are Christ's body, and each of you individually a part of it" (1 Cor 12.27). The bread is a symbol of the many grains joined in the one body of believers: "Because there is one loaf, we—many as we are—are one body" (1 Cor 10.17). That is what Paul means when he says the offender "does not understand what the body is."

Paul's message against the dismemberment of the body of Christ is the same in Corinthians as in Galatians, where the Followers were eating different meals, some still observing kashrut (kosher), others freed from it (Gal 2.12–14). What should have been a celebration of the unity of God's people was a fragmenting of them. The offense in both cases is the same— people eating separately at the agape meal. If the offense had been the desecrating of the real presence of Jesus in the food and drink, surely that would have been referred to. Indeed, Eucharist ("Thanksgiving") in its later sense, of sharing bread and wine as the body and blood of Christ, is never used in the New Testament, not even in the Letter to Hebrews, which alone calls Jesus a priest. Even when the term "Eucharist" came in, as with the letters of Ignatius of Antioch, it was still, as in Paul, simply a celebration of the people's oneness at the "one altar."[15] That meaning for the "body of Christ" would persist as late as the fourth and fifth centuries, in Augustine's denial of the real presence of Jesus in the elements of the meal.

> What you see passes away, but what is invisibly symbolized does not pass away. It perdures. The visible is received, eaten, and digested. But can the body of Christ be digested? Can the church of Christ be digested? Can Christ's limbs be digested? Of course not.[16]

> If you want to know what is the body of Christ, hear what the Apostle [Paul] tells believers: "You are Christ's body, and his limbs" [1 Cor

12.27]. If, then, you are Christ's body and his limbs, it is your symbol that lies on the Lord's altar—what you receive is a symbol of yourselves. When you say "Amen" to what you are, your saying it affirms it. You hear, "The body of Christ," and you answer "Amen," and you must be the body of Christ to make that "Amen" take effect. And why are you bread? Hear again the Apostle, speaking of this very symbol: "We are one bread, one body, many as we are" [1 Cor 10.17].[17]

Believers recognize the body of Christ when they take care to be the body of Christ. They should be the body of Christ if they want to draw life from the spirit of Christ. No life comes to the body of Christ but from the spirit of Christ.[18]

So, to summarize, though there were many charisms of service in the early Jesus movement—many functions, some inchoate offices—there were no priests and no priestly services; no male presider at the agape meal, no re-enactment of Jesus' Last Supper, no "sacrifice of the Mass," no consecrations of bread and wine; nothing that resembled what priests now claim to do. In fact, pagan critics of the Jesus movement said that it could not be a religion at all, since it had no priests, no altars, no designated places of worship.

How, then, did it come about that multiple New Testament texts like Matthew 23.9—"Do not address any man on earth as father, since you have only one Father, and he is in heaven"—should be so ignored by later priests and laity? That happened when a certain class in the church became Holy Men. And why did they become Holy Men? Because they had by then acquired the unique power to change bread and wine into the body and blood of Jesus Christ.

NOTES

1. The followers of Jesus were first called "Christians" by their enemies, as a term of denigration (Ac 11.26, 26.28), and secular writers.
2. Raymond Brown and John Meier, *Antioch and Rome* (Paulist Press, 1983), pp. 8, 108. When Elders of a town were referred to, this seems to mean the heads of the various household churches there (ibid., p. 139). For the home churches of

early Christianity, see Ramsay MacMullen, *The Second Church: Popular Christianity, A.D. 200–400* (Society of Biblical Literature, 2009).

3. For house-church liturgies, see chapter 18. The evidence for the eschatological nature of these meals is collected there. For baptism at the communal meal, see Justin, *Apology* 1.65–66. The earliest writings from the Jesus movement that have come down to us are the letters of Paul, and they quote as pre-existing the hymns at Phil 2.6–11 and Eph 5.14. Other hymns are quoted in the Deutero-Pauline letters—1 Tim 3.16, 2 Tim 2.11–13, and Titus 3.4–7. There are frequent doxology prayers that were already traditional in Rev 1.4–8, 4.8, 11, 5.9–10, 12–13, 11.15, 17–18, 15.3–4. Other hymns were incorporated in the Gospels (Lk 1.46–55, 68–79, 3.4–6, Jn 1.1–14). Thus the earliest voices of the Jesus movement were prayers, and they have the "high Christology" that used to be considered a later development of the Jesus story. *And none of these prayers is one for consecrating bread or wine.*

4. Hans Dieter Betz, "Apostle," ABD, vol. 1, pp. 309–11.

5. Hans Weder, "Disciple," ABD, vol. 2, pp. 207–10.

6. Ac 9.2, 19.9, 23, 22.4, 24.14.

7. For The Housefellows, Gal 6.10, Eph 2.19. For The Called, Rom 1.6, 8.28, 2 Cor 2.17. For The Holy, Rom 12.13, 1 Cor 12.13. For Those-in-Messiah, Rom 12.13, Gal 1.22, Eph 1.1, 2 Cor 5.17.

8. "Shepherd" appears only here in the Gospels to describe anyone but Jesus. It is not known what "caretaking" of the flock is involved here, but there is no reason to think it had to do with the priesthood. In the Acts of the Apostles, all preachers of Jesus are called "shepherds" (Ac 20.28). In the first Pseudo-Petrine letter, all Elders are called shepherds (1 Pet 5.2). The most famous shepherd in early Christian literature (early second century) is the angel who appears as a shepherd to the married freedman Hermas, to reform his life (*Shepherd of Hermas*, Visions 5.3–4, Similitudes 9.33). Raymond Brown points out that when Jesus tells Peter "Feed my sheep" (Jn 21.16–17) this is not a grant of power but an injunction to care for others, as the Good Shepherd seeks the lost sheep at Mt 18.12–14; see Brown, *The Gospel According to John* (Doubleday, 1966), vol. 2, pp. 116–17.

9. For the etymology of *diakonos* as servant, see Hjalmar Frisk, *Griechisches etymologisches Wörterbuch* (Carl Winter Universitätsverlag, 1960), vol. 1, pp. 384–85.

10. Joseph A. Fitzmyer, *The Acts of the Apostles* (Doubleday, 1997), p. 678.

11. Luke Timothy Johnson, *The First and Second Letters to Timothy* (Doubleday, 2001), p. 213.

12. John P. Meier and Raymond Brown, *Antioch and Rome* (Paulist Press, 1983), pp. 75–77.

13. Ignatius, *Letter to the Philadelphians* 4.

14. William R. Schoedel, *Ignatius of Antioch* (Fortress Press, 1985), pp. 10–11.

15. Ignatius, *Letter to the Philadelphians* 4, *Letter to the Magnesians* 7. For the "non-sacramental" language in Ignatius, see Schoedel, op. cit., pp. 116–17, 197–99.

16. Augustine, Sermon 227.

17. Augustine, Sermon 272.

18. Augustine, *In Joannem Tractatus* 26.13.

Holy Men

The most striking thing about priests, in the later history of Christianity, is their supposed ability to change bread and wine into the body and blood of Jesus Christ. "From this unique sacrifice their whole priestly ministry draws its strength" (C 1566). Nothing else about their actions is on that scale—the fact that they can routinely work an astounding miracle. Jesus becomes present in every bit of bread and every bit of wine that is consecrated, and only one thing can make this happen—the words of a priest impersonating Jesus at the Last Supper and saying, "This is MY [i.e., Jesus' though the priest is speaking] body . . . This is the cup of MY blood."

The only person on earth who can do this is a priest, and he can do it all by himself, with no congregation present (in what is called a private Mass). A congregation of believers, no matter how large or how pious, cannot do this if no priest is present. The people of God cannot approach God directly, in this rite central to many Christians, but only through a designated agent. As Thomas Aquinas put it: "A priest, it was earlier said, is established as the mediator between God and the people. A person who stands in need of a mediator with God cannot approach him on his own" (ST 3.22 a4r).

The power to effect transubstantiation is lodged in a priest by the sacrament of ordination, and it cannot be taken from him except by death. He is ordained as "a priest forever," in the line of Melchizedek, whose priesthood had no beginning and no end. Even if a priest is defrocked, discredited, convicted of crimes, and imprisoned, he still has the "character" (imprint) of the sacrament. "Through that sacrament [ordination] priests, by the anointing of the Holy Spirit, are signed with a special character" (C 1563). Get bread and wine to him in a prison cell, and a priest can still make Jesus present there. That was why it was so hard to discipline pedophile priests. Church authorities can take away their "faculties" (permission to act in certain dioceses) but not their priesthood.

Nothing else a priest does matches his Eucharistic power. He can forgive sins—in the confessional and as part of the last rites—but that does not make Jesus himself present in a particular moment and place. He can marry, and bury, and baptize Catholics—but these are lesser matters than the power that gives him all his other dignities. In fact, all these other acts became sacraments as part of the power extending outward from the power to celebrate Mass. That is because the Mass re-enacts the Passion of Christ, from which all graces are derived in the Thomistic system.

The "whisky priest" in Graham Greene's novel *The Power and the Glory* (first published in America as *The Labyrinthine Ways*) is a fornicator with a child born out of wedlock, and the people where he had his affair know all about him. Since the novel takes place during President Calles's fierce persecution of the Catholic Church in Mexico (1924–1934), the priest knows that, simply by being there, he puts the people around him at risk of death for harboring him. But he goes on, even while accusing himself as a vile man, a menace to others, because he thinks he can still make God present when he consecrates bread and wine for the people he endangers. He keeps risking his own life and the lives of others to continue bringing that miracle to them. Nothing else justifies what turns out to be his suicidal mission.

> If he left them, they would be safe; and they would be free from his example; he was the only priest the children could remember. It was from him they would take their ideas of the faith. But it was from him too they took God—in their mouths. When he was gone it would be as if God in all this space between the sea and the mountains ceased to exist. Wasn't it his duty to stay, even if they despised him, even if they were murdered for his sake, even if they were corrupted by his example? . . . He could feel no meaning any longer in prayers like these [for a boy's life]—the Host was different: to lay that between a dying man's lips was to lay God. That was a fact.[1]

There is another priest in Greene's novel, Padre Jose, a man who has given up his mission, married, and submitted to the government. He, too, has the unremovable power to work miracles:

> He was just a fat old impotent man mocked and taunted between the sheets. But then he remembered the gift he had been given which nobody could take away. That was what made him worthy of damnation—the power he still had of turning the wafer into the flesh and blood of God. He was a sacrilege. Wherever he went, whatever he did, he defiled God. Some mad renegade Catholic, puffed up with the governor's politics, had once broken into a church (in the days when there were still churches) and seized the Host. He had spat on it, trampled it, and then the people had got him and hanged him . . . He wasn't so bad a man, Padre Jose thought—he would be forgiven, he was just a politician; but he himself, he was worse than that—he was like an obscene picture hung here every day to corrupt children with.[2]

The miracle of changing bread and wine into the literal body and blood of Christ is so stupendous that the church for a long time tried to minimize its physical actuality. An air of mystery around it was meant to restrain literal thoughts verging on cannibalism. Drinking blood is a rather gruesome concept—indeed, it is forbidden by Jewish Law (Lev 7.26–27)—and chewing human flesh is not much better in the scales of normal behavior. Medieval theologians said that it was a marvelous providence of God that the sacrament was veiled under the semblance of bread and wine, to prevent the *horror cruoris* or the *horror sanguinis*—"revulsion from flesh" or "revulsion from blood." Roger Bacon wrote in the thirteenth century that "the human heart could not endure to masticate and devour raw and living flesh and to drink fresh blood."[3] Thomas Aquinas assured readers that "Nothing repulsive [*horrendum*] occurs in the sacrament. It would only be repulsive if raw flesh were eaten."[4] Peter Damian said that if eating flesh were perceived in the Eucharist it would be a *terribile sacramentum*.[5]

In my childhood, one did not have to consider that one was drinking blood, since the chalice was denied to laypeople—a medieval development that held only priests were worthy of that privilege (women were the first to be denied the cup).[6] Nor did chewing of flesh come into the imagination, since the act was so far as possible dematerialized: a paper-thin wafer was invented to be the Host, something that could melt on one's tongue, obviating the need to chew. What happens to the wafer in the digestive tract was best not thought of, and the Host's practically non-material nature made that virtually unnecessary.

The first miracle, how the wafer became Jesus, was to be followed by an obscure second miracle, how the wafer had to be "de-consecrated" before it became an excretion. Did it turn back into bread at some traveling point toward the toilet bowl? As the theologian Edward Schillebeeckx put it, there had to be a "reverse transubstantiation" to separate Jesus from the "accidents" of bread and wine before they were excreted:

> To explain the real presence of the heavenly Christ, the further miracle of "adduction," "production" or "reproduction" in the bread was necessary. This in turn required a new miracle, to explain how it was possible for Christ to remain in heaven and yet, at the same time, to dwell in the Host, even though this did not take place spatially. This speculation should ultimately have resulted in the problem (which was never in fact sorted out and was not really taken seriously, as the previous questions were) of whether a reverse transubstantiation did not have to take place when the Eucharistic forms passed away, and Christ accordingly returned to heaven—which he had, however, never left.[7]

The consideration of what happens to the Host in the intestines was made a taboo subject, so much so that people who brought up the inconveniencing problem were branded as heretics—"Stercoranists" from *stercus*, meaning "feces."[8] To distance the taking of communion from ordinary eating, all Catholics were ordered to fast from all food and drink from midnight to the reception of the Host. They were also told they could not be in a state of sin while receiving communion, so they had best go to confession before taking the Host.

The Host was made into an object of adoration. It was retained after the Mass where it was consecrated, kept in a tabernacle, carried around in a pyx in case it had to be taken to a dying person, or someone hospitalized, or one otherwise incapacitated. A vigil lamp was kept lit to signal its presence in the tabernacle, and worshipers genuflected to the Host behind the tabernacle door. They also paid "visits" to Jesus in what Thomas Aquinas called an inappropriate incarceration.[9] Periodically the Host was exposed in an ornate gold monstrance, to be venerated at the service called Benediction, with incensings, hymns, and a congregation permanently on its knees. Being excommunicated from the church meant, as the name suggests, that one could no longer receive the Host. Everything revolved around the Host.

In my youth, no one was allowed to touch the Host but the priest, who placed it on a communicant's tongue, not in the hands. The fact that the priest's hands were allowed such intimacy with the Host was symbolized by tying his hands during the ordination service. This set the hands apart from mundane service. The "consecrating fingers" that held the Host during the performance of the service were so important that a man lacking those could not be a priest at all. When Isaac Jogues, the Jesuit missionary to North America, was captured by Mohawk warriors in 1642, he was tortured so extensively that his thumbs and forefingers were cut, burnt, or gnawed away. When Jogues returned to France after his rescue, Pope Urban VIII had to grant him special permission to consecrate the Host with his remaining fingers.[10] The significance of the miracle-working hands is expressed in many ways. When Pope Pius IX kidnapped a Jewish boy who had been baptized during an illness, he showed his determination not to give the boy back to his family by saying, "I know what my duty is in the matter and, God willing, I will let them cut off my hand rather than be found wanting."[11]

One of the deep urges to deny the reality of sexual abuse by priests is probably the fact that pious people thought it inconceivable that the "consecrating fingers," those which touched the Host, could also stroke a woman's clitoris or a young boy's penis. John Chrysostom (c. 347–407 CE) wrote: "How God shows his love for man. He who sits on high beside the Father is held in all priests' hands!"[12] Francis of Assisi said that this cradling of Christ in his hands made the priest resemble Mary his mother, who bore him in her womb and nursed him at her breast.[13] In the twelfth century, Saint Norbert, the founder of the Premonstratensian order of priests, wrote of the priest's re-enactment of the Incarnation, "Priest you are not, because you are God."[14]

The priest was not only allowed to handle holy things. He was a kind of walking holiness himself. According to John Chrysostom:

> Though the priesthood is exercised on earth, its acts rank with those of heavenly beings. And no wonder. For the priesthood is not bestowed by a man, or an angel, or an archangel, or any created force, but by the Paraclete himself, who leads men to act as if they are angels though they are still in the flesh. Thus the man set apart should be as pure as if he already stood in heaven among the ranks of the celestial powers . . . When you see the Lord sacrificed and lying on the altar, and the priest praying over the sacrifice, all the bystanders imbrued with the sacred blood, how can you feel that you are standing on the earth with fellow mortals rather than swept up to heaven, shedding all carnal thought to gaze around at celestial things with pure soul and innocent mind?[15]

Being set apart is always the sign of holiness. Just as the priest's hands were tied during his ordination, his whole body was tied up, as it were, in the special clothes he wore. His everyday wear included a Roman collar, a long-skirted cassock, and a biretta (a hard square hat with projecting vanes). If he belonged to a religious order, he had a distinctive habit—a brown Franciscan robe and cowl, with cincture (and sometimes a large rosary dangling from it), or a Dominican white and black habit, or a Benedictine black habit and cowl. Abbots of various orders had special capes (mantellettas).

But it was when he prepared to perform the ceremony of the Mass that a priest got really dressed up. I used to watch, as an acolyte in the sacristy before Mass, how the priest applied layer after layer of symbolic clothing around his body. The clothes themselves are set apart by being blessed before use. The priest put on an amice, a cloth draped around the shoulders.

Before settling it, he first kissed it and touched it on his head, since the amice was originally a hood. He said a prayer as he did this: "Place upon my head, O Lord, the helmet of salvation for repelling the attacks of the Evil One."[16] He put on an alb, the long white garment that looks like a night-gown but is descended from the white garb of purity worn by the newly baptized (Mormons still wear a version of this under their street clothes). The priest is supposed to make the alb cover all the other clothes, even the Roman collar (it must be tucked over it). The Vatican has granted an indulgence (free time from purgatory) for the prayer said about the alb: "Purify me, O Lord, and make me clean of heart, so that, washed in the blood of the Lamb, I may possess eternal joy."[17]

A maniple is a fabric band, over a foot long and over two inches wide, worn on the left arm. In Roman times it was thought to be an official's fancy instrument for touching things, like a substitute glove or handkerchief. In Christian times it became a symbol of the bonds that held Christ.[18] A stole is an elongated piece of fabric worn like a scarf over the alb, both ends hanging in front of the priest. It is about six inches wide and reaches below the knees until it is crossed over the breast and held in place by a cincture (a silken rope).

Once the priest is wrapped and tied up like a package, over it all comes the chasuble, a fancier poncho that is known in the Western church as a fiddleback because it is open at the sides, and the back portion has the shape of a cello. This is a specially ornate vestment, often with gold threads and rich needlework. The liturgy treats it as a symbolic yoke, and the priest prays as he puts it on: "My yoke is sweet and my burden light—grant that I may so carry it as to merit Thy grace."[19] The color of the chasuble changes seasonally or by the purpose of a specific Mass—purple for Advent and Lent, white or gold for major feasts, green for "ordinary time," red for Pentecost and martyrs' feast days, pink for Gaudete Sunday in Advent and Laetare Sunday in Lent, black for funeral Masses. This extensively change-able wardrobe was satirized by the ecclesiastical fashion show in Fellini's movie *Roma* (1972). Instead of a chasuble a priest can wear an even more elaborate and voluminous cape called a cope, which he uses at Benediction or when carrying the Host in processions.[20]

Thus bundled and blazoned, the priest entered the sanctuary to perform the Mass. On entry there, he wore his biretta, which he dropped with a plop on the altar steps. The sanctuary was prepared with lit candles on the altar, and the altar was often incensed from a bronze thurible, before the priest himself was incensed. The altar boy rang a nest of bunched bells at the consecration of the Host and of the chalice. Everything about the priest and the sanctuary (which could not be entered but by the priest and his acolytes) proclaimed that this was a very special person, made different by the special task he had to perform. That is why he was wrapped and enclosed like a human treasure.

As he rose in the hierarchy, a priest's clothes, manner, and action became even more set apart and "holy." A priest can use a fascia, or sash, to tie his cassock at the waist. As one reaches higher office, the fascia gets wider and longer. Like that of the chasuble, its color changes, but this time for the rank, not for the season; and the quality of the fabric also changes:

> There are five colors for the fascia: white (watered silk for the pontiff, cloth for religious habits), scarlet (watered silk for cardinals), violet (silk for patriarchs, primates, archbishops, bishops, apostolic protonotaries, and prelates of honor), purple (wool cloth or faille for chaplains of His Holiness), and black (wool cloth or faille for priests and seminarians).[21]

A monsignor could have a colored lining to his cassock or his biretta, a purple sash, a colored cape.

A bishop's cassock acquired a collar and became a simar. He also acquired a scarlet biretta and zucchetto (skullcap), a mitre for his head, and a crozier (ornate shepherd's crook) for his hand. For liturgical occasions, he wore special gloves with a large ring outside them, which the faithful kissed while genuflecting. He might also wear a lace shawl, the rochet (pronounced ro-*shay*), when assisting at ceremonies where he was not the chief celebrant.

When attending on the pope, a bishop could wear the mantelletta, a large overgarment open on the side and front. Otherwise he was permitted a mozzetta (elbow-length cape buttoned in front).

Cardinals can also wear the mozzetta, when they are not wearing a watered silk cape called the ferraiolo. Archbishops are given a pallium by the pope. This is a Y-shaped band that hangs from the shoulders before and behind the archbishop, over his other vestments. It is woven of white wool from Trappist farms, and fastened with pins of three precious metals (purportedly to recall the three nails used in the Crucifixion).[22]

Popes had until recently a range of special wear—a subcinctorium suspended from the cincture, a falda (long skirt worn under the alb), a mantum (long cope), a white zucchetto, a staff tipped with a cross, a special mozzetta, and red shoes. Before Paul VI, the pope wore a huge crown (actually three crowns nested together) called the tiara:

> The triple tiara represents first, the Vicar of Christ's universal episcopate; second, his jurisdictional supremacy; and third, his temporal power. The tiara has also been described as representing the pope's power—militant, penitent, and triumphant—and his role as priest, pastor, and teacher. In heraldry, the *triregno* is always depicted as having a white "beehive" form, with three gold and jeweled diadems. The tiara is surmounted by an orb and a cross. The *infulae* (ribbands suspended from it in back) are depicted as red-lined, gold-fringed, and gold-backed.[23]

Until recently the pope used to enter Saint Peter's on a *sedia gestatoria*, a throne borne on the shoulders of twelve footmen while two attendants used the flabellum, a large ceremonial fan made of white ostrich feathers. Despite suspension of its use, the *sedia* has not been formally renounced.[24]

All this fuss and finery far outdoes what Jesus condemned in the Pharisees. "Everything they do is done to impress people. They enlarge their tefillins and lengthen their tassels" (Mt 23.5–6). If, as Acton said, power tends to corrupt, so does the show of power, the sense of power, the display of power. And holiness can be a form of power. Everything around the priest proclaims holiness. His workplace, the sanctuary, was what its name suggests, a church Holy Place (*sanctum*), one compared to the Holy of Holies in the Jewish Temple. A communion rail cordoned it off from the rest of the church—a vestige of the "rood screen" that used to hide the chancel from lay vision.[25] That the priest faced the altar, with his back to the congregation, did not matter when the rood screen kept him invisible from the nave in any event.

For a long time, women could not enter the sanctuary. Even the nuns who washed the altar linens had to have them handed out to them by a male acolyte. When I was young, women could not even enter the main body (nave) of the church without a hat on. Girls at my grade school used to satisfy this requirement by fixing a tissue to their heads with a hairpin. At the altar itself, consecrated vessels proclaimed their exalted use—the silver or gold paten for the Host, the jeweled chalice for the wine, the crystal cruets for diluting the wine, the ornate little temple called a tabernacle for depositing the unconsumed Hosts, the brass pyx for carrying the Host. A large altar stand radiated gold beams from its frame, which contained a little window where the Host was displayed at Benediction. The altar stone with relics in it, the candles lit on the altar, the bells rung at the consecration of the Host and the chalice, the incense often wafted toward and around the altar—all proclaimed the special status of the space where the transformation of bread and wine into the body and blood of Jesus regularly happened.

And the sanctuary is not the only sacred space surrounding a priest. Spreading out from it is the whole church—the cathedrals and basilicas and the smaller imitations of them, with their great gates, stained glass windows, spires above, and statues lining their interiors. All these, too, pay tribute to the central Eucharistic act that calls for them, and for the man performing that act.

When that act occurred, it did so because of words spoken by the priest, and for centuries the words were (in the Western church) Latin, another way of separating what went on there from ordinary human transactions. Some older Catholics thought the miracle could occur only if the words were the original ones of Jesus (though Jesus spoke Aramaic and Greek, not Latin). Priests used to recite their "Office" from a Latin breviary every day, a relic of singing "the hours" in monasteries. The breviary was also in Latin, and no one could be ordained a priest who did not know Latin (I met religious-order brothers who wanted to become priests but were denied that privilege since they had no Latin). The Office of the day had to be read before midnight. When a priest was driving my high school debate team back from a meet, he had to get out of the car and finish his Office by the headlights. (We imagined a passing motorist telling someone in his car, "That must be one hell of a book!")

Most priests had only rudimentary knowledge of Latin, restricted to rote recitation of the Mass and the breviary, but that was enough to set the priest apart—as did the rule of celibacy. A common argument for priestly celibacy is that it makes a man more open to the community—he is not concerned primarily with his own family. But in fact it created a distance from others, like the rood screen, the communion rail, the special clothes and special language. The holy cannot be the ordinary.

How can men so cosseted, set so on high, deferred to so universally, not think of themselves as exceptional beings? The keeper of a higher order of knowledge can come to believe, gradually, that he is a higher order of being. An awe for priests was instilled, in the parochial grade school I attended, by the nuns who taught us. Though these nuns could be surprisingly spunky in some ways (as when insisting on fairness to our Hispanic classmates), they exemplified and instilled a reverence for the parish priest who dropped by for brief but intentionally awe-inspiring visits to the classroom. These nuns were like the mother who tells refractory children, in a doom-laden voice, "Just wait till your *father* gets home."

The aura around the priest was sensed not only by Catholics. Deference to priests was widely paid, and was reflected in the heroic priests presented in the movies by Henry Fonda, Bing Crosby, Pat O'Brien, Gregory Peck, Spencer Tracy, Frank Sinatra, Karl Malden, Montgomery Clift, Charles Bickford, Donald Crisp, Lewis Stone, Regis Toomey, and others. A wise-cracking critic said of such movies that they were made by Jews about Catholics for an audience of Protestants. The holiness exuded by movie priests made John Ford, when he transferred Greene's *The Power and the Glory* to a film called *The Fugitive*, remove the whisky from the whisky priest. The fornication committed by the priest, and the resulting child, now belonged to the persecuting secular policeman, who is made to be a hypocrite, though Greene created him as a sincere fanatic.

I observed the deference to priests as a boy when I caddied at a golf course. If a regular player known to be a priest showed up with his golf bag, men already prepared to tee off let him go ahead of them. It was presumed that he had to get back to his spiritual tasks. Priests came to expect such favors. Once, when a priest drove me to the airport to pick up a friend, he stopped in a no-parking area just outside the entry and started to come in with me. I pointed to the no-parking sign, and he told me he had a clerical sticker on his car (granted to give him immediate access to the sick or others needing his spiritual service) so he would never get ticketed or towed. (This was before terror threats tightened security at airports.) Priests caught speeding were routinely given a pass. Years of such exemptions lay behind the reluctance of authorities to credit accusations of sexual molestation by priests. The "good father" could not be such a monster.

The fact that priests give up marriage and a family was used by some of them to take compensatory rewards in the form of luxurious cars, state-of-the-art sound systems, and other "creature comforts." The dynamics of such compensation are wittily detailed in J. F. Powers's novel *Morte d'Urban*, whose priest (Father Urban) jockeys for rich men's favors. Expecting privileges is a habit into which a priest can all too readily fall. John Chrysostom, after all, said that a priest should be honored more than a king, since a king cannot turn bread and wine into the body and blood of Jesus.[26] Some bishops were egregiously expansive in their lifestyles, as I saw when I visited Bishop John Wright at his episcopal palace in Pittsburgh.

Sometimes the fact that a priest has no family of his own can make him presume that other people's families should serve his convenience. My wife and I once knew a priest who invited himself to our house every Saturday to watch his favorite TV shows. He asked that our kids be kept quiet, and he ate the special meal my wife provided—without ever thanking her. He obviously assumed it was just his right. At the time we were generally dining on fish and vegetables, for health reasons. He joked, after a bit of this, that if we did not serve him meat soon he would have to eat our little dog. We took him out after that for a pepperoni pizza. Eventually, but after many weeks, my wife said she would no longer put up with it, and we started saying we would be away on Saturday when he called to tell us he was coming. Of course, we were lucky that our friend's hedonism was confined to food and comfort. As we know from many victims' stories, some priests who molested children got access to them by befriending and visiting their parents on a regular basis, using a surrogate family as a stalking horse for designs on its children. Those parents felt doubly betrayed.

Of course I have known humble and hardworking priests, men who shamed me by their devotion to others. But there are enough of the other kind to make one appreciate the words of Jesus when he told his Followers not to strive for pre-eminence (Mk 9.33–37). Or when he sent his disciples out to preach the Gospel, saying, "Provide yourselves no gold or silver or copper in your belts, or traveler's pouch, or second pair of tunics or sandals" (Mt 10.9–10). Saint Peter's Basilica and the Vatican Palace cannot claim true descent from that pair of sandals and that single tunic.

NOTES

1. Graham Greene, *The Labyrinthine Ways* (Viking, 1940), pp. 89, 205.
2. Ibid., p. 39.
3. *The Opus Majus of Roger Bacon*, translated by R. B. Burke (University of Pennsylvania Press, 1928), vol. 2, p. 822. Other medieval texts in this vein are cited by Caroline Walker Bynum, *Christian Materiality: An Essay on Religion in Late Medieval Europe* (Zone Books, 2011), p. 146.
4. Thomas Aquinas, *Commentary on the Sentences of Peter Lombard*, book 4, distinction 10, question 1, article 4c.
5. Caroline Walker Bynum, *Wonderful Blood: Theology and Practice in Late Medieval Northern Germany and Beyond* (University of Pennsylvania Press, 2007), p. 298.
6. Ibid., pp. 94–96.

7. Edward Schillebeeckx, *The Eucharist*, translated by N. D. Smith (Sheed and Ward, 1968), p. 91.

8. Bynum, *Wonderful Blood*, p. 138.

9. Ibid., p. 88.

10. Francis Parkman, *The Jesuits in North America in the Seventeenth Century* (Library of America, 1983), pp. 555–67; Francis X. Talbot, *Saint Among Savages: The Life of St. Isaac Jogues* (Harper and Brothers, 1935), pp. 218–26, 350.

11. David I. Kertzer, *The Kidnapping of Edgardo Mortara* (Vintage, 1998), p. 157.

12. John Chrysostom, *Priesthood* 3.4.

13. Francis of Assisi, "Letter to a General Chapter of the Franciscans," quoted in Caroline Walker Bynum, *Holy Feast and Holy Fast* (University of California Press, 1987), p. 57.

14. Ibid., p. 57.

15. Chrysostom, op. cit., 3.4.

16. James-Charles Noonan, *The Church Visible: The Ceremonial Life and Protocol of the Roman Catholic Church* (Viking, 1995), p. 346.

17. Ibid., p. 338.

18. *Catholic Encyclopedia*, s.v. "Maniple."

19. Noonan, op. cit., p. 342.

20. Ibid., p. 343.

21. Ibid., p. 295.

22. Ibid., p. 362 (and *Catholic Encyclopedia*, s.v. "Pallium").

23. Noonan, op. cit., p. 189.

24. Ibid., p. 413.

25. Bynum, *Holy Feast*, p. 57.

26. Chrysostom, op. cit., 3.5.

THREE

The Eucharistic Miracle

The priest is made powerful because of the Eucharist. That explains him. It is what he does, what makes him what he is. No one else can do this—consecrate the Eucharist. But what exactly is the Eucharist? The miracle of changing bread to Jesus is so staggering that many people through the ages have felt they had to explain it, or show its importance, with secondary miracles—like seeing the Host bleed, or an image of Jesus on or above the Host or in the chalice. In legend after legend, people gave the Host visible powers (like levitation). The validity of such Eucharistic miracles was endorsed by theologians during the eleventh-century controversy over the real presence of Christ in the Eucharist. They said that if Christ were not really present in the Host, how could it work such miracles?[1]

Thomas Aquinas saw some danger in these miracles. He felt he had to explain them in such a way that they would not detract from the authenticity of the main miracle, the presence of Jesus in the Eucharist. He noted that some see a spectral Jesus on or over the Host when no one else does, or only in glimpses. Or only an innocent child sees the priest lifting the baby Jesus in his hands, not the Host.[2] He called this a fleeting and subjective visual effect (*immutatio oculorum*), not affecting the Eucharistic presence. But when a whole group sees a continuing vision of the Lord, he says this is a spectral indication of what is properly present only in the Eucharist—and in that sense to be welcomed, as confirming rather than challenging faith (ST 3.76 a8r).

Thomas did not try to persuade people that the visions were not there, simply that they did not replace the reality of Jesus, who is present physically only in heaven, or sacramentally only in the Host and chalice. He must have known there was no way to stop people from supplementing what they *believe* about the Eucharist with what they could *see*, or think they see. There are thousands of such ancillary miracle stories around the Eucharist.[3] Sometimes the Host flies from the hand of an unworthy recipient. Sometimes it comes unscathed through fire—like the "miraculous Hosts" of Wilsnack, which made that town in Germany the fourth most popular goal of fifteenth-century pilgrims (after Rome, Jerusalem, and Compostela).[4] Or the Host floats, rather than becomes saturated, in water. Or it paralyzes the tongue of an unworthy recipient.[5] Or a child who has had pagan food in its mouth before receiving the Host has to spit it out.[6] Or it turns to ashes when carried off by someone trying to desecrate it.[7] Or it heals a sick person with its touch. Or, carried in procession, it wards off an enemy attack. Or it was carried out to the fields to cause fertility.[8] It even raised the dead.[9]

Perhaps the most famous story is "the miracle of Bolsena." In 1263, it is claimed, a priest in Bolsena, Italy, who did not believe in the real presence, broke the large Host held in his hands and the sacred blood ran down onto the corporal (the white linen cloth on which the paten and chalice are placed during Mass). The stained corporal became a prized relic and was installed in a special monstrance at a special altar in the nearby Orvieto cathedral, where it has been worshiped by pilgrims ever since. Still on display, it has been visited by popes. The miracle was commemorated in many paintings, the most famous of which, by Raphael, fills one wall in the Vatican's Room of Heliodorus.[10] Many red-stained corporals became holy items after that.[11]

The second most famous Eucharistic miracle, and one of the oldest devotions in Italy, is the miracle of Lanciano, dating from about 700 CE. Again a priest who doubted the real presence of Jesus found himself holding a piece of the flesh of Jesus and looking into a chalice with five globules of his blood. The flesh, looked at with a little imagination, is roughly shaped like a heart. It and the five globules of blood are still displayed, in a monstrance for the flesh and a tear-shaped crystal vessel for the drops of blood, to be venerated close up by pilgrims who climb stairs behind the altar in Lanciano.[12] This was so well known an event that Aquinas referred to it in his discourse on secondary miracles, singling out the appearance of "flesh or blood [of Jesus]," *caro aut sanguis* (ST 3.76 a8r). He says these cannot be part of the glorified body of Jesus (*propria species Christi*), which exists only in heaven. If these were bits of Jesus in his earthly state, putting them in a ciborium or tabernacle would be putting the glorified Jesus in prison instead of heaven! Since these apparitions are neither the heavenly nor the sacramental body, they are not a really present Jesus, says Aquinas, though they are rightly reverenced as aids to piety.[13]

The appearances of Jesus in connection with the Eucharist, appearances that Thomas honored while saying that they should not replace the reverence for the Host, were encouraged by the very process of making the Host. Hot plates pressed the Host, in its baking stage, into a form with a raised image of the crucified Christ on it. One example of these baking plates, from the seventeenth century, was on exhibit at the Art Institute of Chicago in 2011. The catalogue of the exhibit explained the widespread use of such Hosts:

> The embossed imagery . . . may have been responsible for some of the Host-related visions documented throughout the medieval and Renaissance periods, as consecrated wafers were much more likely to be seen to emit blood if they already bore the raised image of Christ's death on the cross.[14]

Despite the strictures of people like Thomas Aquinas, a sight of the Host and chalice seemed to stimulate rather than suppress the longing for more visualizable forms of the body and blood of Jesus.

The many relics of the true cross were considered "first-class relics" because they were thought to have traces of Jesus' blood on them, or simply to have touched the body of Jesus while he lived on earth. Such relics were the pillar to which he was bound while scourged, the chains binding him there, thorns from his crown of thorns, nails used to fasten him on the cross.[15] There were several pillars kept as relics.[16] It applied to the ropes that supposedly bound Jesus, or the sponge that was lifted up to him on the cross.[17] The lance that stabbed Jesus' side, shedding his salvific blood, was discovered in Antioch by troops on the First Crusade and helped the bearers of this relic take Jerusalem.[18] It was even true of the Holy Stairs in the Lateran, which Jesus is supposed to have climbed toward his trial by Pontius Pilate after he had been scourged. The hope that Jesus left traces of his blood and sweat from the Passion animated the cult of "Veronica's veil" used to wipe his face as he went to the cross, or the shroud of Turin used to wrap his body as it came from the cross.[19] If Jesus could leave bits of his blood on the instruments of his torture, why could not some of the blood itself have been preserved? Many pilgrimage sites claimed to have quantities of Holy Blood, saved from the Crucifixion by Mary Magdalene or the converted soldier Longinus, or saved after the Crucifixion by Nicodemus and/or Joseph of Arimathea, the men who buried Jesus.[20]

Two recent books have shown how the blood was fetishized in waves of hysterical devotion.[21] Nicholas Vincent prints maps showing the distribution of shrines claiming to possess the Holy Blood.[22] Caroline Walker Bynum lists the shrines that were given ecclesiastical sanction in the form of indulgences.

> Authentic indulgences indicate that something called blood was shown for veneration at Beelitz, Wasserleben, Bernstein, Cismar, Braunschweig, Schwerin, Marienfliess, Krakow am See, and Guestrow in the hundred years before Wilsnack. Gottsbueren had a lively pilgrimage at least fifty years before, and in Mark Brandenburg itself, the three Cistercian convents of Zehdenick, Marienfliess, and Heiligengrabe offered competing blood cults (with very different kinds of holy objects) in the years around 1300. There were plenty of examples to inspire Johannes Kabuz [the priest-impresario of pilgrimages to Wilsnack], just as the success of his enterprise encouraged subsequent efforts at Zehdenick and Sternberg, Heiligengrabe, and Berlin.[23]

Blood from the Passion led to theological debate over the authenticity of liquid as opposed to dried blood (since divine blood should not decompose).[24] Thomas Aquinas denied that blood from the Passion could be left behind on earth, since the integrity of the risen body (*veritas corporis*) made Jesus whole in both his forms, heavenly and Eucharistic (ST 3.54 a3). But

Franciscan defenders of traditional relics said that a superficial amount of blood—like Jesus' sweat, spit (*sputum*), or other effusions—could have been left on earth, while the essential blood was retained in the *veritas corporis*. The idea of the disposable sweat of Jesus was used to defend the authenticity of Veronica's veil and the shroud of Turin—and if traces of Jesus' sweat remain, why not of his blood as well?

> Franciscans . . . with their stress on the event of Christ's death, could theorize Eucharistic wonders or bodily relics as revelations of God's substance in the wafer, as miracles created by God, or as remnants—inessential but real—of the body cared for long ago by Mary Magdalen, Longinus, or Joseph of Arimathea. If the blood pointed to the death on the cross, its presence was of utmost utility in arousing and sustaining devotion. Visible manifestations were important because they point beyond.[25]

Bynum shows that by the fifteenth century, "theological arguments concerning bleeding Hosts and those concerning blood relics have fused into the question whether there can be *Blut Christi* on earth."[26]

Lucrative pilgrimages like that of Wilsnack made theologians hesitant about denying the validity of these blood miracles. Thomas Aquinas was firm that the blood was not that of Jesus, but the miracles were valid, since God provided some substitutes (*similia*) for the authentic blood, to confirm the reality of transubstantiation.[27] In the *Summa Theologiae* he says: "The blood recognized in certain churches as relics did not flow from the side of Christ, but is said miraculously to have spurted from some penetrated image of Christ," *miraculose dicitur effluxisse de quadam imagine Christi percussa* (ST 3.54 a3 ad3). He seems to be thinking of blood from stabbed crucifixes or Hosts, blood which would proliferate in the coming centuries. As Caroline Walker Bynum writes: "The status of blood, both as integral to (*integer*) and as separated from (*effusus*) Christ is central to the theology of the fifteenth century."[28]

The idea that superficial bits of Christ's body could be shed and left behind on earth buttressed the claim of some shrines to have a baby tooth of Jesus, lost forever from the mouth that replaced it with a grown-up tooth, saved by Mary and passed on to early disciples.[29] Only the adult teeth rose with Jesus at the Resurrection, so the baby teeth could continue to be revered in reliquaries. Guibert of Nogent wrote a savage attack on a rival monastery that drew pilgrims to its tooth relic.[30] The same monastery he was attacking claimed to have a bit of the umbilical cord from Jesus' birth (a double relic, of both Jesus and Mary).[31]

Even more popular were the many sites that proclaimed they had the holy prepuce cut away when Jesus was circumcised. A famous example of this was preserved in the pope's own treasury of relics in the Sancta Sanctorum of Rome.[32] Saint Catherine of Siena was often painted with Jesus putting a ring on her finger in a "mystical marriage," but she said in letter after letter that the true marriage with Jesus was sealed with the ring of his circumcised flesh on the spouse's fingers.[33] If these "disposable" parts of Jesus could exist apart from his risen body, why not deciduous parts of his blood?

The common element in devotion to the Host, to relics, and to holy objects was a belief that Jesus was physically present, and even harmable, in all of them. A stabbed crucifix could bleed, just like a stabbed Host. Bloody corporals were common after Bolsena.[34] The concern over this continuing physicality of Jesus on earth went along with an obsession over his mistreatment. The idea of a Host detached from its Mass context led to a new series of reported miracles, like those wherein a mad or disaffected person gets hold of a Host and tries to desecrate it by making Jesus suffer again—after which the malefactor is punished in some spectacular way. The normal villains in these were Jews, and the supposed desecration led to very real persecutions, like the famous German ones in Sternberg (1492) and Berlin (1510). Both events left extensive trial records and led to worship of Hosts allegedly attacked by Jews.

In Sternberg, a priest named Peter Dean was convicted of trading some Hosts to get back an iron pot he had pawned with some Jews. The Jews stabbed the Hosts and tried to drown them. When they would not sink, they buried them. When some clergymen found the Hosts, sixty-five Jews were arrested and tortured. After their trial, twenty-seven were executed by burning. So was the priest. The church at Sternberg displayed the miraculous Hosts, along with the table where they had been stabbed, and the stabbing instruments, and the pot the priest had pawned.[35]

Think for a moment what this meant. The persecutors seemed to reason (if at all) in terms like these: Jews, who were accused of being Christ killers in the first place, were trying to repeat their crime; but this time they were caught and they were the ones killed. In other words: If they could have apprehended the first Jews who turned Jesus over to Pontius Pilate, they would have caught and killed Annas and Caiaphas—even though Jesus told Peter not to resist the soldiers arresting him. In a kind of delayed blood-thirstiness, Jews were killed en masse for trying to harm Jesus—though the Host seemed perfectly able to care for itself, in the telling of the very men trying to avenge it. This attempt to amend history, or redress it, defied Jesus' own submission to suffering as the Father's will. The whole exercise was so illogical as to make its Christian perpetrators the truly diabolic actors, not the Jews. Yet such mass murders were repeated again and again.

In Berlin, a man stole a pyx with consecrated Hosts in it. Caught and tortured, he claimed to have sold one Host to a Jew in Spandau. When the Jew was brought to Berlin and tortured, he confessed that he had tried to defile the Host, but it spontaneously parted into three segments. He distributed these to other Jews in other towns for further desecration. When these Jews were rounded up and tried, thirty-nine were burnt and two were beheaded. The man who stole the monstrance was torn apart with fiery tongs. Later anti-Jewish propaganda embroidered this tale. It said that one of the parted Host segments had been ground into a red powder, but the Host vindicated itself when the powder healed a possessed woman.[36] The tale was as undying as the Hosts.

We should not let ourselves think of Eucharistic superstitions as quaint, as so many folktales or remnants of the Middle Ages. The Host could be, and was, a bringer of death across the years.

NOTES

1. Jaroslav Pelikan, *The Christian Tradition: A History of the Development of Doctrine*, vol. 3, *The Growth of Medieval Theology (600–1300)* (University of Chicago Press, 1978), pp. 200–201.

2. Guibert of Nogent, *Monodies and On the Relics of the Saints*, translated by Joseph McAlhany and Jay Rubenstein (Penguin Books, 2011), p. 199.

3. They are still being counted online by the Real Presence Eucharistic Education and Adoration Association.

4. Charles Freeman, *Holy Bones, Holy Dust: How Relics Shaped the History of Medieval Europe* (Yale University Press, 2011), p. 192.

5. Caroline Walker Bynum, *Christian Materiality: An Essay on Religion in Late Medieval Europe* (Zone Books, 2011), p. 142. A holy person, according to the twelfth-century abbot Guibert of Nogent, saw angels putting hot coals on the tongues of sinners who took the sacrament; see Guibert, *On Relics*, p. 239.

6. Guibert, *On Relics*, p. 234.

7. Ibid.

8. Freeman, op. cit., p. 196.

9. Pelikan, op. cit., p. 201.

10. Ingrid Rowland, "The Vatican Stanze," in *The Cambridge Companion to Raphael*, edited by Marcia B. Hall (Cambridge University Press, 2005), pp. 112–13.

11. Bynum, *Christian Materiality*, pp. 143–44.

12. In 1887, Pope Leo XIII granted an indulgence to those worshiping at the altar of the miracle; see "Lanciano, 700's A.D.," on the Web site of the Miracle of the Rosary Mission.

13. Ibid.

14. Suzanne Karr Schmidt, *Altered and Adorned: Using Renaissance Prints in Daily Life* (Yale University Press, 2011), pp. 69–71.

15. Guibert, *On Relics*, pp. 87, 150.

16. One of the famous scourging posts is in the Treasury of San Marco in Venice. Another is in the baldachino over the altar of Saint Peter's Basilica in Rome.

17. Pelikan, op. cit., pp. 183–84.

18. Guibert of Nogent, *The Deeds of God Through the Franks* (Echo Library, 2008), pp. 91–92, 97. Part of the lance itself is supposed to be contained in the reliquary above Bernini's huge statue *Saint Longinus* (three times life-size and made of four huge marble blocks) at the sanctuary crossing of Saint Peter's Basilica in Rome.

19. The "veil" with which Veronica wiped the face of Jesus on his way to the cross was revered in Rome, put on display at special events, and was contained in the reliquary above the huge statue of Veronica—planned by Bernini but executed by Francesco Mochi—in the sanctuary crossing of Saint Peter's. Dante marked the exposure of "our Veronica" (*Veronica nostra*) in the Holy Year of 1300

(*Paradiso* 31.103–8), where the onlooker's rapt look is compared with Dante's own awe in the presence of Saint Bernard in Paradise. Mochi makes the "veil" of his statue as big and rippling as a tablecloth—which led to a toreador's pass with the full cape being named "the veronica."

20. Nicholas Vincent, *The Holy Blood* (Cambridge University Press, 2001), pp. 88–89, 115; Caroline Walker Bynum, *Wonderful Blood: Theology and Practice in Late Medieval Northern Germany and Beyond* (University of Pennsylvania Press, 2007), pp. 129, 309.

21. Bynum, *Wonderful Blood*, and Vincent, *Holy Blood*.

22. Vincent, op. cit., pp. 52, 68.

23. Bynum, *Wonderful Blood*, pp. 75–76.

24. Freeman, op. cit., pp. 193–94; Bynum, *Wonderful Blood*, pp. 124, 147–48.

25. Bynum, *Wonderful Blood*, p. 129.

26. Ibid., p. 109.

27. Thomas Aquinas, *Commentary on the Sentences of Peter Lombard*, book 4, distinction 10, question 1, article 4c.

28. Bynum, *Wonderful Blood*, p. 111.

29. Guibert, *Monodies*, p. 268.

30. Ibid., p. 251. Guibert mocked the notion that Jesus "littered the earth with particles of his own body, like some trail of leftovers, and took the rest to heaven."

31. Ibid., pp. 253, 257. Relics of Mary's body were harder to come by than those of her son, since she was thought to have been assumed bodily at her death, and there were no convincing protectors of her childhood teeth, etc. But samples of her milk were displayed—why did it not curdle, Guibert asked (*Monodies*, p. 162), and bits of her clothing were treasured. The most precious relic at Chartres Cathedral was Mary's veil. Mark Twain mocked the milk relics in *Innocents Abroad*, chapter 55 (Oxford edition, 1996), pp. 601–2.

32. *Treasures of Heaven*, edited by Martina Bagnoli et al. (British Museum Press, 2010), p. 71. For other sites possessing the foreskin, see Vincent, op. cit., pp. 85–86, 103, and Bynum, *Christian Materiality*, pp. 138, 155–56, 210, 240, 245, 345, and *Wonderful Blood*, p. 122.

33. Caroline Walker Bynum, *Holy Feast and Holy Fast* (University of California Press, 1987), pp. 174–75, 376–77. Other women with a devotion to the holy prepuce were Bridget of Sweden and Agnes Blannbekin of Vienna (ibid.).

34. Bynum, *Christian Materiality*, pp. 15–16, 144.

35. Bynum, *Wonderful Blood*, pp. 69–70.

36. Bynum, *Christian Materiality*, p. 211.

FOUR

Explaining the Miracle: Aquinas

Theologians, especially Scholastic theologians, while admitting that bread and wine could become the body and blood of Jesus only by a mystery and a miracle, kept trying to put that miracle in some kind of conceptual framework that would make it more acceptable if not more understandable. William of Ockham (c. 1288–c. 1346), also known as Occam, wrote a long treatise on the *Sacrament of the Altar*. There he admitted (because the dogma of the Resurrection demanded it) that the glorified body of Christ in heaven was material. But the sacramental body of Christ was non-material, therefore non-spatial, like that of an angel. It could be present in a *punctum*, a point.[1] The Scholastic theologians are often derided for debating how many angels could dance on the head of a pin. That is not a thing they would ever discuss, since their angels are non-spatial and pins are spatial, so never the two could meet. The mockers simply did not know what was meant by *punctum*, a non-material (Euclidian) "point."

Since a *punctum* can be anywhere in the Eucharist, there was no need to replace the substance of bread with the substance of Christ (transubstantiation). Occam preferred to think of the Eucharist as *con*substantial, having both bread and Christ present together, the one as spatially material, the other as a mere *punctum*.[2] The Council of Trent later condemned any form of consubstantiality in the Eucharist.[3] Occam submitted, formally, to church terminology and said he could refer to this as transubstantiation, since he was always on the run from church authorities condemning him.[4] This is a clever approach to the Eucharist, and it influenced Martin Luther as a way of professing the real presence of Christ in the Eucharist while avoiding the Catholic doctrine.[5] But it does not make the mystery more manageable.

It does not solve the angels-on-a-pin problem, since bread is as material and spatial as a pin, while the *punctum* is neither. The *punctum* does not have a *where*, while the bread, like the pin, has a *where*, and never the material and the immaterial shall meet. But Occam does solve what might be called the crumbs problem. Since the *punctum* can be anywhere in the bread, when part of the bread falls as a crumb, it is only bread. But when the substance of bread has been wholly replaced by the substance of Jesus, as in the theory of transubstantiation, every crumb that falls is God. As the Council of Trent put it, "Christ, whole and entire, is contained not only under either species [of bread or wine] but also in each particle of either species"[6]—each crumb or droplet. That is why the priest so hastily tried to retrieve every bit of the Host any time he cracked the large Host held up for display after consecration. He was required to break it, as a symbol of Christ's death (though John 19.32–36 said that no bone was broken in Christ's body). But crumbs rarely fell in the church of my youth, since the Host was baked as a tight-textured cracker that would not fray when broken.

A variant on the *punctum* school might be the atom school. Galileo and others held the Democritan view that all matter is made up of minute and invisible atoms—so an atomistic body of Christ could co-exist with the atoms of bread and wine. The various atoms could compenetrate one another, as an Inquisition document attacking Galileo put it.[7] This, no less than Occam's theory, was condemned as "consubstantiality," though Occam's *punctum* was non-material and Galileo's atoms were a form of "thin" material.

The Scholastic theory that won out as the consensus Catholic position was that of Thomas Aquinas, who used the Aristotelian distinction between substance and accidents to make the Eucharist seem philosophically respectable. Thomas had been condemned in Paris for his reliance on the pagan Aristotle, but he finally made the Greek polymath the church's philosopher of choice. (Freethinkers of Florence and other Italian cities daringly preferred Plato.) Aristotle had distinguished substance (*ousia*, "essence") from accident (*symbebēkos*, "what accompanies")—which became in Thomas's Latin *sub-*

stantia ("underlying") and *accidens* (*ad cadens,* "falling in with").[8] The substance "dog" does not depend on whether the dog is sitting or running, healthy or unhealthy, male or female, wild or tame, small or large, black or white. Those are all accidents. According to Aristotle, they do not affect the substance. No matter whether the dog is or is not being or doing any of these things, it remains a dog. None of them can make it cease to be a dog.

Though Aristotle distinguished substance from accident, he did not (could not) separate them. A dog cannot exist without accidents like size. And there cannot be "a large" or "a white" standing alone without a substance. It has to be a large or a white *something.* An accident "comes along with" (*symbainei*) the thing that is its essence. Thomas admitted this natural truth: "An accident assumes what it is from its substance" (ST 3.77 a1r). But for the Eucharist, he posited a miraculous disruption of the natural order. He took the radical step of claiming that a substance can exist without its proper accidents, and accidents can exist without their proper substance, though only by a special action performed by God every time the priest says the words of consecration. The substance of Christ's body is in the Eucharist without that body's accidents, and the accidents of bread can exist without its proper substance, and the two separate things can be joined in the Eucharist. The Eucharistic Host looks like bread, tastes like bread, feels like bread, though it is not bread.[9] And the liquid consecrated in a chalice looks, tastes, and feels like wine without being it.

Thomas admits that God is upsetting the natural order when he makes one substance's accidents unite with another substance that lacks its own accidents:

> It happens, necessarily, that in this sacrament accidents are present without their substance. It takes divine power to make this happen. Since everything derives more from a first cause than a secondary one, God, as the first cause of both substances and accidents, can by his infinite power keep in existence an accident, even in the absence of the substance that maintains it as an immediate cause. That is how, without natural causes, he makes things happen that are normally impossible

without natural causes, as when he formed a human body in the womb of the Virgin without male insemination. (ST 3.77 a1r)

Although in the ordinary course of nature, an accident may belong only to a substance, here by a special dispensation following the provision of divine grace, accidents are present in the sacrament without their substance . . . In this sacrament the accidents do not subsist without their substance by any effect peculiar to them, but by the intervention of divine power. So they do not cease to be accidents, they cannot be defined as less than accidents, nor does this make them their own substances. (ST 3.77 a1 ad2)

Thomas did not quite say that God, as first cause, was creating something new in the freestanding accidents and substance, nor that he was changing bread into Christ in the sense of natural change that Aristotle gave that term (where a potentiality has to precede the act of change). Though there were elements both of creation and of change operating in this unique miracle, Thomas wanted to warn people away from anything so simple as saying that "bread becomes Christ," or "bread is changed into Christ." But if the bread and wine are not changed into Christ, what happens to them? Do they simply go out of existence—a position held by so-called annihilists?[10] Thomas did not like the idea of the Creator becoming a Destroyer.

It should be granted that this alteration from bread to the body of Christ in some measure approximates a new creation and in some measure resembles a natural process of change, while in some measure differing from both. All three describe a process, a "before and after." In creation, first there is non-being, and then being. In the sacrament, first there is bread, and then the body of Christ. In natural change, by Aquinas's physics, things like air turn into fire. These processes are not, all of them, the same. Still, in none of the three cases is the final state the same as the original one. Thus we cannot link them by using a verb in the present tense—to say, for instance, that non-being *is* being, or bread *is* the body of Christ, or oxygen *is* fire. Still, because of the preceding-and-followingness of the process, we can use the temporal word "after." So being comes after non-being, or the body of Christ comes after the bread, or the fire comes after the oxygen (ST 3.75 a8r).

Thomas found the substance-accidents concept useful for explaining other aspects of the Eucharist. For instance, how can the body of Christ be in every Host all around the world at the same time? He argues that locale is an accident, not a substance (ST 3.76 a6 ad3). The dog is a dog whether he is on the lawn or in the doghouse—though in real life if he is in the doghouse he is not at the same time on the lawn. Well, Thomas says, this is just another case of God not merely distinguishing substance from accident, but absolutely separating them by a miracle. This also helps with the problem of the Host's digestion and excretion in the human body. Thomas says that only the accidents of bread decompose, while the substance is separate from such accidents and continues to exist in all other Hosts (ST 3.77 a4 ad5).

The Thomistic approach somehow made the Eucharist appear more explicable, though it just shifted the terms of what was miraculous in any account of it. And there were certain disadvantages to his approach. For one thing, what if one did not understand or accept the Aristotelian categories? Edward Schillebeeckx points out that the Fourth Lateran Council, in declaring transubstantiation true doctrine, did not include Aristotelian definitions of substance and accident.[11] In other words, the Council did not declare Aristotle infallible—and a good thing, too, since many philosophers no longer accept Aristotle's metaphysics (or the physics on which it is based).

Another disadvantage of Thomas's method is that many of the faithful do not understand it. I have tested this on intelligent Catholics, who often have the foggiest (if any) notion of what transubstantiation means. I do not recall a single sermon preached in a Catholic church to explain the term, even after the term has been repeatedly used. That does not mean that the concept has not indirectly affected church life. For one thing, declaring that the substance of bread has totally disappeared, never to reappear, leads to a fetishizing of the Host. Since there is no bread left in the Host, it is all and only the body of Jesus—in each of its parts (ST 3.76 a3).

Once consecrated, so long as it does not decompose naturally, the Host cannot be de-consecrated. The priest has a formula for bringing the body of Christ down on the altar. He does not have a formula for sending it back to heaven. He is like the sorcerer's apprentice, who cannot undo his spell. If he is in a place without a tabernacle (say a field altar for an army congregation) and he consecrates more Hosts than the community consumes, he must eat them all himself.

The un-de-consecratable Host, which is entirely and nothing else but the body and blood of Christ, poses again the fallen-crumbs problem, but this time in an embarrassingly complicated way. Thomas himself spells out all the ramifications of this problem. What, for instance, if the priest is sick and vomits the Host and/or the blood right after taking them into his mouth? Or what if a fly or spider drops into the chalice after its substance has been changed? Or what if a poisonous insect falls there, or a priest's enemy puts poison in the wine? Do the accidents of poison carry over with the accidents of the wine? Or is poison itself a substance? What if a mouse nibbles on a consecrated Host, unaware that it is eating God? These are the literal examples Thomas gives in his deadpan way (ST 3.83 a6 ad3 ad7).

Thomas's solutions to these problems are given in some detail. If a fly is in the consecrated cup, one must capture it daintily (*caute*), wash it thoroughly (*diligenter*), burn it, then put the ashes and the water used for washing it inside the tabernacle. Who knew that fly washing would turn out to be a priestly skill? If there is poison in the cup, the blood must be poured into a closed vessel and deposited in the tabernacle. It may be poisoned, but it is still the blood of Christ. It cannot be thrown away since it is still, in substance, the blood of Christ, even if wine's accidents are joined with the substance of poison. If the accidents of bread and wine are visible in a priest's vomit, they must be burnt and the ashes buried under the altar. This part of an altar was called a tomb (*sepulchrum*) for reburying Christ.[12] What a mouse has eaten from a Host will presumably be disintegrated in its system, just as in a human recipient's. The un-nibbled part of a Host, if the priest cannot consume it, should be burnt and the ashes buried under the altar, because "so long as the accidents are still there, the body of Christ is still there" (ST 3.83 a6).

Thomas was forced to go to such lengths in caring for damaged Hosts because alternatives to transubstantiation were condemned by the church. One such alternative was offered in the ninth century by Ratramnus of Corbie, who said that Jesus was present in the Eucharist only symbolically (*in figura*), not physically. Ratramnus was rebuked by his superior, Paschasius Radbertus, who insisted on the real presence of Jesus in the Eucharist—which made Ratramnus's student Gottschalk of Orbais claim Paschasius was advocating cannibalism.[13] The view of Paschasius was the dominating one for the next two centuries.

But then, in the eleventh century, the charismatic and ascetical Berengar of Tours renewed in a more sophisticated way what Ratramnus had argued for, that the Eucharist is Christ *in figura* (in symbol). Relying on Augustine's philosophy of the sign, Berengar said that a sign does not stand alone. It has to have a signifier and a recipient of the sign. The whole system cannot function without this transaction. For him, the Eucharist was a dynamic system, in which the riches of salvation were offered to those with the faith to receive it.[14] Lanfranc of Bec worked energetically less to refute Berengar than to haul him before various church tribunals. Berengar was condemned by the Synods of Vercelli and of Rome. He was forced to burn his own books, though he kept reasserting his condemned views.[15]

Guibert of Nogent ventured into Berengar's dangerous territory until he ducked for cover.[16] He began from a theological conundrum of his time: Did Judas receive the Eucharist at the Last Supper? Many thought a damned soul could not carry the Savior within him.[17] Guibert concluded that the sacrament was invalid unless it is received with faith. So if a dog or a mouse consumed a Host, it remained mere bread: "If it burns or decays or is chewed or licked, such glory withdraws, having suffered no misfortune."[18]

This view ran up against a long-standing dogma of the church. When Donatists claimed that a sinful bishop could not validly baptize, or ordain priests, or consecrate the Eucharist, Augustine answered that an intent to perform the sacrament, along with the proper words and actions, was enough to guarantee the effect. The maxim enforced afterward was that sacraments are validly performed *ex opere operato, non ex opere operantis*— "from the work done, not from the worker doing it." Berengar and Guibert would say that faith was necessary not only for the one performing the Eucharist but for the one receiving it. They reversed and expanded the old adage, saying the effect was, indeed, *ex opere operantis, sed etiam ex opere recipientis*—validated from the worker doing it *as well as* from the one it was being done for. Guibert understandably anticipated, and ducked out from under, condemnation by the church.

So Thomas was trapped into searching out every fragment or droplet of the body of Christ, once its substance lodged under the accidents of bread and wine. The consecration stood irreversible in every particle of the no-longer-bread and no-longer-wine. The miracle was performed, even outside the transaction of the Mass or the interaction of worshipers, as if by a magic power. That is why legends could be told in my school days of a priest going into a bread shop and changing it all with the abracadabra *Hoc est enim corpus meum*. Caroline Walker Bynum notes that the miracle of transubstantiation standing on its own led to devotions and worship of the Host apart from the Mass.

Emphasis focused on the elevation of the newly consecrated Host in the priest's hands, even more than the moment of consecration or distribution of it.

> The new emphasis on "seeing" God is reflected in the increasing number of miracles connected with elevation [of the Host] rather than reception. In orders (e.g., Franciscan nuns or tertiaries) where communion was infrequent, ecstasies tended to come at the elevation.[19]

It is indicative that Pope John Paul II, in his long encyclical on the Eucharist, wrote: "The gaze of the Church is constantly turned to her Lord, present in the Sacrament of the Altar, in which she discovers the full manifestation of his boundless love."[20]

The cult of the Host as an object of worship was celebrated in Raphael's Vatican fresco of the *Disputa* (Argument for the Eucharist), where the center of the picture is a little Host inside a monstrance lifting it high above the altar. The crowd of onlookers distributed throughout the foreground, buttressed with massive books they have studied, directs all eyes or hands toward the Host—and not toward the Trinity hovering in the upper half of the painting. God is present to the crowd, not as the glorified Son along with the Father and the Spirit, painted as endorsing the Eucharist, but only in the visible Host, this tiny thing at the center of the universe, all forces natural and supernatural radiating from it or bending back toward it, a glowing white thing outside the natural order, a kind of benevolent kryptonite. Pietro Redondi gives an excellent analysis of Raphael's painting and its deep significance:

> The observer's gaze cannot avoid concentrating on this transparent Host. The quiet "still life" seems to emit vibrations of its ineffable inner light. On it, in fact, converge from right and left the gazes of theologians, doctors of the Church, saints, prelates, popes, and the faithful— all convoked here to testify for us that the Eucharistic mystery is the focal point of faith.[21]

Even when the Host was not exposed in a monstrance, it was felt to be present within the altar tabernacle, its divinity signaled by a vigil lamp— not a sheltered matter of bread and wine but an abiding divine person to whom one "paid visits," worshiping, genuflecting, and praying to it. Alexander Nagel points out that, increasingly, from the fourteenth to the sixteenth century, the tabernacle became larger and more central to churches.[22] Part of this was a result of the Vatican Council's artistic reforms, though the tendency began even earlier. It was felt that altar frontals and altarpieces should be cleared away from the main altar, along with prized relics and the saints being honored in them, to make the focus on the repository of the Host.[23] Tabernacles became great centers for the eye, built higher and higher on the altar. Some were even suspended in the air, as in stories of the levitating Host.[24] The Host, as a separate object of worship, outside and apart from the Mass, had become the whole point of the faith. It was God among us.

NOTES

1. *The De Sacramento Altaris of William of Ockham*, edited by T. Bruce Birch (Lutheran Literary Board, 1930), parts I–III.
2. Ibid., part V.
3. Council of Trent, Thirteenth Session, Canon II.
4. *De Sacramento*, part IV.
5. Ibid., Introduction, pp. xxiii–xxvi.
6. *Enchiridion Symbolorum et Definitonum* 1641.
7. Archive of the Sacred Congregation, Series AD EE, folios 292–93. Reprinted in Pietro Redondi, *Galileo Heretic*, translated by Raymond Rosenthal (Princeton University Press, 1987), pp. 333–34.
8. Aristotle, *Metaphysics* 4.1025a14–33.
9. Occam said that some of these "accidents" are in fact substances (op. cit., parts XXXIII–XXXIV).
10. Caroline Walker Bynum, *Wonderful Blood: Theology and Practice in Late Medieval Northern Germany and Beyond* (University of Pennsylvania Press, 2007), pp. 88, 138.
11. Edward Schillebeeckx, *The Eucharist*, translated by N. D. Smith (Sheed and Ward, 1968), pp. 58–76, 102.
12. Bynum, *Wonderful Blood*, p. 96.
13. Jaroslav Pelikan, *The Christian Tradition: A History of the Development of Doctrine*, vol. 3, *The Growth of Medieval Theology (600–1300)* (University of Chicago Press, 1978), pp. 74–80; Rachel Fulton, *From Judgment to Passion: Devotion to Christ and the Virgin Mary, 800–1200* (Columbia University Press, 2002), pp. 11–14.
14. Pelikan, op. cit., pp. 186–202; Fulton, op. cit., pp. 118–40; H. Liebeschueltz, "Berengar of Tours," in *The Cambridge History of Later Greek and Early Medieval Philosophy*, edited by A. H. Armstrong (Cambridge University Press, 1967), pp. 600–607.
15. Pelikan, op. cit., p. 187; Fulton, op. cit., pp. 126, 129.
16. Jay Rubenstein, *Guibert of Nogent: Portrait of a Medieval Mind* (Routledge, 2002), pp. 133–71.
17. People quarreled over Matthew quoting Jesus (26.27) as saying, "Drink, all of you," and Mark (14.23) saying, "They all drank," though John (13.26–30), who does not have the Eucharistic institution, lets Judas slip out, perhaps before eating anything other than the crust (*psomion*) Jesus dipped in the dish with him.

18. Guibert of Nogent, *Monodies and On the Relics of Saints*, translated by Joseph McAlhany and Jay Rubenstein (Penguin Books, 2011), p. 236.

19. Caroline Walker Bynum, *Holy Feast and Holy Fast* (University of California Press, 1987), p. 328.

20. John Paul II, *Ecclesia de Eucharistia* (2003), par. 1.

21. Redondi, op. cit., pp. 203–6.

22. Alexander Nagel, *The Controversy of Renaissance Art* (University of Chicago Press, 2011), pp. 221–60.

23. Pelikan, op. cit., p. 184.

24. Nagel, op. cit., pp. 243, 258.

FIVE

Explaining the Miracle: Augustine

Transubstantiation defines the meaning of the Eucharist in official Catholic dogma. The Fourth Lateran Council (1215) declared:

> Jesus Christ is himself both priest and sacrifice, and his body and blood are really [*veraciter*] contained in the sacrament of the altar under the species of bread and wine, the bread being transubstantiated into the body and the wine into the blood by the power of God.[1]

The Council of Trent (1563) joined eleven pronouncements of excommunication to the formula of transubstantiation. The second of the eleven reads:

> If anyone saith that in the sacred and holy sacrament of the Eucharist, the substance of the bread and wine remains conjointly with the body and blood of our Lord Jesus Christ, and denieth that wonderful and singular conversion of the whole substance of the bread into the body and of the whole substance of the wine into the blood—the species only of the bread and wine remaining—which conversion indeed the Catholic Church most aptly calls transubstantiation, let him be anathema.[2]

In 2003, Pope John Paul II's encyclical *Ecclesia de Eucharistia* repeated the dogmatic definition:

> This sets forth once more the perennially valid teaching of the Council of Trent: "The consecration of the bread and wine effects the change of the whole substance of the bread into the substance of the body of Christ, our Lord, and of the whole substance of the wine into the

substance of his blood; and the holy Catholic Church has fittingly and properly called this change transubstantiation."[3]

That this dogma still holds in the church can be seen in the Vatican-approved *Catechism of the Catholic Church* (1994), which declares: *"By the consecration the transubstantiation of the bread and wine into the Body and Blood of Christ is brought about"* (1413).

Not only is the dogma officially declared, but its most prominent articulator, Thomas Aquinas, has been made by many popes the official theologian of the church.[4] At the Council of Trent Thomas's *Summa Theologiae* was the only theological volume honored with a place on the altar alongside Holy Scripture.[5] Innocent VI said of Aquinas's teachings: "Those who hold to it are never found swerving from the path of truth, and he who dares assail it will be suspected of error."[6] Pius X and Pius XII prescribed Thomism for all seminaries.[7]

It is no wonder that Catholics generally accept the doctrine of transubstantiation as if there were no other view of the Eucharist. They would probably be surprised to hear that there is any other theory of the Eucharist—and no wonder: other theories have been repeatedly condemned, as were those of Berengar and Occam. But there has been a recurrent challenge to the official view, voiced softly or surreptitiously, that dates back to Augustine of Hippo. I mentioned earlier that Augustine did not believe in what is called "the real presence" of Jesus in the Eucharist, and quoted several places where he said that. Here is his most explicit claim that what is changed in the Mass is not the bread given out but the believers receiving it:

This bread makes clear how you should love your union with one another. Could the bread have been made from one grain, or were many grains of wheat required? Yet before they cohere as bread, each grain was isolated. They were fused in water, after being ground together. Unless wheat is pounded, and then moistened with water, it can hardly take on the new identity we call bread. In the same way, you had to be

ground and pounded by the ordeal of fasting and the mystery of exorcism in preparation for baptism's water, and in this way you were
watered in order to take on the new identity of bread. After that the
water of baptism moistened you into dough. But the dough does not
become bread until it is baked in fire. And what does fire represent for
you? It is the [post-baptism] anointing with oil. Oil, which feeds fire, is
the mystery of the Holy Spirit . . . The Holy Spirit comes to you, fire
after water, and you are baked into the bread which is Christ's body.
That is how your unity is symbolized.[8]

This Augustinian view of the Eucharist's real meaning did not die with
him, though the church made long efforts to dismiss it. In 1944, the French
Jesuit Henri de Lubac published a book, *Corpus Mysticum*, that traced a line
of theologians in the first Christian millennium who drew on Augustine to
provide a theory of the Eucharist opposed to transubstantiation.[9] Publishing the book was an act of spiritual courage to match the political courage
he was showing at the same time as an underground member of the French
resistance, opposing the Nazi regime of Vichy.[10] It went against the authori-
tative prounouncements making Aquinas the only approved expositor of
the Eucharist.

Many of the theologians de Lubac cited, like Berengar and Ratramnus,
had been repudiated by the church. Naturally, as a Jesuit theologian teaching at the Catholic University of Lyon, he had to tread very carefully, pointing out how the condemned teachers had sometimes stated their case in
flawed ways.[11] Six years passed before the Vatican pressured de Lubac's
Jesuit superiors to dismiss him from his faculty post, remove his book from
their houses, and forbid its dissemination elsewhere. De Lubac's fellow
theologian Hans Urs von Balthasar wrote of him:

He was deprived of permission to teach, expelled from Lyon and driven
from place to place. His books were banned, removed from the libraries
of the Society of Jesus, and impounded from the market . . . It was a
silent ostracism that drove the sensitive man into complete isolation.[12]

Perhaps Rome's delayed reaction was caused by the disturbances of the Second World War and its aftermath. More likely, the Vatican was waiting for Pope Pius XII to lay the groundwork for repression in his 1950 encyclical *Humani Generis*. De Lubac understandably called this papal document a lightning bolt, since he was its principal target. De Lubac received one notice from Rome saying:

> The corrections necessary for the publication of *Corpus Mysticum* cannot consist merely in the suppression or the modification of a few passages. Those passages that are the most open to criticism have extended ramifications in the author's development of the subject. The book would have to be profoundly changed in order for it to appear.[13]

After *Humani Generis*, directives for punishment were issued from Rome—silencing not only de Lubac, but Jean Daniélou, Yves Congar, Marie-Dominique Chenu, Karl Rahner, Teilhard de Chardin, John Courtney Murray, and other leading liberal thinkers.[14] Under Pope John XXIII these men emerged from the shadows to bask in the warmth of the Second Vatican Council, where they became leading lights.[15] Pope Paul VI even tried to make de Lubac a cardinal in 1976, but at the time one had first to be a bishop, and de Lubac revered too much the historic role of bishops as the leaders of dioceses to take a nominal episcopacy. In 1981, Pope John Paul II gave de Lubac a dispensation (the first) from the requirement of becoming a bishop, and made him a cardinal. (His fellow suppressed authors, Fathers Congar and Daniélou, also became cardinals after their reinstatement.)

Even during de Lubac's silencing (1950–1959), his book made its surreptitious way through the ranks of progressive theologians. He would later note that there was "a little black market" for it.[16] But after he was named an expert (*peritus*) for Vatican II by Pope John XXIII, many of his ideas permeated the proceedings—in, for instance, the definition of the church as "the people of God."[17] *Corpus Mysticum* was not only a brave book to be published under Pius XII. It was a stunningly original work of scholarship.

It went exhaustively through the writings of the fathers and early medieval theologians, showing how often they had recourse to Augustine and how pervasive was the early use of the term *Corpus Mysticum* to refer to the body of believers in conjunction with the Eucharist. These texts had mainly been forgotten, ignored, or misrepresented in favor of the official teaching on transubstantiation. De Lubac did not directly attack transubstantiation; he just subtly showed how much more ancient and better grounded was the view of the Eucharist-cum-church as a single *Corpus Mysticum*. Augustine himself had been distorted to make his views consistent with the official teaching.[18]

To show how thoroughly de Lubac turned the situation he first met upside down, we have to remember that in 1944 the normal view was that the Eucharist was the *Corpus Verum* (true body) of Christ and church members made up the *Corpus Mysticum* (a view Pius XII had proclaimed in an encyclical just a year before de Lubac's book appeared).[19] But de Lubac proved with ample testimony that the reverse had been the case for nearly a thousand years of the Christian tradition. The church was the physical and perceptible phenomenon, the first thing to come to mind when one said "the body of Christ," something Paul had established from the beginning (1 Cor 12.12–14). The Eucharist, by contrast, was the body of Christ as a sign addressed to believers, confirming what they *were*.[20]

The complete reversal of this relationship, making the Eucharist the true body and the church a weakened "mystical" body of Christ, made itself felt beginning in the eleventh century.[21] There was a reconfiguration of three entities: the glorified (risen) body of Christ in heaven, the earthly continuation of Christ in his body of believers, and the sacramental body in the Eucharist. The risen body and the Eucharist were increasingly identified with each other, and the ecclesial body more and more dissociated from them.[22] The relation went from this general figure

Risen Christ
Sacramental Christ–as–Church

to a new schema

> Risen Christ
> Eucharistic Christ apart from Church.[23]

The priest was now separated from believers by a rood screen. He faced away from his fellow Christians, spoke a language they did not understand, and addressed God in Christ's name, in a vertical relationship not truly shared by the congregation.[24] This broke the mutually strengthening bond between Eucharist and believers that de Lubac saw through the earlier days of the church. As he phrased it in a complete summary of his position:

> Since the body of the church takes its life from the Spirit, the communal body must literally be the body of Christ, to be celebrated as the body of the church, a church perfected as the body of Christ. But the Eucharist is the mysterious basis of this miracle, at work in a permanent way as its font forever springing up. Fed by the body and blood of the Savior, his believers are all steeped in one Spirit, so as to be one body. Literally, then, the Eucharist *creates* the church, creates its inner reality. By its secret working, the body's members achieve their unity with one another, making them even more the members of Christ, since their mutual union seals their union with their sole Head. This union of the Head with the entire body, the unity of Christ with his church—Himself the head, it the body—is more than what is generally referred to as "the church's body in itself," or even "Christ's body in itself." It makes up a true reality. It is what Alger of Liège [1055–1131] meant by "the complete body of Christ," the "inclusive body of Christ":
>
>> Since the sacrifice at the altar, by symbolizing the union of the church with Christ, is the sacrament of the inclusive body of Christ, Christ alone is not celebrated there but the inclusive Christ is celebrated. Therefore the Eucharist does not occur without the grace pervading the whole body of Christ.[25]

In de Lubac's book on Origen, published just before his silencing in 1950, he expanded his thoughts on the Eucharist.[26] To the triad, Risen Body–Church–Eucharist, Origen added a fourth embodiment of the Logos—the body of sacred writings. Just as the Logos became flesh in Jesus, it was incorporated in the church, in the Eucharist, and in the revelation of the Logos through Scripture. Augustine compared the "breaking of the bread" (Lk 24.30) in which the disciples recognized their Lord to the breaking open of the deep meanings in Scripture. De Lubac quotes Origen:

> Thus the bread is the Word of Christ, made from that wheat which, falling into good earth, has produced abundant fruit. For it is not this visible bread that he holds in his hands [at the Last Supper] that the divine Logos said was his body; but was the Word in the mystery of which this bread was to be broken. And it was not this visible beverage that he designated as his blood, but the Word in the mystery of which this beverage was to be shed. In fact, what else can the body or the blood of the divine Logos be but the Word that nourishes and the Word that rejoices the heart?[27]

For Origen, too, the church is the *Corpus Verum* of Christ, as opposed to the mystical incorporations of the Logos in Scripture and the Eucharist—because the last two are transitory, revelations along the church's way through time, but the church, perfected in heaven by completed union with its Head, will continue after time ends.[28] Since the Eucharist and believers and Scripture are all aspects of the same incorporation of the Logos, Origen anticipates the later claim that non-believers, those not recognizing the Word in Scripture, do not receive the body of Christ, even if given it in the Eucharist.[29]

The Second Vatican Council began to change the celebration of the Mass in response to the findings of de Lubac and Congar and the generally Augustinian understanding of what the Eucharist is.[30] This broke the vertical emphasis of the priest isolated at the altar speaking to God in Latin. It opened this esoteric rite horizontally out toward the people. The altar was turned around to let the priest communicate with his fellow members of the body of Christ. According to the Council document, *Sacrosanctum Concilium*, vernacular languages were permitted as well as Latin (54, 57). The laity were granted reception of the chalice as well as the Host (55). The same document decreed:

26. Liturgical services are not private functions, but are celebrations of *the church which is "the sacrament of unity"* [Cyprian, cited by de Lubac]— namely, the holy people united and organized under their bishops [no mention of priests]. (Emphasis added.)

48. The Church, therefore, spares no effort in trying to ensure that, when present at this mystery of faith, Christian believers should not be there as strangers or silent spectators. On the contrary, having a good grasp of it through the rites and prayers, they should take part in the sacred action, actively, fully aware, and devoutly.

37. Even in the liturgy, the church does not wish to impose a rigid uniformity in matters which do not affect the faith or the well-being of the entire community. Rather does it cultivate and foster the qualities and talents of the various races and nations. Anything in people's way of life which is not indissolubly bound up with superstition and error the church studies with sympathy and, if possible, preserves intact.

30. To develop active participation, the people should be encouraged to take part by means of acclamations, responses, psalms, antiphons, hymns, as well as by actions, gestures, and bodily attitudes.

It is not surprising that some people, accustomed to a silent and passive spectatorship of what they were told was a sealed mystery, should resent a hyperactive intrusion into their devotions. I can understand that. The nuns who taught me said that after communion one should kneel with eyes closed in private prayer. All that mattered was one's communication with the God inside oneself. One nun told me that when someone went straight out from communion to the street, still carrying God within, another person should race along beside him, holding a sanctuary light to signal the presence of a Host in that mobile shrine.

I grew up in those days of a kind of secret Mass. As a seminarian, I rose in time to serve as acolyte at a 6:30 Mass with no one attending but me and the priest, who was the famous Jesuit semiotician Walter Ong. He would come to a side altar in the darkened morning church while I was lighting the altar candles. We said nothing to each other but the Latin of the Mass, and then we wordlessly parted. Some people thought this was the ideal way to celebrate Mass. Not only were we not interrupted in our private devotion, but the more Masses said in such isolation, the more "sacrifices" offered for the souls of others, the greater piling up of graces would occur. It was such a waste to have many people attending only one Mass. That is why conservatives also opposed "concelebration" (two or more priests presiding at the same Mass).

William F. Buckley strenuously objected to the Vatican Council's emphasis on the Mass as a communal event: "I never thought of the Mass, when only I was present (and such things happened, every blue moon), as an incomplete experience for want of fellow worshipers."[31] He much preferred that kind of Mass to the one which thrust upon his attention the people of God, what he called

the fascistic static of the contemporary Mass, during which one is either attempting to sing or attempting to read the missal at one's own pace, which we must not do athwart the obtrusive rhythm of the priest or the commentator; or attempt to meditate on this or the other prayer or sentiment or analysis or exhortation in the Ordinary or in the Proper of the Mass, only to find such meditation is sheer outlawry, standing in the way, as it does, of the liturgical calisthenics devised by the Central Coach, who apparently judges it an act of neglect if the churchgoer is permitted more than two minutes and 46 seconds without being made to stand if he was kneeling, or kneel if he was standing, or sit—or sing—or chant—or anything if perchance he was praying, from which anarchism he must at all costs be rescued.[32]

The novelist Evelyn Waugh would also rather not see others at the Mass. He complained of an altar that people encircled: "If they raise their eyes they will be staring at one another. Backs are often distracting; faces will be more so."[33] Buckley, too, wanted to see the priest's back, not his face: "The priest was the executor of the transubstantiation. He stood, appropriately, with his back to the parishioners, the better to absorb himself in his divine mission."[34] Buckley especially resented "the handshake of peace" with one's fellow members of the body of Christ. This spread out to the laity what had been the formal "kiss of peace" exchanged by priests and deacons at High Mass. The new rite said that the congregation were celebrants of the Mass, not mere attendees.

De Lubac had said that the bonds within the body strengthened the bonds with its Head—this had been the original meaning of "communion," as in "the communion of saints" in the Creed.[35] Buckley was glad that Waugh was not submitted to the indignity of greeting his fellow members in Christ:

> I somewhere opined that Evelyn Waugh's death on Easter Sunday in 1966, the Sunday before the reformers promulgated the Kiss of Peace, was evidence that the Holy Spirit was in fact behind it all, but merciful in His afflictions: no imagination is so vivid as to visualize Mr. Waugh yanked from prayerful thought to clasp the hand of the pilgrim to his right, to his left, ahead, and behind him.[36]

The rudeness of forcing Waugh to acknowledge not one or two of his company but at least four (those ahead and behind him as well as to either side) was an affront to Buckley's sensibilities.

One might think this discomfiture at having community forced upon the individual is a tic of certain prickly people like Waugh or Buckley. But a resistance to the communalizing of the Mass had a more weighty expression in the words of Pope Benedict XVI when he was still Cardinal Ratzinger. What Buckley called fascistic, Joseph Ratzinger called democratic or communalist—almost as denigrative in the papal vocabulary. He criticized "assigning all kinds of liturgical functions to different individuals and entrusting the 'creative' planning of the liturgy to groups of people who like to, and are supposed to, 'make their own contribution.'"[37] The cardinal liked the old silence, along with the old Latin, and having the priest facing away from the congregation. To have him face those present with him gives the mistaken notion that the Mass is a meal.

> The Eucharist that Christians celebrate really cannot adequately be described by the term "meal." True, the Lord established the new reality of Christian worship within the framework of a Jewish Passover meal, but it was precisely this new reality, not the meal as such, that he commanded us to repeat. Very soon the new reality was separated from its ancient context and found its proper and suitable form . . . This new and all-encompassing form of worship could not be derived simply from the meal.[38]

The authority of a cardinal was not the only one to be marshaled in favor of the objectified Eucharist. Even the pope who presided over the later sessions of the Second Vatican Council, Paul VI, felt that the Host should be treated as an object, not a means for the body of Christ to communicate with itself in all its members. In his encyclical on the Mass, *Mysterium Fidei* (1965), Paul wrote:

> The Catholic Church has always displayed and still displays the *latria* [worship of God] that ought to be paid to the Sacrament of the Eucharist, both during Mass and outside of it, by taking the greatest possible care of consecrated Hosts, by exposing them to the solemn veneration of the faithful, and by carrying them about in processions to the joy of great numbers of people . . . In fact, the faithful regarded themselves as guilty, and rightly so as Origen recalls, if, after they had received the Body of the Lord and kept it with all reverence and caution, some of it were to fall to the ground through negligence.[39]

Paul VI also attacked the idea that a priest's solitary Mass is less meaningful than one said with a congregation present:

> For each and every Mass is not something private, even if a priest celebrates it privately . . . There is no reason to criticize but rather only to approve a Mass that a priest celebrates privately . . . For such a Mass brings a rich and abundant treasure of special graces to help the priest himself, the faithful, the whole Church and the whole world toward salvation—and this same abundance of graces is not gained through mere reception of Holy Communion.[40]

The laity, you see, is capable of "mere reception" of the Eucharist. It is the priest alone who pours out endless graces by consecrating the species.

The fact that Benedict XVI has encouraged a return to the Latin Mass shows that church officials have not abandoned the Thomistic understanding of the Eucharist, even after Vatican II moved toward Augustinian views. The popes insist that the Mass is not a meal because it is a sacrifice: "Just as Moses made the Old Testament sacred with the blood of calves, so too Christ the Lord took the New Testament, of which He is the Mediator, and made it sacred through His own blood."[41] This belief in the sacrifice of the Mass as a fulfillment of animal sacrifices in the Old Testament is derived mainly from the Letter to Hebrews, which treated Jesus as a priest "in the line of Melchizedek," offering himself as an animal sacrifice. It is time to start investigating that odd claim.

NOTES

1. Fourth Lateran Council, Canon I.
2. *The Canons and Decrees of the Sacred and Œcumenical Council of Trent*, edited and translated by J. Waterworth (Dolman, 1848), Thirteenth Session, pp. 75–91.
3. John Paul II, *Ecclesia de Eucharistia* (2003), par. 15.
4. Leo XIII, *Aeterni Patris* (1879), par. 21.

5. Leo XIII (ibid.) listed the papal endorsements up to his time—by Clement VI (bull *In Ordine*), Nicholas V (address to Dominicans), Benedict XIII (bull *Pretiosus*), Pius V (bull *Mirabilis*), Clement XII (bull *Verbo Dei*), Urban V (brief to University of Toulouse), Innocent XII (brief to University of Louvain), Benedict XIV (brief to Dionysian College in Granada). Since then one should add Pius XII (*Humani Generis*, 1950, par. 31). Leo described Thomas this way:

> With his spirit at once humble and swift, his memory ready and tenacious, his life spotless throughout, a lover of truth for its own sake, richly endowed with human and divine science, like the sun he heated the world with the warmth of his virtues and filled it with the splendor of his teaching. Philosophy has no part which he did not touch finely at once and thoroughly . . . Reason, borne on the wings of Thomas to its human height, can scarcely rise higher. (*Aeterni Patris*, par. 17–18)

6. Innocent VI, Sermon on Saint Thomas.
7. Pius X, *Pascendi Dominici Gregis* (1907), par. 45; Pius XII, *Humani Generis* (1950), par. 31.
8. Augustine, Sermon 227.
9. Henri de Lubac, *Corpus Mysticum: L'Eucharistie et l'église au moyen âge; étude historique* (Aubier, 1944). The English translation by Gemma Simmonds, C.J., edited by Richard Price and Christopher Stephens (University of Notre Dame Press, 1949), is of the revised 1949 edition, and it omits citations from Greek and Latin in the footnotes. I cite page numbers from the 1944 original.
10. While in hiding de Lubac and others published the underground opposition paper *Témoignage Chrétien*. Some of those involved were captured and executed.
11. Berengar, for instance, is said to have manifested "an emphaticness [*insistance*] and a troubling univocalness" (De Lubac, *Corpus Mysticum*, p. 165).
12. Hans Urs von Balthasar, *The Theology of Henri de Lubac*, translated by Joseph Fessio, S.J., and Michael M. Waldstein (Ignatius Press, 1991), pp. 17–18. De Lubac's account of his days on the run from Vichy agents is at pages 53–54 of *At the Service of the Church: Henri de Lubac Reflects on the Circumstances That Occasioned His Writings*, translated by Anne Elizabeth Englund (Ignatius Press, 1993).
13. De Lubac, *At the Service*, p. 74.
14. John W. O'Malley, *What Happened at Vatican II* (Harvard University Press, 2008), pp. 86–88.
15. Ibid., pp. 118–22.
16. De Lubac, *At the Service*, p. 74. He was not formally notified that he could teach again until June 1959 (ibid., p. 91). As late as 1965, he reminded a surprised member of the Holy Office that *Corpus Mysticum* was still listed as banned by his Congregation (ibid., p. 303).

17. Vatican II, *Lumen Gentium*, chapter 2, par. 9. In the early draft of the document on the church, its members were called the "subjects" (*subditi*) of church rulers. "The strong horizontal line implicit in 'People of God,' with its stress on the fundamental equality of all members of the church, replaced the strong vertical line of ruler-subject" (O'Malley, op. cit., p. 174).

18. De Lubac, *Corpus Mysticum*, pp. 254–57, 292–96. It was even asserted that Augustine believed in "the real presence" but could not clearly assert it because of the *disciplina arcani* keeping the secrets of the faith from outsiders (p. 292).

19. Pius XII, *Mystici Corporis Christi* (1943).

20. De Lubac, *Corpus Mysticum*, pp. 9–23.

21. Ibid., pp. 118–27.

22. Ibid., pp. 133–35.

23. Ibid., p. 294.

24. By a ludicrous choice, the Notre Dame Press translation of *Corpus Mysticum* has on its cover a vivid picture of a Mass celebrant with his back to the nave of the church, lifting the Host to God in a strongly vertical gesture. There could not be a more emphatic rejection of the meaning of the book inside the cover.

25. De Lubac, *Corpus Mysticum*, pp. 102–3. My translation. Sister Simmonds sometimes transliterates more than translates, as here, where she renders "celebrate the sacrament" (*conficere sacramentum*) as "confect the sacrament."

26. Henri de Lubac, *Histoire et esprit: L'intelligence de l'écriture d'après Origène* (Éditions Montaigne, 1950). Translation by Anne Englund Nash, *History and Spirit: The Understanding of Scripture According to Origen* (Ignatius Press, 2007).

27. De Lubac, *History and Spirit*, p. 410 (Origen, *Commentary on the Gospel of Matthew* 85).

28. Ibid., p. 425.

29. Ibid., p. 420.

30. I cite the Council documents from Austin Flannery, O.P., *Vatican Council II, the Basic Sixteen Documents: Constitutions, Decrees, Declarations* (Costello Publishing Company, 2007).

31. William F. Buckley, Jr., *Nearer, My God: An Autobiography of Faith* (Doubleday, 1997), p. 104.

32. Ibid., p. 98.

33. Evelyn Waugh, "The Same Again Please: A Layman's Hopes of the Vatican Council," *National Review*, December 4, 1962.

34. Buckley, op. cit., p. 104.

35. De Lubac, *Corpus Mysticum*, pp. 23–27.

36. Buckley, op. cit., p. 104.

37. Joseph Ratzinger, *The Spirit of the Liturgy* (Ignatius Press, 2000), p. 80.

38. Ibid., p. 78.

39. Paul VI, *Mysterium Fidei* (1965), par. 56, 58.

40. Ibid., par. 32.

41. Ibid., par. 28.

II

Jesus the Non-Priest

SIX

Killer Priests

Jesus was a radical Jewish prophet. And like many Jewish prophets, he was against the Jewish ruling structures of his time. Not all prophets, admittedly, opposed the reigning authority—there were some "court prophets" and "Temple prophets" who supported the Jewish monarchy and (later) ritual administrators like the priests.[1] But "the classical prophets," as they are called, were normally harsh critics of ritual that was only ritual. That is what prophecy meant, then—not predicting the future, as the word has come to be understood subsequently. Prophets were originally God's messengers, called to rebuke those who were forgetting or defying his commands, deserting his Pact (Covenant) with his people. Sometimes this involved warnings about the consequences of deserting the Lord— which is why they came, simplistically, to be considered as predictors of doom.

In the treaty terms we call the Ten Commandments, the Jewish people recognized Yahweh's sovereignty, and he in return promised his protection if the people kept their side of the Pact. When they did not do that, he let them know that the treaty was broken and his protection could be withdrawn. His instrument for informing the people of this was a long line of prophets carrying his message. The remedy for what Abraham Heschel called the "absolutizing of the Law and its cult" was a prophet's call back to the intent and spirit of the Law: "The prophets disparaged the [Temple] cult when it became a substitute for righteousness."[2] Ritual can become mechanical, a matter of rote repetition, until life is breathed back into it with the fresh urgencies of the prophet. That is why the revelation of God's will was twofold, given in "the Law *and the prophets*."

The Law was beneficial but static. The prophets gave it new life in a dynamic series of pointed, provocative messages. Bruce Vawter writes of the prophetic role:

> When the prophets condemned the priesthood, as they often did, it was not for what the priests were teaching but rather for what they were not; they had rejected knowledge and had ignored the law of God . . . Certain of the prophets would have had at best a minimal interest in the Israelite liturgy,[3] which does not necessarily mean that they made a fetish of opposing rites the observance of which had become a fetish for others . . . The prophetic attitude to the cult was like the prophetic attitude to everything—one in which forms were always secondary to the realities they signified. It was only when forms no longer signified anything that he [the prophet] demanded condemnation.[4]

The office of prophet was, paradoxically, both institutionalized and spontaneous. The credentials of the prophet had to be established from moment to moment. They rested on the authenticity of concern for God and for his people, for justice and for the poor. They could also depend on literary power and on dramatic enactment. This extraordinary kind of authority was bound to run into difficulties with the established powers. It fit Max Weber's thesis on charismatic power vs. institutional power: "We shall understand prophet to mean a purely individual bearer of charisma, who by virtue of his mission proclaims a religious doctrine or divine commandment."[5] Joseph Blenkinsopp develops this Weberian notion:

> Weber located prophecy in the context of charismatic authority and defined the prophet as "a purely individual bearer of charisma." This was taken to imply that the prophetic-charismatic figure is legitimated not by virtue of a socially acknowledged office like the priesthood, but solely through extraordinary personal qualities. The prophet is therefore neither designated by a predecessor nor ordained, nor installed in office, but *called*. The claims staked by the prophet, or on the prophet's behalf by others, would tend inevitably to set him (less commonly her)

in opposition to dominant elites dedicated to preserving the status quo. This kind of prophecy would therefore, according to Weber, play a destabilizing rather than a corroborative role in society.[6]

Weber and Blenkinsopp compare Israelite prophets to seers and "ecstatics" in other cultures. But Abraham Heschel argues that this underestimates the unique quality of prophecy in Israel.

Prophetic incidents, revelatory moments, are believed to have happened to many people in many lands. But a line of prophets, stretching over many centuries, from Abraham to Moses, from Samuel to Nathan, from Elijah to Amos, from Hosea to Isaiah, from Jeremiah to Malachi, is a phenomenon for which there is no analogy . . . Where else was there a nation which was able to emulate the prophetic history of Israel? . . . Neither Lao-Tzu nor Buddha, neither Socrates nor Plotinus, neither Confucius nor [the Egyptian] Ipuwer spoke in the name of God or felt themselves as sent by Him; and the priests and prophets of pagan religions spoke in the name of a particular spirit, not in the name of the Creator of heaven and earth.[7]

John Bright agrees with Heschel: "Regardless of its antecedents, the phenomenon of prophecy as it developed in Israel was unique, without a real parallel."[8]

The prophets put their message in visible metaphors, as when Jeremiah broke the clay vessel (Jer 19.7) or wore a yoke (Jer 27.2). Or when Habakkuk wrote his message on placards visible far off (Hab 2.1).[9] They engaged in what sixties radicals would call "street theater." Isaiah went "naked as a sign" of Egypt's fate (20.2–4). They could also put the humiliation of a rebellious people in vivid sexual terms, as when Jeremiah said that God was raping his own wife (13.26–27).[10] The image of the people's infidelity to their Pact with God was given its most vivid expression when Hosea was called to marry a whore, "for like a wanton this land is unfaithful to the Lord" (1.2). Jesus, too, acted out his radical message—by healing or feeding on the Sabbath, by writing on the ground to ignore the crowd calling for a prostitute's death, by cursing the fig tree, or by weaving a lash and driving money changers from the Temple. This last action, which prevented the carrying of money to pay for the animals to be sacrificed, suspended for a time the very possibility of performing the sacrifices at the center of Temple worship.

The prophets had a tradition of saying that sacrifice without moral reform is an empty gesture. This often put them at odds with the Temple and its ministers. When Jeremiah was banished from the Temple for predicting its demise, he had to have his disciple Baruch read his message in the sacred precinct.[11] Here, for instance, is Amos:

> I will not delight in your sacred ceremonies.
> When you present your sacrifice and offerings
>   I will not accept them,
>   nor look on the buffaloes of your shared-offerings.
>   Spare me the sound of your songs;
>   I cannot endure the music of your lutes.
>   Let justice roll on like a river
>   and righteousness like an ever-flowing stream. (5.21–24)

Or Hosea:

> Therefore have I lashed you through the prophets
>   and torn you to shreds with my words;
>   loyalty is my desire, not sacrifice,
>   not whole-offerings but the knowledge of God. (6.5–6)

Or Isaiah:

> Your countless sacrifices, what are they to me?
>   says the Lord.
>   I am sated with whole-offerings of rams
>   and the fat of buffaloes;

I have no desire for the blood of bulls,
   of sheep and of he-goats.
Whenever you come to enter my presence—
who asked you for this?
No more shall you trample my courts.
   The offer of your gifts is useless,
the reek of sacrifice is abhorrent to me.
New moons and sabbaths and assemblies,
sacred seasons and ceremonies, I cannot endure.
I cannot tolerate your new moons and your festivals;
   they have become a burden to me,
      and I can put up with them no longer.
      When you lift your hands outspread in prayer,
I will hide my eyes from you.
Though you offer countless prayers,
   I will not listen.
There is blood on your hands;
   wash yourselves and be clean.
Put away the evil of your deeds,
   away out of my sight.
Cease to do evil and learn to do right,
pursue justice and champion the oppressed;
give the orphan his rights, plead the widow's cause. (1.11–17)

Or Micah:

Am I to approach him with whole-offerings of yearling calves?
   Will the Lord accept thousands of rams,
      or ten thousand rivers of oil?
   Shall I offer my eldest son for my own wrongdoing,
      my children for my own sin?
God has told you what is good;
   and what is it that the Lord asks of you?
   Only to act justly, to love loyalty,
   to walk wisely before your God. (6.6–8)

Or Psalm 50 (12–14):

> If I were hungry, I would not tell you,
> for the world and all that is in it are mine.
> > Shall I eat the flesh of your bulls
> > or drink the blood of he-goats?
> Offer to God the sacrifice of thanksgiving
> and pay your vows to the Most High.

Or Jeremiah:

> What good is it to me if frankincense is brought from Sheba and fragrant spices from distant lands? I will not accept your whole-offerings, your sacrifices do not please me. (6.20)

No one could be more scathing against the religious establishment of the Jews than another Jew, the prophet Malachi:

> If I am a master, where is the fear due to me? So says the Lord of Hosts to you, you priests, who despise my name . . . I will accept no offering from you . . . And now, you priests, this decree is for you: if you will not listen to me and pay heed to the honoring of my name, says the Lord of Hosts, then I will lay a curse upon you. I will turn your blessings into a curse; yes, into a curse, because you pay no heed. I will cut off your arm, fling offal in your faces, the offal of your pilgrim-feasts, and I will banish you from my presence. (1.6, 10, 2.1–3)

Jesus was acting in the prophetic tradition when he cleansed the Temple, driving out the money changers. The weaving of a lash recalls God's "lashing" of priests through the prophets at Hosea 6.5. And his words, "My house shall be called a house of prayer, but you are making it a robbers' cave" (Mt 21.13) recall Jeremiah (7.11), "Do you think that this house, this house which bears my name, is a robbers' cave?"

The prophets attacked those who used power against the poor. As Isaiah said (10.1–2):

Shame on you! you who make unjust laws
and publish burdensome decrees,
depriving the poor of justice . . .

The prophets, as a menace to those in power, were regularly treated as troublemakers. They were threatened, called crazy, driven away, isolated, or murdered. Amos was banished (7.11). Priests called for the death of Jeremiah (Jer 26.11). Elijah says: "The people of Israel have forsaken thy covenant, torn down thy altars and put thy prophets to death with the sword. I alone am left, and they seek to take my life" (1 Kings 19.10). Jeremiah spoke the same way: "'Come, let us decide what to do with Jeremiah,' men say. '. . . Let us invent some charges against him; let us pay no attention to his message' . . . Well thou knowest, O Lord, all their murderous plots against me" (18.18, 23).

Jesus suffered the fate of other prophets. His own family thought him crazy (Mk 3.21). Men called him a bastard (Jn 8.4–1), unclean (Lk 11.38), a glutton (Lk 7.34), a devil (Jn 7.20). They tried to throw him off a cliff (Lk 4.29) or stone him (Jn 8.59). Men schemed to get him into trouble with the Roman authorities by criticizing the taxes paid to them. They tried to get him into trouble with religious authorities by criticizing the death penalty or divorce as prescribed by the Law. King Herod plotted to kill Jesus, just as he had killed the Baptist (Mk 3.6).

As Jesus traveled through Galilee and Palestine, he was constantly harried. His foes used the Law to oppose his acts of healing and helping the poor. Jesus could say with the prophet, "You have turned into venom the process of law and justice itself into poison" (Amos 6.12). In Matthew's Gospel Jesus says such leaders are descended from the men who killed prophets:

"Alas for you, Scribes and Pharisees, you hypocrites, who raise tomb monuments for the prophets and adorn their memorials, protesting that 'If we were living in the prophets' times we would have had no part in shedding their blood'—which is a confession that you are the descendants of the prophet-killers. Complete their record . . . Take note that I send more prophets and sages and Scribes. Some of them you will kill, some crucify, some scourge in your gatherings, and others chase from city to city, so that the guilt of all the just men's blood shed on earth belongs to you, from the blood of the just Abel to that of the just Zachary the son of Barach, whom you murdered between the sanctuary and the altar . . . O Jerusalem, Jerusalem, you who murder the prophets and stone the emissaries sent you, how often I yearned to gather your children to me, as a hen gathers its brood within her wings, but you would have none of it." (23.29–37)

Luke, in the Acts of the Apostles, gives us the fulfillment of what Jesus was saying about those who murdered prophets. He describes the first Christian martyr, Stephen, accusing his executioners: "Which of the prophets did not your fathers persecute?" (Ac 7.52).

In the Gospels, opposition to Jesus the prophet came from four sources—all of them conceiving themselves as upholders of the Law of Yahweh: Sadducees, Pharisees, Scribes, and Priests.

1. The *Sadducees*, who claimed descent from the priest Zadok, were aristocrats, according to Josephus.[12] By the time of Jesus, the Sadducees had become comparatively secular and were in "sympathy with the foreign occupying power."[13] The Synoptic Gospels claim that Sadducees denied that there is life after death (Mt 22.23, Mk 12.18, Lk 20.27). Despite disagreements in their past, the secular Sadducees joined the religious Pharisees in testing Jesus (Mt 16.1), who warned his Followers against "the leaven of the Pharisees and Sadducees" (Mt 16.6). The Acts of the Apostles treats the Sadducees as allies of the chief priests (4.1, 5.17). They were a conservative force worried about troublemakers like Jesus.

2. The *Pharisees*, or "the Separated," were adherents of the strictest readings of the Law, as that was defined in continual oral refinements.[14] Raymond Brown writes of them:

The Pharisees began as a liberalizing movement which, through appeal to oral tradition, sought to make contemporary the real thrust of the written Law of Moses. The problem in [the Gospel of] Matthew's eyes (and here he may reflect Jesus) was that this oral interpretation had now become as rigid as the written tradition, and was at times counterproductive. The Jesus who says, over and over, "You have heard it said, but I say to you" (Mt. 5.21, 27, 31, 33, 38, 43) is, then, preserving the purpose of the Law by making certain that past contemporization of God's will is not treated as if it were exhaustive of that will.[15]

Since pride in their lore made the Pharisees even more demanding than the Law, they kept up a running criticism of Jesus for boundary-crossing relations with the "unclean," whether lepers, the insane, the possessed, a menstruating woman, prostitutes, tax gatherers, or Samaritans. They also thought he was not sufficiently observant of the Sabbath or of fasts. They collaborated with Herod's scheme to kill Jesus (Mk 3.6).

The Pharisees are threatened by Jesus' teachings and reject him because none of the authorities (*archontes*) or Pharisees have believed in him, and the people who have do not know the Law (Jn 7.48–49). Only once do the Pharisees directly debate with Jesus (Jn 8.13–20); usually they maintain a superior position based on social recognition of their learning, their influence with the people, and their political power in conjunction with the chief priests—and so they refuse to treat Jesus as an equal.[16]

3. The *Scribes* were scholars, lawyers, secretaries, or assistants to the priests. Scribes were praised in the Wisdom Literature (Sirach 39.1–11) for use of all their time in studying the Law and the prophets.[17] Raymond Brown and other scholars think that the author of Matthew may have been a Scribe, as one sees by his meticulous compiling of cognate bits of information and his careful citation of Scripture.[18] But the Scribes who mainly dealt with Jesus seem to have become middle-level officials "mainly in or

from Jerusalem" who were useful to others in power, and are linked with them as assistants, as in the formula "scribes and Pharisees."[19]

4. The *Priests* were the men most dangerous to Jesus. They had the greatest stake in what he was saying about God's justice for the poor. They had the religious establishment to protect from the Roman imperial overlords. They had to contain any challenge to the status quo, to preserve their own standing with Roman officials, as the spokesmen for allowed religion. Jesus, by questioning their authority, could upset the delicate balancing act they performed from moment to moment. They had to convince the Roman rulers that Jesus had no overwhelming popular support or political meaning or religious authority, but was nonetheless a threat to the stability of imperial relations. For years the Pharisees, Sadducees, and Scribes stalked Jesus, discredited him, threatened and harassed him from Galilee to Jerusalem. But when it came time to close in for the kill, they turned the dirty work over to the priests. The priests are the ones who bribe Judas (Mk 14.10–11), who lend Temple police to the arrest of Jesus (Jn 18.3), who make sure that the "high priests, elders, and scholars of the Law" condemn him (Mk 14.53), and who manipulate Pontius Pilate into doing what they had no more authority to do—to execute a criminal (Jn 18.31). "Christ, who inherited the religion and ethic of the prophets, was betrayed by the institutional church in much the same way as the prophets had been betrayed by the ritualistic-legalistic system of early Judaism."[20]

To say that the priests killed Jesus is not to say, with anti-Semites down through the ages, that "the Jews" killed him. The priests are the culpable ones, and if there is any curse upon them, it is the one Malachi called down on priests who betrayed their Covenant with the Lord. How can saying that Jesus suffered the fate of Jeremiah and other prophets be anti-Semitic? This is part of a story that was old and familiar in Jesus' time—once again, Jewish authorities were killing a Jewish prophet. The "Jewish people" as a whole had no part in the transaction, nor had they ever been guilty when prophets met their fate. The priests killed Jesus. That is what they do. They kill the prophets.

NOTES

1. John Bright, *Jeremiah* (Doubleday, 1965), pp. xx–xxi; Bruce Vawter, "Introduction to the Prophetic Literature," NJ, p. 189; Joseph Blenkinsopp, *A History of Prophecy in Israel*, revised and enlarged (Westminster John Knox Press, 1983), pp. 3, 15, 17.

2. Abraham J. Heschel, *The Prophets* (Harper & Row, 1962), p. 250.

3. Cf. Carroll Stuhlmueller, "Deutero-Isaiah and Trito-Isaiah," NJ, p. 345: "Deutero-Isaiah was indifferent to Temple and cult."

4. Vawter, op. cit., pp. 192–93.

5. Max Weber, *The Sociology of Religion*, translated by Ephraim Fischoff (Beacon Press, 1963), p. 46.

6. Blenkinsopp, op. cit., p. 35.

7. Heschel, op. cit., pp. 604–5.

8. Bright, op. cit., p. xix.

9. Blenkinsopp, op. cit., p. 127.

10. Kathleen M. O'Connor, "Reclaiming Jeremiah's Violence," in *The Aesthetics of Violence in the Prophets*, edited by Julia M. O'Brien and Chris Franke (T & T Clark, 2010), pp. 37–49.

11. Blenkinsopp, op. cit., p. 133.

12. Josephus, *Antiquities* 18.16; Gary G. Parton, "Sadducees," ABD, vol. 5, pp. 892–95. Zadok was the high priest under David and Solomon, and those claiming descent from him were sometimes rivals with, sometimes members of, the priestly Levitical line. Cf. William H. C. Propp, *Exodus 19–40* (Doubleday, 2006), pp. 567–74; Jean J. Castelot and Aelred Cody, "Religious Institutions of Israel," NJ, pp. 1256–58; and Stanley E. Porter, "Zadok," ABD, vol. 6, pp. 1034–36.

13. Joseph A. Fitzmyer, "Jewish Movements in Palestine," NJ, pp. 1243–44.

14. Ibid., p. 1243.

15. Raymond E. Brown, *The Churches the Apostles Left Behind* (Paulist Press, 1984), p. 127.

16. Anthony J. Saldarini, "Pharisees," ABD, vol. 5, p. 298.

17. Alexander A. Di Lella, "Sirach," NJ, p. 507.

18. Brown, op. cit., p. 126.

19. Anthony J. Saldarini, "Scribes," ABD, vol. 5, pp. 1012–16.

20. Blenkinsopp, op. cit., p. 17, paraphrasing Julius Wellhausen.

SEVEN

The Melchizedek Myth

All through the New Testament, with only one exception, Jesus is not called a priest—and with good reason. He was a layman. Though he attended the Temple, as any Jewish layman would, he performed no priestly acts there; presided over nothing; did not enter the Holy of Holies; made no animal sacrifice. In fact, he suspended the sacrifices by denying money changers the ability to trade "unclean" Roman denarii (with their idolatrous images and inscriptions) for Jewish shekels, which alone could buy the sacrificial animals.

There was another reason why Jesus could not be a priest. Ancient priesthoods tended to be hereditary, coming from a sacred family. For the Jews of Jesus' time, this meant that priests came from Levi's family. Jesus, who was from the tribe of Judah, did not qualify for priesthood, even if he had wanted it—which seems unlikely, given his frequent criticism of the priests and their deadly designs on him.

The great scholar Julius Wellhausen, in his influential *Prolegomena to the History of Israel* (1882), argued that priesthood was in fact a profession, not a tribal distinction, and that priests became, as it were, honorary Levites.[1] That may be true for the early history of the Israelites, but by the time of Jesus the claim of the Levites was established and assumed, as we see from the Letter to Hebrews itself. Rival claims, like those of the Zadokites, were subsumed under the scriptural authority given the Levites.

The Lord spoke to Moses and said, "Bring forward the tribe of Levi and appoint them to serve Aaron the priest and to minister to him. They shall be in attendance on him and on the whole community before the

Tent of the Presence, undertaking the service of the Tabernacle . . . To Aaron and his line you shall commit the priestly office and they shall perform its duties; any unqualified person who intrudes upon it shall be put to death. (Num 3.5–10)

The prophet Malachi, when he attacked corrupt priests, said they were dishonoring Yahweh's pact with Levi. "You have set at nought the covenant with the Levites, says the Lord of Hosts. So I, in my turn, have made you despicable and mean in the eyes of the people" (2.8–9).

The establishment of the Levites as priests for the whole community was connected with the episode of the Golden Calf during the exodus from Egypt. When Moses came down from Sinai and found the Israelites worshiping an idol (even Aaron had cooperated with them), he issued a call, and only the Levites responded:

He took his place at the gate of the camp and said, "Who is on the Lord's side? Come here to me"; and the Levites all rallied to him. He said to them, "These are the words of the Lord the God of Israel: 'Arm yourselves, each of you, with his sword. Go through the camp from gate to gate and back again. Each of you kill his brother, his friend, his neighbor.'" The Levites obeyed, and about three thousand of the people died that day. Moses then said, "Today you have consecrated yourselves to the Lord completely, because you have turned each against his own son and his own brother and so have this day brought a blessing upon yourselves." (Ex 32.26–29)

Thus dramatically separated from all other Israelites, the Levites seem to confirm what René Girard and others have written about society as founded on an episode of "sacred violence."[2] A revolt against the Levite monopoly on the priesthood was settled by Moses when he had each of the Twelve Tribes put a staff in the Shrine of the Ark overnight, and only Aaron's staff "sprouted, blossomed, and produced ripe almonds" (Num 17.1–8). The "rod of Aaron" was later kept in a favored spot inside the Temple.

How, then, could Jesus be a priest, without being a Levite? The Letter to Hebrews had to find a different lineage for him. It did this by appeal to a minor figure, Melchizedek, mentioned briefly only twice in Scripture, in Genesis and in the Psalms. Who was this Melchizedek? What do we know (or think we know) about him? And how reliable is that knowledge? To ask these questions will lead us, eventually, into thistle-tangles of myth and legend. But we can begin, simply, with the two first (slight) mentions of him in the Old Testament.

Genesis 14.18–20

Melchizedek is first brought up in three verses of Genesis, where he offers hospitality to Abraham as that patriarch returns from slaughtering the men who had stolen his nephew Lot's belongings. Lot had suffered while four kings, in alliance with Kedorlaomer of Elam, fought at Siddim with five kings from the Cities of the Plain (Gen 14.8–9). One of the five kings who were defeated at Siddim was Bera of Sodom, where Lot had settled. So the forces of Kedorlaomer seized Lot and his possessions, along with other flocks and herds belonging to King Bera. Abraham, coming back from the battle where he regained the captured men and property, stopped off at Sodom, where he was thankfully greeted by Bera (Gen 14.17).

But then, suddenly, before Bera and Abraham can have any conversation at all, King Melchizedek comes out from Salem to greet Abraham—and the king blesses Abraham, and receives a tithe from him (14.18–20). After this interruption, Bera is brought back to continue his meeting with Abraham. As Fred Horton says, "Genesis 14.18–20 represents an intrusion into the text of chapter 14 and has but the loosest connection with what precedes and what follows."[3]

If the story of Melchizedek is a sudden interpolation into the framework dealing with Abraham's rescue of Lot, that framework itself is an addition to the text of Genesis. According to many scholars, the entirety of chapter 14 shows no sign of being the work of the prime sources for Genesis—the J (Yahweh), W (Elohim), or P (Priestly) strands. Moreover:

Genesis xiv stands alone among all the accounts in the Pentateuch, if not indeed in the Bible as a whole. The setting is international, the approach impersonal, and the narration notable for its unusual style and vocabulary. There is still much about this chapter that is open to wide differences of opinion. On one point, however, the critics are virtually unanimous: the familiar touches of the established sources of Genesis are absent in this instance. For all these reasons, the chapter has to be ascribed to an isolated source.[4]

If the whole chapter is from a foreign source, that helps explain certain things about the Melchizedek insertion, as that he is a priest without the normal (for Hebrews) priestly lineage—indeed without any of the regular familial identifiers ("X son of Y"). To quote the great Jesuit scholar Joseph Fitzmyer:

The mention of Melchizedek as "priest of God Most High" creates a difficulty: How could anyone be called a priest of God Most High whose genealogy was not known? All this has to be attributed to the fact that the Melchizedek verses were originally an independent description of him as a priest of a Canaanite god called El Elyon.[5]

The fact that Melchizedek invokes a Canaanite god puts him at odds with all later attempts to make him a priest of monotheistic Judaism (including that contained in the Letter to Hebrews). "Canaanite religion in all its manifestations was always polytheistic . . . The supreme Canaanite deity was the god El-Sedek."[6] Melchizedek, indeed, is named for that god in the polytheistic stable of Canaan deities: "The name Melchizedek is Malki-Sedek in Hebrew, meaning 'Sedek is my king'—Sedek being the name of a Canaanite god."[7] A foreign source for the interpolation explains the foreign god. With that in mind, read all that is said of Melchizedek in Genesis:

Then Melchizedek king of Salem brought food and wine. He was priest of God Most High, and he pronounced this blessing on Abram:
"Blessed be Abram

by God Most High,
creator of heaven and earth.
And blessed be God Most High,
who has delivered your enemies into your power."
Abram gave him a tithe of all the booty. (14.18–20)

Why, it may be asked, did the interpolator choose this point in the chapter
for inserting the Melchizedek story? Well, the welcoming of Abraham by
King Bera of Sodom is easily paralleled with the welcoming of Abraham
by King Melchizedek of Salem. Each king generously offers something to
Abraham, and he responds with a similar generosity. For Melchizedek to
bring food to Abraham obviously means feeding all 318 men (Gen 14.14)
he had taken with him on his raid and brought back with him—and feeding, as well, Lot's family and the subjects of King Bera whom (we later learn
from Genesis 14.21) Abraham was also restoring to their native land. This
was no small offering—which is the reason for mentioning it. Abraham
shows his gratitude for such large provisioning by giving Melchizedek a
tenth of his captured goods (14.20).

The parallel for this transaction with a king is the fact that Bera offered
Abraham a similarly generous gift. Abraham had been willing to restore
everything of Bera's that he had captured. But Bera said he would accept
only his rescued subjects, while his flocks and herds rightly belonged to
their new captor. Abraham declines the offer, saying:

"I lift my hand and swear by the Lord, God Most High, creator of
heaven and earth: not a thread or a shoe-string will I accept of anything
that is yours. You shall never say, 'I made Abram rich.' I will accept
nothing but what the young men have eaten and the share of the men
who went with me. Aner, Eshcol, and Mamre shall have their share."
(Gen 14.22–24)

The stories are similar, which explains the further intrusion of foreign
matter into an already inserted story. But the two tales are incompatible. If
Abraham turns over his spoils (the flocks and herds) to Bera, how can he

give a tenth of them to Melchizedek? Was he giving only from Lot's possessions? What right (or desire) had he to do that? And, besides, the insert-in-the-insert says that Abraham gave Melchizedek "a tithe of *all* the booty" (Gen 14.20). If Abraham already had provisioning from Melchizedek, why does he spell out his needs—"the share of the men who went with me"—to Bera? Obviously, the two accounts were originally independent of each other, and nothing has been done to make one avoid contradicting the other.

The Bera encounter is clumsily broken off to slip in the Melchizedek story, and then it is resumed as if the intervening verses had not occurred. Some would say that the three verses about Melchizedek were spliced in here to show that Abraham could give the king of Salem a tenth of his winnings since he had not yet returned them to the king of Sodom. But the meeting with Bera precedes the meeting with Melchizedek, and we are not to suppose that the exchange between them was somehow delayed while Abraham went to meet Melchizedek, as that king came out from a different town, before returning with only 90 percent of his captured goods to turn over to Bera. This is an odd story in many ways, and the Letter to Hebrews will just make it odder.

Psalm 110.4

Genesis is not the only text the Letter to Hebrews builds on. It also relies on Psalm 110. Here we must begin with the whole psalm in the New English Bible translation, since only its entirety can tell us who is being addressed in the key verse 4, "You are a priest forever."

> The Lord said to my lord,
>   "You shall sit at my right hand
> when I make your enemies the footstool under your feet."
> When the Lord from Zion hands you the sceptre, the symbol of
>   your power,
>   march forth through the ranks of your enemies.

At birth you were endowed with princely gifts
    and resplendent in holiness.
You have shone with the dew of youth since your mother bore you.
The Lord has sworn and will not change his purpose:
    "You are a priest forever,
  in the succession of Melchizedek."
The Lord at your right hand
has broken kings in the day of his anger.
So the king in his majesty, sovereign of a mighty land,
    will punish nations;
he will drink from the torrent beside the path
and therefore will hold his head high.

Who is being addressed here? The Letter to Hebrews will say it is (pro-leptically) Jesus, the Son of God. But do we really expect Jesus to be breaking kings in anger and punishing nations? The Letter wants him to be engaged in a very different work, presenting himself as a sacrifice in the heavenly court. Others have different candidates for the king celebrated in the psalm— Abraham, or David, or Hezekiah.[8] There is a consensus that this is a royal psalm, addressed to a king either at his inauguration, or just before or just after a battle. Fred Horton thinks the king is David, but David was never a priest. (Horton tries to make "priest" of Psalm 110 mean "chieftain.")[9]

Those who would prefer that the king of the psalm be David, but who temper the claim because David was not a priest, maintain that the king or prince involved is at least from David's era (tenth century to ninth century BCE)—as opposed to the Maccabees' time (second turning to first century BCE), the principal rival for the dating of the psalm.[10] Some of those in the second camp think that the psalm's subject is Simon Maccabee (reigned 142–134 BCE). This body of opinion seemed to have scored a coup when George Margoliouth and Gustavus Bickell claimed that the first conso-nants of the psalm's verses (if rearranged a little) form an acrostic, spelling "Simeon" from verses 1–4 and some honorific title (the guesses varied) from the other lines. Critics say the uncertain colometry of the psalm's corrupt text makes such a theory far-fetched.[11] Besides, these dissenters claim, the Maccabees would have relied on a priesthood from Aaron, not Melchizedek: "The Maccabeans were born priests of the line of Aaron before they attained sovereignty. They were not instituted as priests by divine oath. It was least of all appropriate to speak of any of them as a priest after the order of Melchizedek, implying not after the order of Aaron."[12]

The late Jesuit scholar Mitchell Dahood, a professor at the Pontifical Biblical Institute in Rome, was a pioneer in the use of Ugaritic parallels to interpret Hebrew poetry.[13] He concluded that Psalm 110 comes from the tenth century BCE, and celebrates some victory of an early Davidic king.[14] If that is so, what sense can be made of Yahweh telling a tenth-century king, "You are a priest forever"? Does that mean he remains a priest even after his death? After the end of the Levitical priesthood? After the end of the nation he rules over? Some want the verse to mean that the Davidic line will be eternal, as is promised in a number of royal psalms. But that is the line of kings, not priests.

It does not help to add, immediately after, that he is a priest forever *in the succession of Melchizedek*" (Ps 110.4). Genesis 14 says nothing about Melchizedek having a "succession." He is brought briefly into the narrative to meet Abraham, once, and then he disappears from the narrative devoted to the patriarch. He and Abraham have an exchange of gifts—their only interaction (one not mentioned in Psalm 110), and then they immediately part company. Verse 4 is a stranded anomaly in the psalm, as Dahood recognized.

Here is the solution Dahood proposed for the problem, one that attributes eternity not to Melchizedek's priesthood but to the Canaanite god he serves as a priest. Dahood's translation of verses 4 and 5 is:

"You are a priest of the Eternal
    according to his pact;
His legitimate king, my lord,
    according to your right hand."

Here is how Dahood justifies his rendering:

> In Genesis 14.8, "Melchizedek king of Salem brought bread and wine,
> since he was *kohen l'el 'elyon*, a priest of El Elyon." In Genesis 21.33,
> however, El Elyon is called *'el 'olam*, "El the Eternal." The case does not
> rest here. The traditional rendering, "You are a priest forever after the
> order of Melchizedek," creates problems of interpretation that have
> proved insoluble. As J. A. Fitzmyer has pointed out in *Catholic Biblical
> Quarterly* 25 (1963), nothing in Genesis indicates that Melchizedek will
> remain a priest forever. But to account for *l'olam* in Psalm 110, Fitzmyer
> labels the phrase a midrashic element introduced into the psalm; our
> translation, however, eliminates the necessity of appealing to later
> interpretive insertions—always a risky procedure.[15]

There are some who want to retain the older translation of verse 4 in
the psalm. They treat it as if it were a foundational text of Christianity.
In one sense, that is not surprising. The psalm's opening verse is "the
Old Testament text most often cited or alluded to in the New Testament."[16]
But outside the Letter to Hebrews, none of these many references to the
psalm makes any mention of its verse 4, the "priest forever" passage. They
concentrate on verse 1. In the Gospel of Mark (12.35–36), Jesus himself
quotes it:

> To answer them Jesus said as he taught in the Temple, "Why do
> expounders of the Law say that the Messiah is David's son? David
> himself said, by the Holy Spirit:
>> 'The Lord said to my Lord [the Messiah]
>>> "Sit at my right hand
>> until I make your enemies
>>> a footstool under your feet." ' "

The Gospel of Matthew (22.45) explains the point: "If David calls him
'Lord,' how can he be David's son?" Luke (20.42–44) repeats the argument.

The Gospel of Mark (14.61–62) has Jesus quoting the psalm again:

> Over again the high priest said, "Are you the Messiah, the Son of the
> Blessed One?" Jesus said, "I am, and you shall see the Son of Man seated
> at the right hand of the Power."

There are many references to Jesus as "exalted to the right hand of God"
(Ac 2.33). At Acts 7.55–56, Stephen, about to die, looked up and "saw the
splendor of God and Jesus standing at the right hand of God." At Mark
16.19, "Jesus the Lord was swept up to heaven and took his seat at the right
hand of God." At Ephesians 1.20, God "raised him from the dead and
established him at his right hand in the heavens." Colossians 3.1 says, "Seek
out the heights, where Christ is seated at the right hand of God." At 1 Peter
3.22, Christ "is now at God's right hand." At Romans 8.34, Christ "is at
God's right hand." At Revelation 3.21, Christ says, "I prevailed, and was
seated with my Father on his throne."

Since this psalm was so familiar and important to the Followers of Jesus
as a messianic text, why do none of the New Testament authors (but one)
cite verse 4 to show that Christ is a priest? The first Christian generation
was obviously not interested in Melchizedek, whom none of them (again,
except one) ever mentions. More important, none of them (obviously)
thought of Jesus as a priest. And why should they? Jesus does nothing
priestly in the Gospels. He does not preside in the Temple. He does not
offer animal sacrifice. He does not speak for the priesthood or the religious
establishment. He does the opposite of all these things. He excoriates
priests, and priests in return contrive his death. It was left to the author of
the Letter to Hebrews to find a circuitous way of claiming a priesthood for
Jesus.

The author of the Letter says that this is something new and difficult for
his audience to understand. And no wonder. No one else in the New
Testament—no one else anywhere, so far as we know—had asserted that
Jesus was a "high priest in common with Melchizedek." The Letter says that

this is something that must be *added to* the basics that the recipients of the Letter had been taught—something they would resist because it went beyond their original instruction:

> On this point I have much to say, though to reason it out in words is hard, since you are now loath to listen. Actually you should, after so much time, be doing the teaching rather than need teaching in the simplest things God first revealed to you—you have gone back to needing milk, not solid food. It is obvious that anyone drinking milk for lack of true doctrine is a child. Only grown-ups eat solid food; they have a trained faculty for telling good from evil. So let us pass over what you first learned about Christ, and press on to the fullness of teaching. Why lay again the groundwork about renouncing acts that lead to death, or what is fidelity to God, or the proper rites for ablution or the laying on of hands, or how the dead rise and are judged eternally. It is time to go beyond that, God prospering us. (5.11–6.3)

What I have translated as "On this point" is, in Greek, *peri hou*, which can mean either "concerning him" (Melchizedek, the last word in the sentence preceding this passage) or "concerning which." Harold Attridge writes:

> The antecedent of the initial relative pronoun (*hou*) is ambiguous. It could be construed either as neuter, referring to the whole subject of the priesthood according to Melchizedek, or as masculine, referring to Melchizedek or Christ, the "High Priest" of verse 10. The first construal is more likely, since the account (*logos*) will begin in chapter 7 with a treatment of Melchizedek and his priesthood.[17]

The author must be referring to the whole argument in the following chapter, since Melchizedek in himself, apart from the Letter's own connection of him with Christ, is not a thing hard "to reason out in words" (*dysermeneutos legein*). The reference to Melchizedek in Genesis is not what needs explaining. It is the connection with Jesus that is unexpected. The author is letting his audience know that a new and difficult mystery lies ahead of them. Its importance is made clear when he says that more basic things—like the Resurrection and Last Judgment!—have to be cleared away to make room for this new and more difficult matter.

This shows that the author thinks he has something more portentous to impart, and it is based on his unusual use of Melchizedek. Before considering what use he made of the "priest forever" of Psalm 110, it is of interest to see what others did with the mythical figure of Melchizedek. Only then can we gauge how the Letter to Hebrews stretched and inflated "the king of Salem" only briefly mentioned in Scripture.

NOTES

1. Merlin D. Rehm, "Levites and Priests," ABD, vol. 4, pp. 297–310.
2. René Girard, *The Scapegoat*, translated by Yvonne Freccero (Johns Hopkins University Press, 1986), pp. 76–94.
3. Fred L. Horton, Jr., *The Melchizedek Tradition* (Cambridge University Press, 1976), p. 14.
4. E. A. Speiser, *Genesis* (Doubleday, 1964), p. 105.
5. Joseph A. Fitzmyer, *The Impact of the Dead Sea Scrolls* (Paulist Press, 2009), p. 123.
6. John Day, "Canaan, Religion of," ABD, vol. 2, p. 831.
7. Fitzmyer, op. cit., p. 125. According to Genesis, Melchizedek was the king of Salem, thought to be an earlier name for the Canaanite Jerusalem. A later king of Jerusalem, perhaps a Jebusite, was Adoni-zedek, also meaning "My lord is Zedek" (Josh 10.1).
8. Paul J. Kobelski, *Melchizedek and Melchiresa* (Catholic Biblical Association of America, 1981), p. 53.
9. Horton, op. cit., pp. 32–34, 45–51. Tremper Longman III and David E. Garland say David was a priest because "David was dressed as a Priest (2 Sam 6.14), was in charge of the sacrifices (2 Sam 6.17–18), and gave a priestly blessing to the people (2 Sam 6.18)." But the first citation is to: "David, wearing a linen ephod, danced without restraint before the Lord"—an ecstatic action Blenkinsopp ascribes to prophets, not priests (and it is not said that David sacrificed, the essential duty of a priest). David was in charge of the Ark when priests sacrificed, and his blessing was something anyone could give. Abiathar and Zadok were *priests* when David was *king*. Longman and Garland, *The Expositor's Bible Commentary: Psalms*, revised edition (Zondervan, 2008), p. 816.

10. Franco Manzi, *Melchisedek e l'Angelologia nell'Epistola agli Ebrei e a Qumran* (Editrice Pontificio Istituto Biblico, 1997), pp. 18–19.

11. Ibid., pp. 19, 112, and Leslie C. Allen, *Word Biblical Commentary: Psalms 101–150*, revised edition (Thomas Nelson, 2002), p. 112.

12. Charles Augustus Briggs and Emilie Grace Briggs, *A Critical and Exegetical Commentary on the Book of Psalms* (Charles Scribner's Sons, 1907), p. 374.

13. Peter Craigie and Marvin Tate, who disagree with Dahood on many points, pay him this tribute:

> Of the numerous scholars who have been engaged in the comparative study of Ugaritic poetry and the Psalms, few have been so prolific, creative, and influential as Mitchell Dahood. Apart from his major three-volume commentary on the Psalms, Dahood has contributed many more than one hundred articles and notes to the topic. With respect to the Psalms alone, Dahood's contribution has been the greatest and most influential since the work of Gunkel earlier in the century. Indeed, some scholars would rate his influence even more highly. W. G. Albright, the most distinguished figure in American biblical scholarship and archaeology in the twentieth century, stated that Dahood had contributed more to our understanding of the vocabulary of biblical Hebrew poetry than all other scholars combined: "Even if only a third of his new interpretations of the Psalms are correct in principle—and I should put the total proportion higher—he has contributed more than all other scholars together, over the past two thousand years, to the elucidation of the Psalter."

Peter C. Craigie and Marvin E. Tate, *Word Biblical Commentary, Psalms 1–50*, second edition (Thomas Nelson Publishers, 2000), p. 51.

14. Mitchell Dahood, *Psalms III: 101–150* (Doubleday, 1970), p. 112.

15. Ibid., p. 117. The text of Psalm 110 is garbled, especially in verse 3, as one can see by the three variants cited in footnotes to the New English Bible version of that verse alone. It may be best to give here Dahood's translation of the whole psalm:

> Yahweh's utterance to my lord:
>   "Sit enthroned at my right hand.
> A seat have I made your foes,
>   a stool for your feet."
> He has forged your victorious mace,
>   Yahweh of Zion has hammered it.
> In the battle with your foes he was your Strong One,
>   your Valiant on the day of your conquest.
> When the Holy One appeared he was your Comforter,
>   the dawn of life for you,
>   the dew of your youth.

Yahweh has sworn,
    and will not change his mind:
"You are a priest of the Eternal
    according to his pact;
His legitimate king, my lord,
    according to your right hand."
He smote kings in the day of his wrath,
    he routed nations;
    he heaped corpses high,
He smote heads across a vast terrain.
The Bestower of Succession set him on his throne,
    The Most High Legitimate One lifted high his head.

16. Allen, op. cit., p. 118.
17. Harold W. Attridge, *The Epistle to the Hebrews* (Fortress Press, 1989), p. 156.

EIGHT

Higher Melchizedeks

Melchizedek, who has such a slight and contradictory presence in the Old Testament, took on glorious raiments and supernatural stature as he was refashioned down through the ages. Shortly before the Letter to Hebrews gave him an exalted relationship with Jesus, the Essene community at Qumran gave him a leading role at the dramatic end of all time.

Qumran

The library of a Jewish sect, unearthed along the Dead Sea shore between 1948 and 1963, was assembled by an ascetic and mystical cult maintained in isolation from most Jewish life. The Essenes no longer honored Jerusalem, or its Temple, or the Levitical priests serving it. They were loyal to sons of Zadok as their priests, and they had separate rituals. For them life was a struggle between the forces of Light and those of Darkness. They did not, like various Manicheans, think of the two forces as entirely independent of each other, and self-subsistent. The Essenes were still Jewish enough to remain monotheists, so both Light and Dark had to come from and be mastered by one God—making Raymond Brown call them "moderate dualists" and Joseph Fitzmyer call them "ethical dualists."[1]

The most important Qumran passage on Melchizedek (11Q13) was discovered in Cave 11 in 1956, and the fragment has been dated to the middle of the first century BCE. It describes a final showdown between the camp of the Sons of Light and the camp of the Sons of Darkness, the forces of Light led by Melchizedek, and those of Darkness led by Belial.[2] Helped by all the sons of God (angels), Melchizedek will save captive

holy ones, as he takes vengeance on Belial and his camp. Here is Geza
Vermes's translation of the Melchizedek section (11Q13, fragments 1–4)
with his reconstructions of lacunae. I italicize the key phrases about
Melchizedek:

> . . . And it will be proclaimed at *the end of days* concerning the captives
> as He said, "To proclaim liberty to the captives" [Is 61.1]. Its interpreta-
> tion is that He will assign them *to the Sons of Heaven and to the inheri-
> tance of Melchizedek;* for He will cast their lot amid the portions of
> *Melchizededek, who will return them there and will proclaim to them lib-
> erty, forgiving them the wrongdoings of all their iniquities.* And this thing
> will occur in the first week of the Jubilee that follows the nine Jubilees.
> And the Day of Atonement is the end of the tenth Jubilee, when all the
> Sons of Light and *the men of the lot of Melchizedek will be atoned for.* And
> a statute concerns them to provide them with their rewards. For this is
> the moment of *the Year of Grace for Melchizedek. And he will, by his
> strength, judge the holy ones of God, executing judgment as it is written
> concerning him in the Songs of David, who said, "Elohim has taken his
> place in the divine council; in the midst of the gods he holds judgment"*
> [Ps 82.1]. And it was concerning him that he said, "Let the assembly of
> the peoples return to the height above them; El will judge the peoples"
> [Ps 7.7–8]. As for that which He said, "How long will you judge unjustly
> and show partiality to the wicked Selah" [Ps 82.2], its interpretation
> concerns Belial and the spirits of his lot who rebelled by turning away
> from the precepts of God . . . And *Melchizedek will avenge the vengeance
> of the judgments of God . . . and he will drag them from the hand of Belial
> and from the hand of all the spirits of his lot. And all the gods of Justice will
> come to his aid to attend to the destruction of Belial . . . And your Elohim is
> Melchizedek, who will save them from the hand of Belial.*[3]

There was great excitement when this fragment was published, since it
gave an exalted role to Melchizedek that parallels the references to Melchizedek in the Letter to Hebrews, written in the following century. It was not
likely that the author of Hebrews was an Essene, or had access to the library
at Qumran. But it might be supposed that the promotion of Melchizedek to

some cosmic status was taking place in a tradition from which both the Letter and the fragment could draw.[4] Second thoughts have largely quenched such speculation. King Melchizedek in Genesis is a man, dealing with Abraham on the same level as King Bera. Though Psalm 110 (in the Septuagint) said that a later king was a "priest in the line of Melchizedek," this still left Melchizedek a human being, like the king who is the subject of the psalm. Even messianic "types," in Christian interpretations, begin as temporally circumscribed human beings.

The Melchizedek of 11Q, by contrast, is a heavenly mediator, not establishing a regal line, but standing above the struggle of the Sons of Light with the Sons of Darkness, rewarding the former and taking vengeance on the misdeeds of the latter. Angels come to his aid as he disposes of the fate of those in his hands—which would suggest that he is superior to the angels (as opposed to the Letter to Hebrews, which allows none but Christ and the Father to be above the angels).

Melchizedek stands in the midst of the divine spirits, the Elohim, who judge men, and he is himself Elohim (the noun is both singular and plural for divine beings). According to Fred Horton,

> Melchizedek is more than a mere human figure, and on the basis of the rest of the text, [even] apart from lines 9–11 [on the Elohim], it would be correct to view him as a heavenly being. When we include lines 9–11 in our consideration, the text takes on more coherence. Melchizedek as Elohim has a place in the divine assembly where he gives judgment.[5]

This will connect him with later uses of the myth, which make him an angel, a god, a Messiah, Christ himself, or the Holy Spirit; but it does not make the Letter to Hebrews depend on Qumran doctrine. Fitzmyer renders a balanced judgment:

> The fragmentary state of the text prevents us from saying whether this midrash has any connection with either Genesis 14.18–20 or Psalm 110, the two places in the Old Testament where Melchizedek is explicitly mentioned. What is preserved is a midrash development which is

independent of the classic Old Testament loci. And this is, in our opinion, the reason for saying that the tradition found here is not the same as that in Hebrews, even though it does shed some light on the more general development [of the Melchizedek myth].[6]

Philo

The myth of Melchizedek was further embroidered by two Hellenistic Jews, the philosopher Philo (20 BCE–50 CE) from Alexandria, and the historian Josephus (37–100 CE) from Jerusalem. Philo treats Melchizedek in three places.

1. *On Gathering to Learn* (*De Congressu*) 99. Here the transaction with Abraham is used to justify tithing to the Temple, a practice Philo calls a divine injunction (*chrēsmos*): "The divine injunction was recorded for the victorious prayer made by Melchizedek, who held a priesthood not taught him [*automathe*] nor in need of teaching [*autodidacton*]—and 'he gave him a tenth of everything'" (Gen 14.20). Why does Philo stress that Melchizedek had no training? Apparently this is to account for the fact that he is given no priestly lineage in Genesis. He was granted a special knowledge by God—which is what Philo says elsewhere of Wisdom (*Sophia*): God infuses it.

2. *On Abraham* 235. After describing Abraham's victory over the forces of Kedorlaomer, Philo writes:

The high priest of the Great God saw him [Abraham] arriving with his trophies, himself unscathed with an unscathed army, since he had lost none of his retinue. Struck by the scale of this deed and reflecting on what it suggested—that this could not have been accomplished without divine insight and assistance—he held up his hands to heaven, made a victory offering, and feasted all those who had fought with him so gloriously. He was as pleased and joyous as if this had been his own success—as indeed, it was, according to the maxim that all things are shared by friends, especially by virtuous friends whose goal is to please God.

Melchizedek is just a man here, as in Genesis. Philo is not really interested in him. The mythical priest is just used to celebrate Abraham's victory with the help of divine insight (*epiphrosynē*) and assistance (*symmachia*).

3. *Allegorical Readings of the Laws* 3.79–82. Melchizedek becomes the subject of Philo's typically allegorical exegesis here. Named as king by God, he stands for Pure Reason (*Orthos Logos*) as opposed to the passions of a tyrant (80). Named by God as priest, he has "The One Who Is" as his companion (82). The strain of allegory is felt most in the exegesis of Genesis 14.18, which says Melchizedek "brought food and wine." Philo contrasts this with the action of the Ammonites (who stand for sensualism) and the Moabites (who stand for arid intellectualism), neither of whom fed the Israelites on their exodus (Deut 23.4, Judg 11.18). Melchizedek combines what was separated in the Ammonites and Moabites, and so his gift of food (senses) and wine (reason) is an ample replenishment of the soul.

> Let, then, the tyrant be called a ruler of war, and the king be called a leader of peace, and let the latter bring out nourishment abounding in contentment and joy. For "he brought out bread and wine"—which, on inspection, neither the Ammonites nor the Moabites were willing to provide. That is why they are excluded from the meeting and the personnel list of God. For the Ammonites take their origin from the mother, which is perception, and the Moabites from the father, which is reasoning, and these forces they take to be constitutive of all reality, leaving no account of God. And therefore, says Moses, they may not join the meeting with god . . . since they did not "greet with bread and water" [Deut 23.3–4] those coming out of Egypt, that is, out of the passions. Let Melchizedek, by contrast, bring out wine, not water, let him slake the soul, let him give pure wine, to give them a divine intoxication, one more sober than sobriety itself.[7]

As Ceslas Spicq, an admirer of Philo, says:

> Arbitrary interpretation sets the pattern for allegorical exegesis. For Philo the Pentateuch is a psychological textbook and a catechism for

behavior. Regardless of history, he sees in Melchizedek an embodiment of Logos, a priest in the order of nature, whose priesthood is a symbol of right reason, who as ruling Mind—*basileus Nous*—bestows peace and justice on men by virtue of just views. (S 2.207)

Flavius Josephus

Josephus was a Jewish general who fought the Romans in the province of Galilee, but after his capture he joined his Roman captors and became an imperial favorite in Rome. Josephus mentions Melchizedek in two places:

1. *The Jewish War* 6.438. Josephus sketches a brief history of the Jerusalem Temple, claiming that Melchizedek built it:

> The original founder was a Canaanite ruler called, in his ancestral tongue, the Just King—which is what he was. Therefore he was the first to perform priestly rites and to build the Temple. He gave the city the name Jeru-salem after its being called Salem. The Canaanites were expelled by David, king of the Jews, who settled his own people there.

Here Josephus seems to be anticipating an argument that some Christians would adopt—that God (Yahweh) instituted a special priesthood for the Canaanite Melchizedek because his kingdom (Salem) was a forerunner of Jerusalem, a point made with a false etymology for the city. But Josephus, though he was born in Jerusalem, was not a celebrant of David's city. As Louis Feldman writes, "Josephus himself was descended from the Hasmonean kings, rather than from the line of David," and he systematically "diminished the importance of David."[8] By emphasizing that Melchizedek was made a priest because of his justice, outside any tribal lineage, Josephus was both pleasing his Roman patrons and propagandizing for his fellow Jews—by showing that Jews honor virtue over tribal ties. Melcizedek is once again a means of escaping the tribal exclusivity of the priesthood.

2. *Jewish Antiquities* 1.180–83. In a paraphrase of the Genesis tales of

Bera and Melchizedek, Josephus tries to erase the contradictions in the two men's stories. Instead of having Abraham approach either of the two kings' cities, he has them meet together at a neutral third place, the Plain of Kings. Thus Bera is present to object to Abraham's tithe for Melchizedek. Abraham, blessed by the just king of Salem, has a more contentious relationship with Bera.

> After Abraham rescued his relative Lot and the captives taken from Sodom, who before his rescue had been seized by the Assyrians, he brought his army back in peace. Then the King of Sodom met him at a place called the Plain of Kings, where Melchizedek, the King of Salem, also received him—Melchizedek whose name means Just King. It was agreed that he deserved that title, which had made him God's priest. Afterward Salem became Jeru-Salem. At that time Melchizedek provisioned Abraham's army, and heaped supplies on it. During the festivities he began to praise Abraham, and to bless God for subjecting his enemies to him. When Abraham gave him a tenth of his spoils, he accepted the gift. But the King of Sodom urged him to keep his spoils, though he begged that his people be given back to him (the ones Abraham had saved from the Assyrians), since they were his subjects. Abraham refused—not that he wanted any personal advantage from the spoils, other than what his men had consumed. But he reserved a share of the proceeds for his fellows in arms, the foremost of whom was called Eschon, then Abner, then Mamre.
>
> God praised him for this virtuous act, but said, "You shall not lose the returns you have earned by your exploits." And he answered, "What good will any returns do me, who have no one to inherit them after me?" He was still childless, but God promised him he should have a son.

In this passage Melchizedek is still just a man, though a just one favored by God. Once again, the emphasis is all on Abraham's virtue, and this occasion is used for God to promise him progeny.

The Rabbis' Melchizedek

Rabbinical sources from an early age solved the problem of Melchizedek having no tribal identity. They believed that Melchizedek of Salem was just another name for Shem, so his father was known—was, in fact, Noah—and he had a long progeny, beginning with Arpachshad. This, apart from some vague mentions of a "righteous priest" for the End Time, is all the rabbinical tradition has to say of Melchizedek.[9]

The Gnostics' Melchizedek

The Gnostic library that turned up in 1945 at Nag Hammadi has a fragmentary treatment of Melchizedek, part of which reads:

> I have a name. I am Melchizedek, the priest of the Most High . . . it is I who am truly the image of the true High-Priest of God Most High . . . I have offered up myself to you as an offering, together with those that are mine, to you yourself, Father of All . . .[10]

From this document, James Robinson (its editor) concludes that "Jesus Christ is Melchizedek," though in a Sethian Gnostic universe.

Even before the Nag Hammadi discovery there was a Gnostic text, the *Pistis Sophia* ("Belief [as] Wisdom"), that gave a dramatic role to Melchizedek. The main codex comes from late in the fourth century, though it incorporates earlier material.[11] Melchizedek is here the Gatherer of Lights, who takes all the Light mixed with matter and returns it to a heavenly place where Lights are refashioned into purified creatures and recycled into the cosmos.

> And Melchizedek, the Receiver of the Light would purify those powers and take their light to the Treasury of the Light, and all the matter of each of the servants of all the archons would gather together, and the servants of all the archons of Heimarmene [the Apportioned] and the servants of the Sphere which are below the archons would make them

into the lives of man and of beast and of reptile and wild beast and bird; and they would send them into the world of mankind.[12]

This Melchizedek is the celestial organizer who keeps the processes of the cosmos running.

The Heretics' Melchizedek

Hippolytus of Rome (170–235 CE) in his *Refutation of All Heresies* identified two heretical beliefs derived from men named Theodotus. The first, Theodotus of Byzantium, taught that Jesus was born just a man and did not become Christ until the Spirit descended on him at his baptism, which gave him special powers but left him still a man. A second Theodotus, this one a baker, began with the view that Jesus was just a man, adding that Melchizedek was a heavenly spirit greater than Christ who descended at the baptism and took on the appearance of Christ.[13] A sect of Melchizedekites is criticized by Epiphanius, the bishop of Salamis (c. 320–402 CE). Around 378 he wrote the *Panarion* ("Universal Cure") for overcoming all heresies. According to him, the claim that Christ was a priest in the succession of Melchizedek meant that Christ was subordinate and inferior to Melchizedek.[14] Epiphanius also attacks the heresy of an Egyptian ascetic called Hierakas, who held that Melchizedek is another name for the Holy Spirit.[15]

Pseudo-Tertullian says that Melchizedek is the mediator between angels and God, just as Christ is the mediator between men and God, once again giving Melchizedek the superior role.[16] This claim, that Melchizedek is the Holy Spirit, was repeated in a fourth-century work falsely attributed to Augustine.[17] Jerome refuted this idea in his Letter 63.

This chapter traces the main lines of embroidery around the modest figure of Melchizedek taken from Genesis 14. He becomes, at the hands of different mythmakers, an angel or a celestial impresario of the End Time, or Christ, or a greater-than-Christ, or the Holy Spirit. Melchizedek was, then, an invitingly blank slate on which the wildest imaginings could be scribbled. Perhaps it is no wonder that the author of the Letter to Hebrews made such odd use of the myth.

NOTES

1. Raymond E. Brown, *New Testament Essays* (Doubleday, 1965), pp. 146–64; Joseph A. Fitzmyer, *The Impact of the Dead Sea Scrolls* (Paulist Press, 2009), pp. 76–78.
2. A fragment from Cave 4 (4Q 'Amram) gives three names to the leader of the Sons of Darkness: Belial, Prince of Darkness, and Melchiresa. Another fragment from Cave 4 (4Q280) says:

   Accursed be you, Melchiresa, in all the . . . May God make you an object of dread at the hands of those exacting vengeance. May God not favor you when you call on him . . . upon you for a curse. May there be no peace for you in the mouth of those who intercede . . . without a remnant; and be damned without salvation.

   These fragments come from a vision of 'Amram, over whose soul two Watchers (angels) are struggling for possession. Cf. Paul J. Kobelski, *Melchizedek and Melchiresa* (Catholic Biblical Association of America, 1981), pp. 78–83.
3. Geza Vermes, *The Complete Dead Sea Scrolls in English*, revised edition (Penguin, 2004), pp. 533–34.
4. For enthusiastic endorsement of the ties between 11Q and the Letter, see Robert Eisenman, *The Dead Sea Scrolls and the First Christians* (Castle Books, 2004), pp. 19–21, asserting the Letter's "evident Qumranisms." Also see Norman Golb, *Who Wrote the Dead Sea Scrolls?* (Simon & Schuster, 1995), pp. 38–81.
5. Fred L. Horton, Jr., *The Melchizedek Tradition* (Cambridge University Press, 1976), p. 77.
6. Joseph A. Fitzmyer, "Further Light on Melchizedek from Qumran Cave 11," *Journal of Biblical Literature* 86, 1967, p. 31.
7. *Les Oeuvres de Philon d'Alexandrie*, edited by Claude Mondésert (Éditions du Cerf, 1962), 3.81–82 (p. 216).
8. Louis H. Feldman, *Josephus's Interpretation of the Bible* (University of California Press, 1998), p. 567, and pp. 537, 541, 562.
9. Horton, op. cit., pp. 114–30.
10. Melchizedek document from Nag Hammadi, translated from the Coptic by Søren Giversen and Birger A. Pearson, in *The Nag Hammadi Library in English*, edited by James M. Robinson, revised edition (HarperSanFrancisco, 1988), p. 442.

11. Horton, op. cit., p. 136. The Coptic is generally accepted as translated from a Greek original, as one sees from the Greek title.

12. *Pistis Sophia*, Book 1, translation by Horton, op. cit., p. 139.

13. Hippolytus, *Refutatio Omnium Haeresium*, edited by Miroslav Marcovich (Walter de Gruyter, 1986), 7.35–36, 10.23–24 (pp. 318–19, 401–20).

14. Epiphanius, *Panarion* 55.1–5.

15. Ibid., 67.3.

16. [Tertullian] *Contra Omnes Haereses* 28.

17. [Augustine] *Quaestiones Veteris et Novi Testamenti CXXVII, Corpus Scriptorum Ecclesiasticorum Latinorum* (G. Freitag, 1908), vol. 1, pp. 257–68.

NINE

Melchizedek and Jesus

The Letter to Hebrews, by an unknown author, was a late entry into the canon of the New Testament, where it was at last added to the letters of Paul. That attribution is untenable now. But I shall be discussing the provenance, date, intended audience, and author of the Letter in my next chapter. Here, in line with other uses of Melchizedek already considered, I shall focus on what the Letter says about Melchizedek, and how it justifies saying it. The Letter is the only place that mentions Melchizedek in the New Testament—but here he is mentioned eight times, a measure of his importance to the argument of the Letter.[1] Yet the rationale for these repeated mentions is fallacious on several layers. Each layer should be examined.

Fallacy One: The Argument from Silence

If Genesis does not name a priestly family for Melchizedek, that very silence must have a higher meaning, according to "one of the hermeneutic principles of the rabbis" (S 1.59), the so-called argument from silence (*argumentum e silentio*). This was often stated as *Quod non in thora, non in mundo*: "If it's not in Torah, it does not exist." Philo Judaeus constantly uses this as a tool of his fanciful exegesis. In Genesis, for instance, the tree of life is said to be in Paradise, but the tree of the knowledge of good and evil is not given a specific location—so Philo concludes that the omission of information is deliberate, lest "one without deep knowledge of the truth should bask in his knowledge."[2] If Torah gives the tree no place, then no place for it exists, and those who pretend to know its place are fools.

In the same way, with regard to the four rivers running from Paradise, three are said to border with or surround or stand off from a country, but the fourth, Euphrates, "is not said to have a relation with any country." Therefore it must symbolize Justice, which does not border, shun, shy away from, or encircle any one country, but apportions what is right to all.[3] If Torah gives the river no place, then no place for it exists.

When Genesis 6.9 introduces Noah for the first time, it gives him no father or mother. If Torah gives Noah no parents, then no parents for him exist. Philo says this is to show that he is begotten not of forebears but only of his own virtue.[4] This is the kind of argument the Letter to Hebrews uses. Genesis does not give Melchizedek a lineage—no begetters, no begottens. It does not even say that he was born or died. The Letter therefore concludes that he had no birth or death. He just appeared, miraculously, outside the order of nature or human succession:

> This Melchizedek, you see, was king of Salem, priest of the highest God, who met Abraham as he came back from slaughtering kings, and blessed him, and Abraham measured out for him a tenth of all he had won. The first meaning of his name is King of Justice, the second is King of Salem (or King of Peace). *Fatherless, motherless, tribeless, with no beginning of his days or ending of his life*, he had a *commonality with the Son of God*, insofar as he was a priest in perpetuity [*eis to diēnekes*]. (7.1–3)

This is carrying the *argumentum e silentio* to a new extreme. Philo said that Noah was not given parents in Genesis. But that did not mean he had "no beginning of his days or ending of his life." It meant that Noah's credentials were not derived from any inheritance, but only from his own virtue. Why does the omission of Melchizedek's tribe not mean something similar? Why leap to the conclusion that his is an immaculate conception, something more than man's, without a "beginning of his days or ending of his life"? As Paul Kobelski writes:

> The use of a tradition that regarded Melchizedek as a heavenly figure, the avoidance of any indication of his being an angel, and the reminder

that he resembles the Son of God suggest that the author of Hebrews considered Melchizedek to be superior to the angels but inferior to the Son of God. Melchizedek, then, would occupy a position between the angels of Hebrews 1 and 2 and the Son of God in chapter 7.[5]

One can go even further than Kobelski does. Why consider Melchizedek inferior to the Son of Man? We have seen that Christian heretics of the early church thought Melchizedek ranked above Christ. The author of the Letter, trying to give Melchizedek a "commonality with the Son of God," has gone too far. He has made his appearance on earth even more miraculous than that of the Son of God, who had no human father, though he did have a human mother. For that matter, Jesus had a "beginning of his days and ending of his life." Melchizedek is above all of those things, according to the Letter's author.

The idea that since no lineage is given for Melchizedek in Torah, therefore he must have no lineage, is absurd. Spicq tries to justify the Letter by saying:

> Admittedly, this mode of reasoning baffles the modern mentality, but its validity as an argument would make its impression on thought in an Alexandrian culture, accustomed by its teacher [Philo] to this sort of exegesis. (S 1.60)

But it does not take a "modern mentality" to resist Philonic arguments like the one that says failure to mention where a tree is means that it must be *nowhere* except in the realm of symbols.

Fallacy Two: Melchizedek's Eternal Priesthood

Since Melchizedek has no "ending of his life," is he still alive now? No, the Letter suggests, it is not his physical life that is extended into perpetuity, but his priesthood (as if that could exist apart from his life). Why single out that aspect of his life for eternity? Melchizedek is also a king. Why is his kingship not called eternal? No ancestors or successors on the throne are named. Melchizedek blesses Abraham. Why does this not make the latter's reign eternal? Why does it not make Abraham a priest, since the Letter says the blessing bestows a priesthood on his descendant, considered as still potential, or "in [his] loins." Why this arbitrary singling out of one aspect of Melchizedek to make it last forever? Most messianic "forerunners" are historically located and confined. But Melchizedek will continue to be a "priest forever" even after the Son of God appears—leaving us, on the heavenly plane, with *two* "priests forever." Myles Bourke underlines the problem:

> Though Melchizedek's "eternity" furnished the author with a typology that suited his purpose, since it provided not only a foreshadowing of Jesus' priesthood but a contrast with that of the sons of Levi, it also creates a problem, viz., are there, then, two eternal priests, Melchizedek and Jesus? W. Loader suggests that the author thought of Melchizedek as a priest who still lived, but without exercising any priestly function. But does a priest who ceases to function fit the Hebrews comparison between Melchizedek and Jesus? And for all the subordination of Melchizedek to Jesus found in the phrase that he was "made to resemble the Son of God," a point on which Kobelski rightly insists, that subordination does not eliminate Melchizedek's eternal priesthood. Perhaps one must conclude that the Melchizedek-Jesus typology, for all its usefulness to the author of Hebrews, raises also a difficulty that he simply ignored.[6]

The two eternal priesthoods make for an odd fit in every way. Jesus is said to be a priest eternal since he does not repeat sacrifices over and over, like the Levitical priests. Does that mean that Melchizedek, too, repeatedly sacrificed? If he did, why is his priesthood eternal, when the Letter says that repeated sacrifices are of no avail (10.11–13)? Are we to think he makes one eternal sacrifice like the other eternal priest, Jesus? If so, did he leave unperformed the priestly duties of his office in Salem? The matter does not bear serious scrutiny.

Fallacy Three: The Power of Blessing

The Letter to Hebrews notes that Melchizedek blesses Abraham, which makes him a being superior to the patriarch from whom the whole Jewish people are descended. How can it prove such an exalted claim for Melchizedek? With this blithe assertion:

> See the scale of this man, to whom the patriarch Abraham gave a tenth of his prize winnings . . . No one contests that one who is lower down is blessed by one who is higher up. (7.4, 7)

But Scripture itself gives examples of the lesser in station blessing the higher. At 2 Sam 14.22, one of King David's subjects, Joab, blesses him. At 1 Kings 1.47, David's householders bless him. At 1 Kings 8.66, his people bless King Solomon. The suffering Job (31.20) says that if he wronged a beggar, the man would have "no cause to bless me"—implying that if he had treated him well, the beggar *could* bless him.

There should be nothing surprising in this. After all, a blessing is implicitly a plea that God will bless its object. In that sense, yes, the higher blesses the lower. But the human doing the blessing is not himself bestowing good fortune (as the Letter assumes), but asking God to bestow it. And anyone, high or low, can do that. The implicit plea is made explicit at 1 Kings 1.47: "'May *your* God *make* the name of Solomon your son more famous than your own and his throne even greater than yours.'" At every step this Letter's flimsiness of argument becomes more evident.

Fallacy Four: Priesthood Certified by Tithing

The Letter claims that Melchizedek is superior to Abraham not only because the former blesses the latter, but because the latter offers a tithe to the former. Tithes were owed to the Levites, in return for their service to the Ark of the Covenant. (Not all Levites were priests, just attendants on the priesthood, so to give a tithe to a Levite did not necessarily make the recipient a priest.)

To the Levites I give every tithe in Israel to be their patrimony, in return for the service they render in maintaining the Tent of the Presence. In order that the Israelites may not henceforth approach the Tent and thus incur the penalty of death, the Levites alone shall perform the service of the Tent, and they shall accept the full responsibility for it. This rule is binding on your descendants for all time. They shall have no patrimony among the Israelites, because I give them as their patrimony the tithe which the Israelites set aside as a contribution to the Lord . . . The Lord spoke to Moses and said, Speak to the Levites in these words: When you receive from the Israelites the tithe which I give you from them as your patrimony, you shall set aside from it the contribution to the Lord, a tithe of the tithe. (Num 18.21–26)

According to the Letter, since Abraham gives a tithe to Melchizedek, who is not a Levite, he is recognizing a priesthood outside Levitical descent.

Now if the priesthood were complete in Levi's line, as was prescribed for the people by the Law, what need was there for a different priesthood in common with Melchizedek, and not in common with Aaron? If the priesthood changes, so of necessity does the Law. Yet the one we speak of was from a different tribe, no member of which officiated at the altar. (7.11–13)

Where to begin with this tangled argument? We are told that a change in the Levitical priesthood (which did not exist in Abraham's time) must mean a change in the Law (which had not been given, yet, through Moses).

Melchizedek, we are told, was not of the tribe of Levi (though the author says he is of *no* tribe, since none is given in Torah). Presumably, he would not be of any Israelite tribe, since he is a Canaanite serving a Canaanite god. Is the author of the Letter saying that no peoples before Moses had priesthoods of their own? Later, will this mean that Jesus exercises a non-Jewish priesthood "in common with Melchizedek"? For that matter, why is tithing before Moses always a *religious* duty? Why not a simple exchange, part of

Abraham's goods given in return for Melchizedek provisioning his army? The whole matter is full of elusive or unrecoverable premises.

Fallacy Five: Loins That Tithe

The author of the Letter is not content to say that Abraham verified Melchizedek's priesthood by tithing. He says that Abraham's great-grandson, Levi, tithed along with his ancestor:

> Even Levi, the receiver of tithes, also paid them through Abraham, since he was already in the loins of his father when Melchizedek met him. (7.9–10)

That is fairly long-distance tithing, one powerful enough to swim upstream through three intervening sets of loins. The argument is so far-fetched that Craig Koester suggests it may have been intended as "a touch of exaggerated humor"—which is, in itself, a far-fetched notion. (K 345).

But the most surprising thing about this claim is that the author of the Letter seems to forget why he introduced Melchizedek in the first place. He wanted to give Jesus a form of priesthood entirely apart from the Levitical lineage. But here he makes Levi acknowledge Melchizedek with a tithe that would make *him* (Levi) a priest "in common with Melchizedek." A kind of two-way traffic is set up between Levi and Melchizedek, each the recipient of tithes, each validating the other. Where does that leave the priesthood of Jesus, inside or outside the Levitical succession? That is a question that must wait for my next chapter. Here I simply want to point out that the Letter is as capricious in its use of Melchizedek as the rabbinical and heretical sources already considered.

Fallacy Six: "Succession" Without Lineage

After establishing that Melchizedek had no lineage, no predecessors or successors, the author of the Letter will say that Jesus somehow followed upon the priesthood of Melchizedek. Some try to distinguish this succession from the normal tribal lineage for priests, saying that Jesus is in the "lineup" (*kata taxin*) of Melchizedek, not in the familial "lineage" (*kata phylēn*, 7.14). *Taxis* refers to any ordering of things, primarily of military formations (whence our English "tactics"). Thus one could say that Jesus was in the ranks of Melchizedek, if there were more than one person in that category. But the uniqueness of Jesus makes "ordering" not easily imaginable—like asking an isolated figure to "line up." Line up with whom or what? The only person he can line up with is Melchizedek, but that suggests that they are equals, like two soldiers in a line; or even that Melchizedek, as the earlier figure, precedes Christ in importance as well as chronologically. If Jesus is following a model of, and thus has lesser dignity than, his "original," we veer toward the heretical view that Melchizedek is superior to Christ.

Kata taxin is variously rendered in English—"in (or according to) the succession" (New English Bible), or "after the order of" (King James), or "of the kind," or "in the line." But since the only thing that Melchizedek has in common with Christ is the claim to an eternal priesthood derived from Psalm 110, I would suggest the most neutral of all translations, "in common with." The same would apply to the statement that Melchizedek is *homoios*, "like Christ," or has "a likeness" (*homoiotēs*) with Christ. Here, too, I would translate, as neutrally as possible, that he has a something *in common with* Christ, or has a *commonality* with Christ.

The attempts of commentators to make sense of these many fallacies is a long parade of contortions. They invoke the argument from silence, or from a statement of what is "in the loins" over four generations, or from the "undoubted" view that blessings are only given by superiors, or from the existence of an "eternal priest" without eternal functions, even from a touch of "exaggerated humor." There is a pious protectiveness about what Christian exegetes say about the Letter's fantastical use of Melchizedek. After all, the Letter is in the canon of Scripture. It must be inspired. This kind of learned fundamentalism is embarrassing. It is time to look at the larger purposes of the Letter.

NOTES

1. The loci are at Hebrews 5.6, 10, 6.20, 7.1, 10, 11, 15, 17.
2. Philo Judaeus, *Allegorical Readings of the Laws* 1.60.
3. Ibid., 1.85–87.
4. Philo Judaeus, *On Abraham* 31.
5. Paul J. Kobelski, *Melchizedek and Melchiresa* (Catholic Biblical Association of America, 1981), p. 127.
6. Myles M. Bourke, "The Epistle to the Hebrews," NJ, p. 932.

III

Letter to Hebrews

TEN

What Is It?

The Author

It is often said that Saint Paul's Letter to Hebrews is not Paul's, not a letter, and not to Hebrews. It cannot be by Paul, since basic Pauline concepts are not in it, and its concepts are not in Paul (especially the idea that Jesus is a priest). Moreover, its language is not that of Paul or of any other author in the New Testament. Its style and vocabulary are unparalleled. Its uses of sentence structure and rhetorical devices are far more polished than those found anywhere else. To take just vocabulary, the Letter uses 152 words not found in all the other texts of the New Testament—all the Gospels and all the epistles.[1] It has, moreover, "over ninety" words used only once elsewhere: "The proportion of unique vocabulary is larger here than in the rest of the epistolary literature of the New Testament, and bespeaks the author's sound literary education."[2]

The striking anomaly of the Letter is its combination of idiosyncratic, indeed eccentric, logic (exemplified in the treatment of Melchizedek and Jesus as priest) and sophisticated language. The author uses a polished Greek rhetoric—alliteration, anaphora, inclusion ("ring composition"), chiasm, and other ornaments.[3] The Letter begins with a striking chain of alliterated words: *Polymeros kai Polytropos Palai ho Theos lalēsas tois Patrasi en tois Prophētais* . . . ("Formerly God spoke Fragmentarily and Figuratively to the Fathers through Features of prophecy . . ."). The text is strewn thick with chiasms (the *A-b-b-A* device), as when Melchizedek is said to have "no BEGINNING of his *days* or of his *life* ENDING" (7.3). Chapter 11 is one long series of sentences launched by anaphora: "By fidelity . . . By

fidelity . . . By fidelity . . ." The Letter's argument is nudged subtly forward
with a flexible use of the postpositive Greek article *gar* (over seventy times
in the Letter), which can mean things as various as "you see," or "naturally,"
or "remember," or "as it were," or "of course," or "obviously," or "consequently,"
or "in fact," or (in anticipation) "first off."[4] In combination with other particles
it can have further meanings (like "in this case" for *toigaroun*). I use all of
these in my translation of the Letter (see Appendix II).

With Paul excluded as the author, there has been a wide and fairly des-
perate range of suggestions for some early Christian as author. Luke has the
best Greek after the Letter, and a wide vocabulary.[5] But he does not have
the sentence structure or rhetorical ornaments of the Letter. Most important, he does not have the key point in the Letter, the assertion that Jesus is
a priest. In the Letter, Jesus continues to be the advocate of his Followers
while seated at the right hand of the Father; but in Luke, Jesus leaves the
disciples but sends the Spirit to be their advocate.[6]

Some critics, if they could not have Paul as the author, shopped around
for people who are mentioned by him or worked with him. For Tertullian,
the author was Paul's early partner Barnabas (Gal 2.1).[7] For Luther, he was
Paul's assistant Apollos (S 1.190). Others, following the nineteenth-century
theologian Eduard Riehm, think the author was Paul's fellow evangelist
Silas (Ac 16.19).[8] For Adolf von Harnack, the writer was Paul's friend Pris-
cilla, alone or in conjunction with her husband, Aquila (1 Cor 16.19).[9] Since
none of these people left writings we can compare with the Letter, they are
blank slates. It is unlikely they would leave no traces in other New Testament documents, echoing the eccentric views of the Letter—that Melchizedek was a priest forever or that Jesus was a self-sacrificer who replicates on a
higher scale the animal sacrifices of the Mosaic Law, or that he was killed
outside the city to repeat the burning of animal remains "outside the camp."
Koester is right to say, "Hebrews is distinctive enough that it cannot be
clearly identified with any known writer" (K 45). Origen said it early: "Who
wrote it, God alone knows."[10] Raymond Brown says all that we can know of
the author:

We have to be satisfied with the irony that the most sophisticated rhetorician and elegant theologian of the New Testament is an unknown. To employ his own description of Melchizedek, the writer of Hebrews remains without father or mother or genealogy. The quality of his Greek and his control of the Scriptures in Greek suggest that he was a Jewish Christian with a good Hellenistic education and some knowledge of Greek philosophical categories. His allegorical style of hermeneutics has parallels in Philo and in Alexandrian interpretation; but that interpretation was taught elsewhere and so the claim that the writer of Hebrews came from Alexandria is unproved. Those from whom he learned about Christ may have had a theological outlook similar to that of the Hellenist moment and its freer attitude toward the Jewish cultic heritage.[11]

The writer was so individual in syntax, rhetorical tropes, mode of arguing, and exotic theses that it is impossible to pin him down in the company of anyone else. He is so anomalous that he could not, for a time, be securely placed in the canon of scriptural writings.

The Genre

Well, if we cannot say who wrote the Letter, can we say with certainty what it is that he is writing? That, too, remains an elusive matter. It is called a Letter in the superscription, but ancient authors did not give titles to their works, and all the scriptural works have titles added later. Obviously, some later editor, looking around in the Letter, deduced from frequent mention of Jewish ritual that it was directed to "Hebrews" (whatever that meant). Paul, however, directed his letters to *places*, to the gatherings at Corinth, or Galatia, or wherever, or to specific *persons* (like Philemon). And he wrote in his own person (with his coadjutors). The Letter to Hebrews has no such directive, no author who says it is Paul doing the writing, or says to whom he is writing. The Letter has no opening greetings and good wishes, which were proper epistolary form: "The standard protocol including salutation and naming of the sender and addressee . . . is common in the epistolography of the Hellenistic and Roman periods generally."[12]

The author calls his message "this supporting address" (*logos tēs paraklēseos*, 13.22), a term used of a sermon at Acts 13.15.[13] He also says he has kept it short, though it is not particularly short for an epistle (only two of Paul's letters are longer).[14] But it is short for a speech, and many have concluded from the strain of exhortation throughout that it is a protreptic oration, encouraging backsliders to renew their Christian commitment. That is why he says he is speaking (2.5, 6.9, 8.1, 11.32) to listeners (5.11). Myles Bourke concludes: "Probably Hebrews is a written homily to which the author has given an epistolary ending."[15] Luke Timothy Johnson and Peter O'Brien find four signs of oral delivery in the Letter, from which Johnson concludes that "Hebrews is a composition that is meant to be heard as a discourse rather than seen as a text."[16] The author has a speaker's awareness of time limits: "What more can I say? Time forbids mention of . . ." (11.32).

It is clear that the author could not deliver this exhortation in person, since he tells us he is absent, though he hopes to join the hearers shortly (13.23). It is also clear, on the other hand—from his references to the community's past troubles, its former heroism, and its backsliding—that he knows his audience very well. Relying on the prior acquaintance that gave him this knowledge, he probably had some trusted friend, or knew of some leader on the spot, who could deliver his "supporting address." Most communications to a gathering were read aloud to it, since papyrus scrolls were difficult to manipulate. Besides, some (perhaps most) in the audience would be illiterate. Paul's letters were read aloud in this way (1 Thess 5.27, Col 4.16).

The Date

The letter had to be written before the nineties of the Common Era, since it is quoted and paraphrased in Clement of Rome's letter of that date. What is the time *after* which it had to be written? It used to be thought that the sixties of the Common Era was plausible, since the Letter refers to animal sacrifices in the present tense (9.6–10, 10.2–3), as if the Temple were still standing (it was destroyed by the Romans in 70 CE). But Philo, Clement of Alexandria, and others refer to Jewish rituals in the present tense after the destruction of the Temple, just stating Jewish Law.[17] But the Letter in fact never refers to the Temple. All the sacrifices it mentions took place in the Mosaic traveling Tent (Shrine, conventionally translated as "Tabernacle"), not the Temple—the importance of which the addressees do not (or do no longer) seem to recognize. This argues for a post-70 date.

Another reason for assigning the Letter to the sixties was the apparent mention of persecution at 10.32–34, which was taken to refer to Nero's killing of Christians in 64 CE. But the author says this was an earlier (*proteron*) trial, and it involved only oppressions (*thlipseis*) and humiliations (*oneidismoi*), confiscations and imprisonment, not death (12.4). This would refer to the precarious position of Christians between Nero's time and the active persecution of Domitian (mid-nineties). Allowing for the influence of Hellenistic thought before Clement, this puts the Letter sometime in the eighties—approximately when the Gospels of Matthew and Luke were written.[18]

The Audience

The Letter is addressed to a Christian audience of the second generation, one that had learned its religion from the Followers of Jesus, not from Jesus himself—a message "confirmed by those who heard it from him, with God's added testimony in the form of signs and portents and every kind of miracle, along with different gifts the Spirit bestowed" (2.3). Despite these signs to confirm their fidelity, and a history of experience with the Holy Spirit (6.4), the community has lost its prior fervor (10.32–34). This has led to internal division (12.15–16), backsliding (10.38–39), and neglect of the community gatherings (10.25). The author attributes this straying from their former course to a hankering back toward the old, toward the reassuring security of God's promises to Moses. The old Pact seems more solid than the new one. The leading contenders for such an audience, it has been agreed, were in Jerusalem or in Rome.

Jerusalem: Though members of the Jerusalem community were demoralized after the Temple's destruction, Ceslas Spicq thinks the letter was addressed to them, and specifically to Palestinian Christians who had been Jewish priests (S 1.226–31). But addressing such hearers in polished Greek rather than Hebrew or Aramaic would not be tactful in dealing with former Jerusalem priests. As Raymond Brown asks, "Why would the author compose in elegant Greek a dissuasive to Jewish Christian priests who would have known Hebrew as part of the liturgy, or to Jewish Christians of Judea, for whom Hebrew or Aramaic would have been a native language?"[19] Koester agrees: "Hebrews was written in Greek using a Greek form of the Old Testament, which does not seem fitting for an audience of Hebrew-speaking Christians based in Jerusalem" (K 172). Most telling of all against the Spicq thesis is the fact that the Letter shows no interest in the Temple, where Spicq's priests would have officiated before 70 CE.

Rome: Raymond Brown and John Meier argue for Rome as the Letter's destination. Brown notes, among other things, that "knowledge of [the Letter to] Hebrews was attested at Rome earlier than at any other place."[20] Meier says that "while there is nothing in the New Testament references to Timothy that would encourage one to associate his name with Jerusalem, in Romans 16.21 Paul made certain that Timothy was the first whose greetings he shared with Rome."[21]

One of the arguments that used to be made for Rome as the place of origin for the Letter, not its destination, is at 13.23–24:

> Be informed that our brother Timothy has been freed, and if he reaches me soon I shall see you with him. Embrace all your leaders and all the saints. Those in Italy embrace you.

The Timothy mentioned here is presumably Paul's important coadjutor. Since he was younger than Paul in the sixties, he could still be alive in the eighties—and in prison, though not in Italy, which was undergoing no persecution in the eighties. Did a greeting sent by "those in Italy" mean that the author is speaking from Rome? If that were the case, why not say "those in Rome" embrace you? John Meier says that *apo Italias* can mean those who *came from* Italy—they have come from different parts of Italy but are gathered in the city (whatever that is) where the author is writing. The inclusive term makes better sense than to say that someone in Rome has collected the greetings from different parts of Italy to send off elsewhere.

Structure

The Letter's leading structural characteristic is that it veers back and forth between theological argument and exhortations to fidelity. A number of attempts have been made to impose an overall framework containing these alternations in one scheme. The most ambitious of these, one frequently invoked, is by the French Jesuit Albert Vanhoye, who proposes a concentric plan around a central part devoted to the sacrifice of the priestly Jesus (5.11–10.39), with the circumferent parts of the Letter arranged chiastically.[22] Spicq argues that his schema is signaled by link-words (*mots crochets*), theme statements (*annonces*), and rhetorical devices like chiasm (*symétrie croisée*)—elements that are all there. But their verbal interplay needs special pleading to align it with the concentric pattern Spicq is arguing for. Such a structure would not be perspicuous to a hearer. It is not even clear in Spicq's labored explication of it. And, in fact, the Letter's argument is linear and cumulative. As Koester writes: "The main arguments were usually not placed in the middle of a speech, but at the beginning and end, where they would have the greatest impact" (K 83). Attridge criticizes Vanhoye in these terms:

> There are also significant points at which even the analysis of the architecture is forced and artificial, particularly in the central expository section. It is no doubt significant that use of the same set of structural principles has resulted in a rather different, and less concentric, structure. Some of the difficulty in analyzing the structure of Hebrews is

due not to the lack of structural indices, but to their overabundance. Hebrews constantly foreshadows themes that receive fuller treatment elsewhere and frequently provides brief summaries that resume and refocus earlier developments. Any structural scheme captures only a portion of this web of interrelationships and does only partial justice to the complexity of the work.[23]

A simpler scheme should be adopted—that the author has crafted a theological argument that will correct the listeners' backsliding toward Jewish precedents, and that he pauses at various points in the argument to apply what he is arguing to the particular situation of his audience, with increasing urgency of exhortation. This accords with good rhetorical precepts, to keep the audience awake and draw attention to the significance of one's overall themes—see especially where he warns that what he is saying is "hard to reason out in words" (5.11).

Canonicity

The acceptance of the Letter into the body of sacred writings was slow in the West (where it was first known) and rapid in the East (where its "high Christology" was welcomed). In Rome, where it had been sent, it was quoted by Clement in the late nineties, but it did not enter the canon for another three centuries. In Alexandria, by contrast, it was canonized as one of Paul's letters not many years after its composition. In Alexandria, the second-century *Corpus Paulinum* made it part of the Bible and it stayed there for use in Eastern Councils. But in the West, even authors who showed respect for the Letter did not consider it canonical—the Shepherd of Hermas, Tertullian, Justin, Irenaeus, Cyprian, Gaius of Rome. It was omitted from the second-century Muratorian Canon (K 23–24). Finally, Jerome and Augustine bowed to the authority of the East, and Hebrews found its niche at the end of the Pauline letters. This was formalized at the Synod of Hippo (393 CE) and the Synods of Carthage (397 and 419 CE).

Raymond Brown summarizes the situation:

A passage from Hebrews is cited in I Clement, written in Rome and thus written within a relatively short time after the writing of Hebrews. In the mid–second century Justin, writing at Rome, shows knowledge of Hebrews. One cannot explain this easily by claiming that Hebrews was known in Rome because it had been sent *from* that city, for writers of the Roman church have views different from those in Hebrews. More probable is the view that Hebrews, designed as a corrective work, was received by the Roman church but not enthusiastically appropriated there. Indeed, such an explanation is almost necessitated by Rome's attitude toward the canonical status of Hebrews. Even though Alexandrian and Eastern knowledge of Hebrews is first attested nearly a century after Roman knowledge, the letter was accepted as canonical in the East rather quickly and attributed to Paul. Apparently Rome did not accept such an attribution, for throughout the second century Roman writers fail to list Hebrews as Scripture or among the letters of Paul. One may theorize that the Roman community which first received Hebrews knew that it did not come from Paul but from a second-generation Christian teacher. Although he was worthy of respect, he did not have the authority of an apostle (an attitude understandable in a church priding itself in having two apostolic "pillars," Peter and Paul—I Clement 5.2–7). Trinitarian controversies helped to change the picture, for Hebrews (especially 1.3) was invaluable in the orthodox defense of the full divinity of Christ against the Arians. Then the opinion that Paul wrote Hebrews won the day in the larger church (circa 400), and Rome was willing to accept it as the fourteenth letter of the apostle.[24]

In summary, then, the "Letter" is a supporting address (13.22) to backsliding (10.38–39) Christians in Rome, who felt the need for reassurance from their Jewish roots, and had therefore grown negligent in attending the house churches and performing the mutual services of the Christian community (13.2–7).

NOTES

1. For a list of these isolated uses (*hapax legomena*) see S 1.157.

2. Harold W. Attridge, *The Epistle to the Hebrews* (Fortress Press, 1989), pp. 20–21.

3. Ibid., p. 20.

4. On the huge range of meanings for *gar* in idiomatic Greek, see J. D. Denniston, *The Greek Particles*, second edition (Oxford University Press, 1959), pp. 56–199.

5. Luke has 1,312 *hapax legomena*, but that is out of his combined Gospel and Acts, amounting to 37,778 words (the largest body of writing in the New Testament). See Joseph A. Fitzmyer, *The Gospel According to Luke I–IX* (Doubleday, 1981), p. 109. The Letter to Hebrews has 152 *hapax legomena* from only 4,942 total words. See Robert Morgenthaler, *Statistik des neutestamentlichen Wortschatzes* (Gotthelf Verlag, 1958), p. 166.

6. David Allen is a dogged defender of Luke as author of the Letter: *The New American Commentary: Hebrews* (B&H Publishing Group, 2010), vol. 1, pp. 46–61, and *Lukan Authorship of Hebrews* (B&H Publishing Group, 2010). Thomas Aquinas attributed the fact that the Letter is so polished to the fact that Paul wrote to Gentiles in their Greek language, but wrote to Jews in "his native tongue," Hebrew. Then Luke translated Paul's Hebrew into a Greek more polished than the Greek of Paul's other writings; see Aquinas, *Commentary on the Epistle to the Hebrews*, translated by Chrysostom Baer (St. Augustine's Press, 2006), prologue, p. 7. There are many problems with this idea. Paul was a Greek-speaker, and he quoted the Old Testament in its Greek translation (Septuagint). Though learned Jews in Palestine would have known Hebrew, many of them, if literate at all, spoke the Aramaic of Jesus and his family, or the lingua franca of the Greek-speaking empire. It was to minister to their needs that the Septuagint was created.

7. Tertullian, *De Pudicitia* 20.

8. Eduard Karl August Riehm, *Der Lehrbegriff des Hebräerbriefes* (Balmer und Riehm, 1859), vol. 2, pp. 890–93.

9. Adolf von Harnack, *Zeitschrift für die Neutestamentliche Wissenschaft* 1 (1900), pp. 16–41. Though the author refers to himself in the masculine singular at 11.32, others have supported the great Harnack's theory; see Attridge, *Epistle to the Hebrews*, p. 4.

10. Eusebius, *Church History* 6.25.

11. Raymond E. Brown, *An Introduction to the New Testament* (Doubleday, 1997), p. 695.

12. Attridge, *Epistle to the Hebrews*, p. 13.

13. The noun *paraklēsis* means action like that of a *paraklētos*, "paraclete"—a person literally "called to one's side," to champion one's cause or fend off criticism. Some have said that the Paraclete's role in the Gospel of John is that of a "defense attorney." Hence I translate a "word of *paraklēsis*" as "this supporting address."

14. Morgenthaler, op. cit., pp. 166–68. Hebrews has 4,942 words. First Corinthians, which may be a composite of several letters, has 6,807. Romans has 7,094.

15. Myles M. Bourke, "The Epistle to the Hebrews" NJ, p. 921. Cf. K 81.

16. Luke Timothy Johnson, *Hebrews: A Commentary* (Westminster John Knox Press, 2006), pp. 10–11; Peter T. O'Brien, *The Letter to the Hebrews* (Apollos, 2010), p. 21.

17. Harold W. Attridge, "Hebrews," ABD, vol. 3, p. 97.

18. Brown, op. cit., pp. 172, 273, 684, 807–9.

19. Ibid., pp. 399–400; Attridge (*Epistle to the Hebrews*, p. 10) notes the Letter's parallels with another "Roman" epistle, 1 Peter.

20. Brown, op. cit., pp. 399–400.

21. John P. Meier, in Meier and Raymond Brown, *Antioch and Rome* (Paulist Press, 1983), p. 144.

22. Albert Vanhoye, *La structure littéraire de "L'épître aux Hébreux," deuxième édition revue et augmentée* (Desclée de Brouwer, 1976). The concentric scheme is outlined on p. 59. The chiastic elements are stressed on pp. 62–63. The Greek text is printed according to his outline on pp. 274–303. Vanhoye has argued for this outline, with slight changes, in publications following the original edition of his main work. See *Traduction structurée de "L'épître aux Hébreux"* (Institute Biblique Pontifical, 1963) and *Le Christ est notre prêtre* (Institute Biblique Pontifical, 1963).

23. Attridge, *Epistle to the Hebrews*, pp. 16–17.

24. Brown, op. cit., p. 700.

ELEVEN

What Does It Mean?

Translations of the Letter to Hebrews make a leap when they supply the definite article, Letter to *the* Hebrews, as if the author had a particular entity in mind. But in fact the word *Hebraioi* is a slippery one, used in different ways at different times by different people. When the Letter was written, *Hebraioi* was already an outmoded term. Some have restricted it to Jews of the patriarchal era, switching to Israelites after God's promises are made to Moses. Craig Koester writes: "By the first century A.D. the term had acquired an archaic quality, since the Old Testament uses Hebrews almost exclusively for the early history of Israel" (K 172). Niels Peter Lemche adds: "The use of this expression is confined to certain parts of the Old Testament . . . Jonah 1.9 . . . is the only place where a person describes himself as a Hebrew; in all other instances they are described as such by other peoples."[1]

Of itself, the word is less an ethnic or historical identifier than a linguistic one, meaning Hebrew-speakers. Not all Jews spoke Hebrew, as opposed to other Semitic languages (like Aramaic) or to Greek, the lingua franca of the Roman Empire. And early Christian history adds to the muddle by distinguishing Christian "Hebrews" from Christian "Hellenists" (Ac 6.1)—a distinction much debated.[2] It may be tempting to let this latter distinction be our guide in dealing with the Letter. The "Hebrews" of the title would then mean Christians who still emphasized their ties to the Jewish Law and Temple. But in fact, the Letter speaks more of the Promise to Abraham than of the Law and the Temple (the latter is not mentioned at all). So the title given the Letter, a later addition to it, is no help at all for understanding it.

All early Christians, including Gentiles, had to ponder and evaluate their relationship with the Jewish revelation. Paul, the first Christian author, known for addressing Gentiles specifically, had only one Bible to preach. There was as yet no New Testament, and he could not conceive of himself as contributing to it. All Followers of Jesus were, for Paul, "the seed of Abraham" (Rom 11.1)—and all rescue comes from the Jews (Rom 11.26). The Jews supply the root and trunk to which the Gentiles have been grafted, and "the branch does not animate the root, the root animates the branch" (Rom 11.18).

The first Christians continued to attend the Temple and the synagogues, but what they claimed there was heresy in the eyes of many Jews—that the Messiah was no longer awaited but had come. Disagreement within the same body of thinkers or believers often provokes a special bitterness, so the very ties that bound Christians to Jews became sources of friction. The early Christian communities did not fall into one attitude in this strained situation. They ran a gamut of love-hate emotions. Raymond Brown sketches briefly the differences within the Christian centers.[3]

1. There were Christians who observed the full Jewish Law, including circumcision. Luke says some of these were Pharisee converts to Christianity (Ac 15.5). Brown finds signs of this Christianity of strict observance not only in Jerusalem but in Ephesus, Philippi, and Rome.

2. Other Christians did not insist on circumcision but retained some Jewish observances, particularly food laws, like the men Paul encountered at Antioch and Corinth, and to whom the Gospel of Matthew shows some sympathy.

3. A third group, typified by Paul, respected Jewish observance, but did not require it. This group felt free to observe or not to observe the Law, so long as one acknowledged its importance in the preparation for Christianity. Needless to say, the first two groups considered this one wishy-washy on its debt to Judaism.

4. The fourth group, typified by Johannine writings, denied any continuing obligation to the Jewish past. Brown sees the Letter to Hebrews as written from the vantage point of this fourth group, but addressed to those in the second group: "The Epistle to the Hebrews would see Jesus as replacing the Jewish high priesthood and sacrifices, and would place the Christian altar in

heaven."[4] The Romans addressed felt the need for extra safety provisions from the old Pact (*Diathēkē*, "Covenant"), which they had formerly observed. The Letter says those assurances are no longer necessary, since the new Pact has fulfilled what was merely hoped for under the old.

> The style of Hebrews is totally different from Paul's, and there is nothing in the Apostle's writings to match the prolonged radical critique of Israelite cult that is at the heart of Hebrews. Indeed, in Romans chapters 9.11 and 15.16, Paul shows himself far more preservative of Judaism and its cultic language than does Hebrews, which would replace the Old Testament sacrifices, priesthood, and Tabernacle.[5]

Of course, the Letter would not be persuasive with those who still respected Jewish cult if it showed outright contempt for that cult. Rather, the author builds on respect for the Mosaic Pact, to show that the second Pact is even more majestic. Was the first one given to Moses through angels? The second one comes directly from God's Son. Did the first one deliver partial and temporary forgiveness for sin? The second one gives permanent and final rescue from it. Did the first one placate God with animal sacrifice? The second one offers God the perfect sacrifice—that of his own Son. The whole Letter is an argument a fortiori. Did the first Pact bring one toward God? How much the more should the second one take men to God along with his Son. The argument is compressed, symbolically, into the contrast between Mount Sinai and Mount Zion.

> You have not, obviously, arrived this time at a material mountain, with burning fire, darkness, gloom, and whirlwind; no ringing trumpet or spoken words, at whose sound hearers begged to hear no more, so did they cringe from the decree, "Let but a beast touch the mountain, it will be stoned to death" [Ex 19.12–13]. So intimidating was what he saw that Moses said, "I am shaking with fear." No, you have arrived at Mount Zion and the city of the living God, heavenly Jerusalem, with thousands of angels in joyous company, and all of heaven's registered

firstborn, and God judging all, and the completed souls of the just, and
Jesus, guarantor of the new Pact, and a blood outpoured more eloquent
than Abel's. (12.18–24)

The attempt to reassure those who miss the Mosaic promises leads the
Letter's author to his most innovative maneuver. Do the faltering Romans
miss the priesthood of the Mosaic dispensation? Then he will supply them
with a startling new priesthood, one not known or referred to anywhere
else in the Christian writings called the New Testament. For an audience
that misses the old institutions, this move is more placatory than provok-
ing. The Letter will call up earlier associations and historical memories,
emphasizing Mosaic description of worship in the Shrine, sacrifice outside
the settlement, and entry into the Holy of Holies. Above all, it will empha-
size the centrality of blood-offering in the worship of God, where the blood
of Jesus trumps the blood of bulls and goats.

All these things, vivid in the Mosaic cult but vanished with the Temple
in Jerusalem, are given a new life in the presentation of Jesus as *both* the
sacrificing priest and the victim being sacrificed. This is a bold concession to
Jewish thought. Early Christians had abolished the priesthood. The Letter
restores it—in a new light, but one that underlines the basic dignity of the
priesthood in all its forms. Aaron is honored, in order to elevate Jesus (with
the help of Melchizedek) even higher in the holy ranks of God.

Some argued that putting Jesus in the mold of Melchizedek made the
prefigurer take the spotlight from the fulfillment. But except for the "priest
forever" line in Psalm 110, Melchizedek does not give us a detailed model
of Jesus' priesthood. We are not told what sacrifice Melchizedek offered
to honor Abraham. Rather, like sacrifices in the Aaronic line, the Letter
stresses a *blood-offering* as what any high priest must perform: "Without
shed blood there is no freeing from sin" (9.22).

With the importance of the priesthood and of blood sacrifice in mind,
we can trace the progress of the Letter's argument, in eight main steps, with
an exhortation, sometimes long, sometimes short, after each step.

1. Superiority of the New Pact (1.1–14)

A modern reader, with the long history of Christology in mind, may wonder why the Letter begins with the messianic Psalm 110 to prove that Jesus is superior not only to Moses but to angels. But we should remember that it was popularly thought that angels were cooperating agents in the inscription of the tablets of the Law on Sinai (K 205). Ceslas Spicq says that this belief is common in Jewish apocrypha, as well as in secular authors like Philo and Josephus (S 1.54–55). It is easy to see how even some passages in the Old Testament could have suggested this idea—for instance, Deuteronomy 33.2:

> The Lord came from Sinai
> and shone forth from Seir.
> He showed himself from Mount Paran,
> and with him were myriads of holy ones
> streaming along at his right hand.

The angels may stream along at Yahweh's right hand. But they are not asked to sit at his right hand, as the Son of God is. They may be winds and a burst of flame (1.7). But this is far below the dignity of the Son.

> And to what angel did he ever say,
>> Sit at my right hand,
>>> till I make your enemies your footstool?
> Are not all angels [merely] helping spirits, to attend those who will inherit the rescue? (1.13–14)

The author has set up one pole of his argument a fortiori, by saying the new Pact is contracted not by Moses, with or without angelic help, but by the Son of God.

This argument is applied in the *exhortation* (2.1–4). If one had to heed the old Pact, mediated by angels, *how much more* should one be faithful to the new one, revealed by the Son of God himself.

2. A Mediator Who Shares Our Humanity (2.5–3.19)

It is a surprising turn for the author, after arguing that the Son of God is higher than the angels, to quote Psalm 8 on mankind as lower than the angels and to apply it to Jesus. He is preparing the way for insisting that Jesus was fully man as well as fully God—the reason the Eastern fathers, with their debates on the Incarnation and Trinity, were so ready to adopt this Letter. As man, Jesus showed mercy toward men as his brothers. This is part of the mission given him by his Father, to which mission he demonstrates his fidelity (as the *pistos archiereus*, 2.17).

The *exhortation* (3.1–19) says that, as fellows in the humanity of Christ, we should have the same fidelity to our calling that Jesus demonstrated in his fidelity to the Father's assignment. It is important to translate *pistis*, and its adjectival form *pistos*, not as "faith" but as "fidelity." Modern "faith" usually means belief. But Jesus does not *believe* in the Father, or in the Pact with men. He shows fidelity on his side, so we should reciprocate with fidelity to the Pact that ties us to the Father: "Focus your minds on the emissary and high priest we profess, on his fidelity to the one who sent him, like the fidelity of Moses to his house" (3.1–2). Moses does not *believe in* his house; he retains fidelity to the charge he was given over it. The first Pact failed, not because God lacked fidelity to it, but because the people "did not keep together in fidelity with those who heeded it" (*sugkekerasmenoi en pistei*, 3.19). This shows that fidelity is not simply an individual duty but the social calling of the people of God. They were made one in the Pact, but they failed to observe their own oneness.

3. The New Pact Is the Promised New Day (4.1–16)

God, who rested after his own labors, promised peaceful rest to his people. When Joshua did not provide lasting peace (*katapausis*, "lasting rest") after he took the people into the Promised Land (Josh 21.43, 22.4), David said there would be a *new* day to find peace (Psalm 95.7), predicting the second Pact. Since *Iēsous* can stand either for Joshua or for Jesus, some have translated it as Jesus in 4.8. But since that discusses the failure of peace under the first Pact, it cannot be Jesus. Joshua was the foretype of Jesus, and the "rest" promised (*pausis*) becomes a final rest (*katapausis*), or peace, under the new Pact.

The *exhortation* (4.14–16), signaled as so often by a hortatory subjunctive (4.11), says, "Let us press on, then, toward our peace," and holds people to fidelity by a stress on God's mind as evaluating (*enthymēseōn*) the inmost thoughts of the human heart (4.13). *Logos* here is normally translated "word," but the enunciations of the Lord, whether in Scripture or direct command, are not what evaluates the heart, but what commands it. Evaluation is done by *logos* as the pondering faculty. "To him we must turn our mind" (*Pros hōn hēmin ho logos*, 4.13).

4. A Priest with Our Frailties (5.1–6.12)

The comparison with Aaron's priesthood means that Jesus is called, as Aaron was; and like Aaron, he can speak for human frailty ("sin apart," 4.15). This passage, more than any other in the New Testament, shows how Christ prayed to avoid death, how "he used pleading and supplication to the one who could rescue him, with a piercing scream and tears" (5.7). This is setting up the later claim that Christ not only performed sacrifice, but he *was* the sacrifice. Aaron sprinkled the blood of slaughtered animals. Christ offered his own slaughtered body.

The *exhortation* here (5.11–6.12) is anticipatory. The author has just mentioned Melchizedek, and he is about to give a long defense of this new point. Its utter newness is emphasized when the Letter says that "to reason it out in words is hard" (5.11), especially since the audience is "loath to listen." This new teaching goes beyond what the audience has already learned—including such "basics" as the Resurrection and the Last Judgment! (6.2). This is a harsh section, saying that those who have turned back from their commitment to God cannot be pardoned (a point debated by other early Christians, but here settled in the camp of the strictest school).

5. In Common with Melchizedek (6.13–8.6)

The long minatory passage is followed by a long expository passage. The last argument had pointed out Jesus' similarities with Aaron, as priest sharing weaknesses with his people. This section stresses the differences from Aaron derived from Jesus' earlier and higher tie to Melchizedek, who lived in the patriarchal period before the first Pact, where he was somehow "a priest forever." Those in Aaron's line are not priests forever. They perform transitory and repeated sacrifices, and receive tithes, and then die (7.8, 7.20). These Levites *receive* tithes, but through Abraham's loins they *gave* tithes to Melchizedek (7.9–10). The Levites are not confirmed in their priesthood by an oath, but Melchizedek and Jesus were both assured by the Lord's word in Psalm 110.4 (7.20–28). Here the argument gets thin. Melchizedek is not only a priest forever, but one whose foreverness is attested by God under oath!

The *exhortation* (8.1–6) calls listeners to a higher fidelity, commensurate with the higher priesthood Christ holds as guarantor of the new Pact, of which the first Pact was merely an earthly foretype. Christ presides in the heavenly reality, and we should rejoice in the surety he provides.

6. The Old Pact Is Canceled (8.7–10.39)

The Letter says that Jeremiah (31.31) had prophesied that there would be a new Pact because the people broke the old one (8.9). The old Pact had its aura (9.1–5), but the author shows how the new one excels the first. What is left of the old Pact in the time of the Letter is no longer animal sacrifice, but minor points like the food code (9.9–10). Under the old Pact, priests had to go repeatedly into the Shrine (9.6), but Christ goes only once into the heavenly Holy of Holies (9.25–28), offering not the blood of bulls and goats but of himself (9.18–22). The author notes even minor differences in the two priesthoods—for example, that earlier priests offered sacrifice standing (10.11) while Christ sits in his eternal act of sacrifice (10.12–13).

On the other hand, there are surprising similarities between the two priesthoods. The Levitical high priest purified the Holy of Holies when he entered it, so Christ, with a nobler sacrifice, must (*anagkē*) purify the heavenly holiness when he enters it (9.23–24). Why the heavens were defiled before this, and needed purification, stymies the commentators. (See chapter 12.) Ceslas Spicq rightly says: "The idea of prior impurity makes no sense where the heavenly sanctuary is concerned" (S 2.267). The author seems to have let the search for parallels between sacrificial rites under the old Pact and the new Pact run away with him. The two rituals must be different enough to assure the superiority of Christ to Aaron; yet they must be similar enough to make comparing them a sensible project.

The *exhortation* (10.19–39) notes that, under the old Pact, the people were left outside the inner veil when the high priest entered there. The Letter urges hesitant Christians to go boldly as high as Jesus is leading them, since his flesh is the veil through which they enter the heavenly sanctuary (10.20). There is no excuse left for backsliding (10.38), just as there is no forgiveness if one rejects the light (10.26–31).

7. Fidelity to the Old Pact a Model for Fidelity to the New (11.1–12.17)

After being harsh on the theme of non-forgiveness to backsliders, the author tries to ingratiate himself with those honoring their Jewish past with a roll call of great Jewish heroes. This is the chapter where "fidelity" for *pistis* is most important. This may not be apparent from 11.3: "By fidelity we realize how history [*hoi aiōnes*] was put together [*katartisthēsan*] by the Word of God [*logos*], how visible things arose from things invisible." With "faith" as the translation, this used to be taken as belief in creation and the supernatural. But the examples given show that it is trust in the providential Promises of God that guided patriarchal heroes and their descendants. Fidelity to the unseen is exemplified in Noah, who was "divinely warned [*chrēmatistheis*] of dangers not yet visible" (11.7). But what about 11.6? "Without fidelity one cannot please God, since to approach God one must trust [*pisteusai*] that he is and that he rewards those seeking him." That, too, is a matter of lived experience under the *logos* of God, the plan he reveals through his promises.[6]

How, one might wonder, can the patriarchs have fidelity to a Pact that was not yet given? For those living before Moses was given the Pact, the promises (*epaggeliai*) given the patriarchs, and especially to Abraham, offer a lodestar for fidelity (11.9, 17). The author says that the promises to Abraham and his descendants were forebears of the Pact.

It must always be remembered that belief or unbelief was not the issue for the Letter's audience. It believed too much in the old Pact, making it backslide from the new one. In line with the a fortiori argument running throughout the Letter, one must discern the point of this chapter. If God rewarded fidelity to the old promises and Pact, *how much more* should the faltering Romans maintain their fidelity to the new one? After all, those of old did not even see the fulfillment of the promises, as we have (11.39). Their completion came only with us (11.40). We should not let them down, from our easier place in the plan of God.

The *exhortation* (12.1–17) takes the ordeals of those under the old Pact (11.35–38) as models for the tests and trials the Romans are experiencing. The hortative subjunctive—"Let us run . . . the course" (12.1)—gives way to imperatives: "Bear it as training" (12.7). "Seek peace" (12.14).

8. The New Pact More Majestic (12.18–13.25)

I quoted earlier the contrast between Mount Sinai and Mount Zion as the author's argument for the superiority of the new Pact. Here this brief argument is followed by a long and final *exhortation* (12.25–13:25). This is marked by direct imperatives (12.25, 13.7, 9, 16, 18, 23:25) and hortatory subjunctives (12.28, 13.13, 15). Despite this overall "paraenetic" tone, there are some teaching elements in the mix—the use of Haggai 2.6, for instance, to say that God's judgment will be final this time, the decree that establishes an everlasting city (12.26–28). Also, the author's desire to draw parallels between the old and the new priesthoods leads him to an aside on the place where the sacrificial animals were slaughtered: "The animals, whose blood is brought into the sanctuary by the high priest for sin-offerings, have their carcasses burnt outside the camp—just as Jesus, in order to sanctify the people with his own blood, suffered outside the city gate. Let us go to him outside the camp . . ." (13.11–13).

This aside raises difficulties that will take some considering in my next chapter. Here it is enough to remind the reader that Hebrews is not discussing the Temple in Jerusalem, but the itinerant Shrine carried by the Israelites on their journey through the desert toward the Promised Land. The Shrine of the Ark was moved along from one "camp" (*parembolē*) to the next. The sons of Levi had to carry the Shrine throughout this exodus, dismantling it in one place and setting it up at the next site, where the priests could sacrifice before the Ark. This distance from Temple liturgy shows how entirely literary and escapist was the yearning back to Moses' time by the Letter's audience. Its members were not actually sacrificing at the Shrine anymore—much less at the Temple that replaced it and was destroyed in 70 CE; instead, they were clinging to vestigial elements of the Law like the food code (13.9). Jesus has replaced Aaron as a more exalted priest than the people of God had ever known before.

The Letter ends with an attempt to reintegrate its listeners into their former social bonds—urging that they return to the house churches, welcome other Christians there, care for one another, pray for one another, love one another, and take pride in the Pact that unites them in shared fidelity to their Rescuer (13.1–17).

NOTES

1. Niels Peter Lemche, "Hebrew," ABD, vol. 3, p. 95.
2. Joseph A. Fitzmyer, *The Acts of the Apostles* (Doubleday, 1997), pp. 346–48.
3. Raymond Brown, in John P. Meier and Brown, *Antioch and Rome* (Paulist Press, 1983), pp. 1–9.
4. Ibid., p. 7.
5. Raymond E. Brown, *The Churches the Apostles Left Behind* (Paulist Press, 1984), p. 25.
6. Greek *logos* has a wide range of meanings, depending on context. To take the first dictionary sense, "word," in all its occurrences, is to defy this range. It can

mean "argument" or "rationale" or "sense" or "list." *Ho Logos* can mean Wisdom (*Sophia*, as in *Verbum Dei*). I translated it earlier as "mind" (4.13). Here it is clearly the program or plan of God, which lies behind all the providential maneuvers for his people. The broad sweep of the word is related to its root, *leg-*, where *legein* means to "gather," "assemble," "sort," "consolidate," and so forth. See Hjalmar Frisk, *Griechisches etymologisches Wörterbuch* (Carl Winter Universitätsverlag, 1960–1970) s.v. "*lego.*"

TWELVE

A New High Priest

Later tradition has incorporated the assertions of the Letter to Hebrews, making the priesthood an accepted institution in some branches of Christianity. This fact masks the novelty of what was attested nowhere outside the Letter among the early writings. But unless we see that the Letter was making a new case for Jesus as priest, using the rejected Jewish institution as a model, we cannot evaluate the selective reading of the ceremonies Jewish priests performed, the substitution of human sacrifice for animal sacrifice, and the attempt to smuggle the priesthood back through the side door of Melchizedek. So important is the title of high priest to the Letter—though that title comes not from Melchizedek but from the Aaronic priesthood—that Christ is called our high priest seven times in Hebrews (2.17, 3.1, 5.10, 6.20, 7.26, 8.1, 9.11).

We also have to pay close attention to what the Letter does *not* claim. It nowhere says that the priesthood would be a continuing institution for Christian men (or women). In fact, it says the opposite. Jesus is the last priest, whose onetime offering makes all other priesthoods obsolete. Like Melchizedek, Jesus has no lineage before or after him, just the single and isolated act of one all-accomplishing sacrifice. It was only after the Letter had insinuated the new concept of Jesus as a priest that other aspects of Jewish practice could make their way into Christian gatherings—including the idea of a continuing line of priests who were not Jesus themselves but prolonged the repetition of his unrepeatable act.

The Letter would not spell out at such length what Jesus validates from Jewish practice if it were not presenting something novel, something meant to reassure the Roman Christians who yearned back toward their Jewish roots. It was laying a new foundation for an altered belief. No wonder the

Letter calls it something *added to* old and accepted teachings—old teachings like the resurrection of the dead and the Last Judgment. This new thing is hard to reason out in words (*dysermeneutos legein*, 5.11), though the Letter makes an energetic effort to do just that. Here is the Jewish foundation being laid for the higher priesthood of Jesus (9.1–10):

> The first Pact, it is true, had rules for worship, and a sanctuary in the created order. There a Shrine was prepared; in it were the lampstand, and the table, and the place for grain offering—it was called the Holy Place. But beyond a second veil was the Holy of Holies, with the gold incense-altar and the Ark of the Pact cased in gold. Here were the gold jar keeping the manna, the staff of Aaron that blossomed, the tablets of the Pact, and the Cherubim of Splendor hovering above the Purgation Site—things it is now impossible to describe exactly.
>
> Given these arrangements, the priests continually enter the first Shrine to perform the sacred acts, but into the second only the high priest enters, and only once a year, and not without blood to offer for himself and for the people's unrecognized sins. As the Holy Spirit makes clear, the way into the sanctuary cannot be revealed while there is still validity in the first Shrine—which is a symbol for its time, where gifts and sacrifices are offered without the power to restore the inner self of the one performing them, affecting as they do food and drink and ablutions, fleshly requirements imposed before the moment of their being put right.

The modern reader may well be puzzled by the fact that the high priest offers sacrifice for sins that are "unrecognized" (*agnoēmatōn*, 9.7). But the purity rules for Jewish observance and for proper ritual were so extensive and complex that it was easy for those wanting to be part of any ceremony to have omitted some requirement without knowing it (K 206, 397).[1] So the priest must first purify the impure before their sacrifice can be accepted. Ritual performance must, by its very nature, be carried out punctiliously. As the scholar Hugh Lloyd-Jones says of similarly exigent classical Greek ritual: "The recital of details which might seem boring to the uninitiated person is in fact absolutely necessary . . . immense importance [is] attached to the proper performance . . . [including] the ritual silence which the proper performance of sacrifice required."[2] The Jewish priests had even higher stakes for their performance. Jacob Milgrom explains:

> Israel, like its contemporaries, was of the opinion that the slightest deviation from the prescribed ritual would not only nullify the ritual but arouse the wrath of the deity . . . The sanctuary would not be purged, leaving the prospect that the Lord would abandon it and his people to their doom.[3]

Such punctiliousness is signaled in the first Pact's "rules" (*dikaiōmata*, 9.1). These presumed (*gar*) that the outer Shrine be "prepared" (*kateskeuasthē*) for worship "in the created order" (*kosmikon*, as opposed to the heavenly sanctuary soon to be mentioned). Given such precision, it comes as something of a surprise that the Letter does not everywhere conform to the prescriptions in the "rule books" of the Pentateuch (K 395–96). The Letter says that the jar of manna and Aaron's staff were contained inside the Ark (9.4), though Scripture says they were placed outside it (Ex 16.30, Num 17.10). The Letter says the incense-altar was placed inside the Holy of Holies (9.4), though Scripture says it was outside it (Ex 30.1–10).[4]

Koester reasons that there were probably different traditions about ancient arrangements (K 395), which may be why the Letter says that the situation "is now impossible to describe exactly" (9.5). It was important for the Letter's author to describe what his target audience thought about Jewish practices, since he is going to make a careful comparison/contrast with the new dispensation brought by Jesus. This fact reinforces what is clear from the Letter taken as a whole—that the author, though not present in Rome at the time of writing, had been there before and knew intimately the people he is addressing. He has to stick to what his audience thought about Mosaic Law.

Having set the template for the old (discontinued) procedures in the

Shrine of the traveling Ark, the Letter now draws the contrast with what Jesus offers to the backsliding Romans:

> Christ, however [*de*], is now at hand [*paragenomenos*], high priest of blessings that are to come in a greater and final Shrine, one not made by hands, indeed not in this order of creation. He has made a one-time [*hapax*] entry into this Holy Place, pioneering [*heuronemos*] an all-time [*aiōnion*] rescue, not by virtue of goat blood or calf blood, but by his own blood. If, after all, the blood of goats and bulls, and the sprinkled ashes of a heifer, make holy the unclean, purifying even the flesh, how much more does Christ's blood, unstained, offered in the timeless Spirit, cleanse the inner self of deathly activity to serve the God of life? (9.11–14)

Here begins the point-by-point contrast between sacrifice under the old Pact and sacrifice under the new.

> The old took place in a structure made by hand, in the created order.
> The new takes place in a non-material sanctuary outside the created order.
> The old had a daily service in the outer Shrine, and an annual ceremony in the Holy of Holies.
> The new offering takes place only once, and its effect lasts forever (*aiōnion*).
> The old sacrifice had to purify the sacrificer himself from his sins.
> The new one is offered by one unstained (*amōmon*) by sin.
> The old cleansing went only as deep as the flesh.
> The new one restores innocence to the inner self (*syneidēsis*).
> The old Pact went by the times of calendrical prescription.
> The new one is offered through the timeless (*aiōnios*) Spirit.

This first comparison sketches the outline of the Letter's argument. The author is about to go deeper into the contrasts, and to go deeper into trouble. The odd legalistic turn of the author's mind now turns sacrifice into a testamentary *bequest*.

> This is what makes him the guarantor of a new Pact, so that—a death having taken place for release from offenses committed under the first Pact—those designated might receive the everlasting inheritance that was pledged them. Where inheritance is concerned, the death of the testator must be certified; it has no force so long as the testator is alive. Thus even the first Pact was not initiated without blood. After every requirement of the Law had been promulgated by Moses to the entire people, he took the blood of calves, along with water and scarlet wool and hyssop, and sprinkled the book itself and all the people, saying, "This is the blood of the Pact that God has put into effect for you." And the Shrine and all the instruments of worship he sprinkled in the same way with blood. That is why nearly all purifications under the Law are by blood, since without shed blood there is no freeing from sin. (9.15–22)

When the Letter moves the category of Christ's action from sacrifice to bequest, the author makes what at first is a surprising assertion—that for Christ to certify the bequest he must first die. This is surprising because the Letter had earlier made Melchizedek's priesthood superior to that of the Levites because the latter all die while Melchizedek does not (7.23–24). Of course, though Jesus dies to fulfill the requirement of his bequest, he rises again to eternal life (in legal terms, would that invalidate the bequest?). He is the sacrificial victim in the *shedding* of his blood, but the sacrificing priest in his *offering* of that blood. The Jewish template that was first invoked and then transcended leads to difficulties. It is not easy to make Jesus the priest *and* the victim of a sacrifice that leaves a bequest to those not the recipients of the sacrifice. Believers in Jesus receive the bequest, but the Father receives the sacrifice.

The slaughter that supplied the necessary blood for sacrifice under the first Pact was carried out by the priests or their agents—they must kill the sacrificial animal to have a claim on it before surrendering it to Yahweh.

Does Jesus have to kill himself in order to possess the victim for offering to the Father, having *become* the victim after killing it? As we shall see later on, the idea that Jesus as priest had to kill the sacrifice (himself) perturbed later Christian thinkers. They labored at nervous and convoluted denials. Besides, the remains of the sacrificed animals were disposed of by burning—a far cry from Jesus' being seated at the Father's right hand as a perpetual victim/priest. If what Jesus is doing is making out a bequest, the receivers of the bequest are not the receivers of the sacrifice—which is offered to the Father, who can get no benefits from the bequest.

The Letter is tangling itself in increasingly intricate consequences.

Now if the copy of the heavens must be purified by such sacrifices, heaven itself must be purified by sacrifices that are higher still. Christ, you know, entered no Holy Place of human construction, the mere reflection of what truly is, but into the reality itself, standing face to face with God as our representative—not to offer himself over and over, as the high priest enters the sanctuary annually to offer blood not his own. Doing that would mean, for Jesus, his own repeated dying down through ages. Instead, when the wait of ages ended, he came on the scene a single time, to erase sin by sacrificing himself. And whereas a single death is set for all men, and after that judgment, correspondingly Christ made a single offering to forgive the sins of many, and after that will he appear again, without sin, to rescue those waiting for him. (9.23–28)

The first sentence of this passage has led to tortuous exercises in explication. Paul Ellingworth counts eight entirely different interpretations of verse 9.23. David Allen counts nine. And there are more.[5] The Letter has, up to this point, been arguing that heaven is a far more sacred "sanctuary" than the pale replica of it in the Shrine's Holy of Holies. Yet now it says that even heaven needed purifying by higher "sacrifices" (plural) than those carried out in the Shrine. What made it need this re-holying of the holiest place? And how was it to be purified? I have already quoted Ceslas Spicq as saying, "The idea of prior impurity makes no sense where the heavenly sanctuary is concerned" (S 2.267). Then how does he treat the passage? He considers four possibilities, in an ascending order of acceptability (S 2.266–68).

Spicq

1. Since the church is a temple of God, *it* is the thing being purified—a reading he calls "quite arbitrary."

2. Patristic authors wrote that the angelic rebellion began in heaven, so Christ completes the purifying of all diabolic traces of the place from which they fell—he calls this more acceptable (*plus satisfaisant*).

3. Even better is the idea that the blood of Christ is a kind of "immunization" against sin—as the high priest was purified by blood *before* he entered the Holy of Holies. Since Jesus himself needs no immunizing against sin, this must apply to "the body of Christ made up of believers," a body of which he is the head. So he purifies those he is taking with him to heaven.

4. Spicq mainly prefers to take "purify" as meaning "dedicate"—so Jesus dedicates heaven to a new purpose, for receiving those he has redeemed. Ellingworth accepts this reading, though there are no real parallels for "purify" meaning "dedicate."[6]

Koester

Since the Shrine is an antitype to the type in heaven, lower purifications should echo higher ones: "Christ did not purify the heavenly sanctuary because he was bound to follow the Levitical pattern; rather, the reverse is true" (K 427). But this goes against the argument of Hebrews, that Jewish sacrifice is the foreshadowing of the heavenly. By Koester's logic, the lower should not need purifying because the heavenly is already pure.

Attridge

Since "cultic cleansing is a matter of the heart and mind," it is the conscience of believers that is purified as they participate in Christ's rise to represent them in heaven.[7] But the text says nothing about believers, just about

Christ's entry into heaven as purifying heaven. Peter O'Brien, David Allen, and F. F. Bruce agree with the Attridge argument.[8]

Lane
William Lane, against almost all other commentators, takes the text literally, which Spicq said would be "monstrous." He argues: "Sin as defilement is contagious . . . reaching even to the heavenly things themselves."[9]

Bourke
Myles Bourke assumes that there were two chambers to heaven, corresponding to the outer Shrine and inner Shrine on earth. Then the purifying of heaven would apply only to "the intermediate heavens, which correspond to the outer part of the earthly tabernacle."[10] There is no biblical support for multiplying heavens in this way.

Johnson
Luke Timothy Johnson thinks that the parallel between purifying the Shrine and purifying heaven just shows carelessness on the author's part: "This may be a case where grammatical choice is governed by the logic of the image rather than by the logic of the argument."[11] Before we dismiss such a conclusion, we should remember that Myles Bourke said something similar about the difficulties the Letter got into when it ended up with two "priests forever" and did not know what to do with the first one (Melchizedek) when the second one (Christ) returned to heaven.[12] Bourke thought that when the Letter lined up two things parallel with each other, it seized one point of similarity between the two and then overlooked all the crippling differences that this entailed.

A perfect example of these strained parallels is still to come in the Letter, in an aside contained in its final chapter.

Do not veer off after fancy and unusual teachings—since it is well, you know, for the heart to be steadied by God's favor, not by food codes that did no good for those observing them in the past. We have an altar where officiators at the Shrine are not allowed to eat. The animals, whose blood is brought into the sanctuary by the high priest for sin-offerings, have their carcasses burnt outside the camp—just as Jesus, in order to sanctify the people with his own blood, suffered outside the city gate. Let us go to him outside the camp, to share his humiliation, since we have no lasting city here but are on a quest for that to come. (13.9–13)

There is a dizzying sequence in that passage, made up of connections that hurry by (Thomas Aquinas called them "quite finespun," *valde subtilis*). Consider the flow of the argument:

(a) It is a novelty to revert to Jewish eating codes, but

(b) we have an eating code to which others have no access, since

(c) Jesus was not sacrificed inside the sanctuary; rather,

(d) he was killed outside the city, and

(e) we should stay outside the earthly city, looking toward a heavenly one.

Take these slippery steps one at a time:

(a) Against "Novelty"

In a bit of rhetorical one-upmanship, the Letter says that reverting to Jewish legalism is, in the context of the Pact Jesus initiated, following ideas that are "fancy" (*poikilai*) and "unusual" (*xenai*). As opposed to such giddy itchings, the heart should stay steady (*kardia bebaia*) with God's help, not by legalisms that failed in the past. It is ironic that the "new" teaching is shown to be a "past" failure.

(b) Proper "Eating"

Against the false "novelty" of Jewish eating codes, the Roman Christians should eat at the new Pact's altar, from which others are interdicted. What is the altar, and who are the others? It has been easy for later Christians to think this verse refers to the Eucharist, eaten at the Mass. That is especially appealing since the Genesis account of Melchizedek says he gave Abraham "food" (14.18). From the late second century, when Clement of Alexandria applied this verse to the Eucharist, this has been part of the Melchizedekian priesthood (K 26). But *the Letter omits the mention of bread and wine* when it describes the meeting of Melchizedek and Abraham (7.1–3). Clearly the author did not connect Melchizedek with the Eucharist, as Spicq confirms (S 2.245–47). In fact, nowhere does the Letter refer to the Eucharist (K 569).

Then what is the altar referred to in Hebrews, from which some are barred? Start with the latter point. Those interdicted are called "officiators" (*latreuantes*) at the Shrine of Moses. But there were no such worshipers, any more than there was a Shrine. It had long ago been replaced by Solomon's Temple, and then by Herod's Temple—and both of *those* were gone. That seems to be the point of the Letter. The Judaizing Romans were longing back to a failed first Pact. Even if the survivors of that ritual world were still around, they could not be part of the altar of the new Pact. The Letter says they could not eat at the altar of the new Pact. What does "not" mean? The author is running the parallel with the failed food code of verse 13.9—just as he made the careless coupling of eternal priesthood in the Melchizedek-Christ comparison, or in the Shrine-heaven coupling. What Bourke and Johnson said about his failure to think through a comparison, after noting some salient aspect of it, is true here as well.

The "eating at the altar" is, by the logic of the Letter, a way of receiving the benefits of the new sacrifice made by Jesus, one that is just as efficacious as the old Pact's requirements had been feckless. Spicq (2.45), Koester, and many others follow Thomas Aquinas in saying, "The altar referred to is either Christ's cross, where Christ was offered up for us, or Christ himself, in whom and through whom we direct our prayers."[13]

We must remember that the author is writing for a specific audience. He did not think he was writing for the ages, or putting a new item in the inspired canon. He thinks always of what will work with the Romans who were yearning back to Jewish eating (and other) habits. He says that the

Jews, even when they had the Shrine from Moses, did not have what believers in the new Pact have—the final eschatological feast with Jesus in heaven (the feast referred to in the Lord's Prayer).[14]

(c) Where Jesus Was Sacrificed

By a leap in thought backward, the author says that the old Pact's sacrifice was made in the Holy of Holies, but the sacrifice of Jesus did not take place in what, so far, the author has treated as the antitype-type pairing with the Holy of Holies—namely, heaven—but outside the camp. In a kind of bait-and-switch, the camp of the Mosaic exodus has become Jerusalem in Jesus' time. The Letter is making one of those imbalanced balancing acts between sacrifice under the old Pact and under the new. The supposed equivalents line up this way, comparing the high priest's Yom Kippur sacrifice with Jesus' offering to the Father:

Offering in Holy of Holies	Offering in Heaven
High Priest	Son of God
Annual	Eternal
Goats and Bulls	Jesus
Temporary Forgiveness	Lasting Forgiveness

Now measure the specific events (13.10–12) against this abstract template, putting in ordinary type what is expected from the logic of the schema and in uppercase what must be added:

Slaughter of Victims	Crucifixion
Offering in Holy of Holies	Offering in Heaven
BURNING OF CARCASSES	CRUCIFIXION

Why is the Crucifixion, out of logical and chronological order, repeated before and after the offering? The burning of the carcasses, in the first column, is a mere afterthought to dispose of the *unsacrificed* parts of the animal. The animal is slaughtered in the outer court of the Shrine by laymen, then its sacred blood is splashed on the altar of atonement by the high priest, and then the unclean residue of the sacrifice, its physical remnants, are burnt "outside the camp," and the choice animal parts are burnt on the altar for God's acceptance. Only then are the unsacrificed (and so unclean) parts of the animal taken out to unsanctified ground and burnt. Nothing these late verses of the Letter introduce into the picture fits with the argument prepared so far.

Why has the Letter put the Crucifixion in this chronologically late and ritually subordinate position? The sacrifice of the animals must be of perfect and unblemished male parts (Lev 1.3, 10). The carcasses disposed of later are of unclean and unimportant remains. Jesus is the unblemished victim of the Letter (9.14). His death should be paired with the death of the unblemished animals, not with their unclean remains. What has led to the strange linking of the Crucifixion with the last and least treatment of the animal remains?

There can be only one reason. The author has seized on a superficial point—action "outside the camp," to be paired with "outside Jerusalem" (for the Crucifixion)—and ignored all the other components of the larger argument. This is the very pattern Bourke and Johnson found elsewhere in the Letter. It also reflects the Letter's tendency to use, forget, or distort Jewish cult when it serves any one of several different purposes.

Consider this, for instance: the bones and skin burnt outside the camp were not part of what was sacrificed. That was completed inside the camp, when the high priest took the fats and innards into the Holy of Holies to be offered to God. Many people make the false association that Ellingworth does: "The killing of animals outside the gate thus foreshadows the death of Jesus outside the walls."[15] The animals were not *killed* outside the walls, but in the outer Shrine, the Holy Place. But it is impossible to keep the parts of the comparison in any logical kind of alignment. As Hans-Josef Klauck notes:

The paradox of this work is that it uses a thoroughly cultic language to make a deeply uncultic statement . . . Death on the cross was basically a noncultic affair, despite all the cultic terms employed . . . In this non-cultic place Jesus shed his redeeming and atoning blood for all.[16]

(d) "Go Outside" and (e) "Stay Outside"

In the next verse, the Letter says that, since Christ was taken outside the gate to be crucified, Christians should *stay* outside and not go back into the city. The author has already forgotten the reason animals were burnt out-side the camp—because the camp is sacred ground and the carcasses are unclean. Though they could be slaughtered in the camp, their remains cannot be burnt there. Jesus, too, had to be crucified outside of Jerusalem, because Jerusalem is the holy city, and unholy acts like crucifixion should not take place there. But now the Letter is saying Christians should stay outside the sacred camp/city in that place of defilement!

Koester, oddly, says that "staying outside the city allows Christians to minister to strangers, the afflicted, and prisoners who live outside the main-stream of urban life" (K 571). He wants to equate the mainstream of urban life with secular authority, since he had earlier claimed that they were the ones who could not eat of the Christian sacrifice: "The principal threat came from government officials, not the Law" (K 570). But how could hostile offi-cials be "officiators at the Shrine" (13.10)? This just shows how even as acute a student of the Letter as Koester can become confused in the whirl of con-tradictory leaps and doublings back in this passage.

He is not alone in this quandary. Ceslas Spicq says that the verse (9.13) calls on Christians to be voluntary exiles either from the pagan world or from the realm of Moses (2.427–28). Needless to say, the two are hardly identical, or even reconcilable. And how can the Letter be saying that Christians should have nothing to do with Moses when the high priesthood of Jesus is of the kind (though a superior kind) of sacrifice carried out by high priests following Mosaic Law?

F. F. Bruce sees the problem and then dodges it. He says the city is actually the sacred, the outside, the profane. Then why are the believers to stay out in the profane sphere?

> Were they to leave the sacred precincts and to venture onto unhallowed ground? Yes, because in Jesus the old values had been reversed. What was formerly sacred was now unhallowed, because Jesus had been expelled from it; what was formerly unhallowed was now sacred, because Jesus was there.[17]

But Jesus does not stay at Calvary. He takes his offering up to heaven, what was symbolized by the Holy of Holies, by the inmost sacredness.

Paul Ellingworth comes close to just throwing up his hands and surrendering the effort to make sense of this conclusion to the whole puzzling sequence:

> Problems arise when attempts are made to specify in greater detail the logical steps in the argument . . . On the one hand, it [verse 13.13] is understood as an exhortation to leave this world and seek Christian heaven (so Cambier, Nitsche). On the other hand, it is taken as an appeal to leave the cultic world for the secular (so, e.g., van der Bergh, van Eysingen, J. A. Sanders). Between these extremes, there are a variety of other explanations: the readers are to abandon Judaism; they are to "go out" in meditation to meet their Lord (Bruce); they are to leave worldly delights for asceticism; they are to flee the material for the spiritual (so Philo). The matter cannot be settled by appeal to the immediate context alone: verse 14 is quoted in support of an "otherworldly" interpretation, while verse 16 clearly suggests that the readers still have duties in this world. To understand this passage as an appeal to abandon Judaism for Christianity is foreign to the whole scope of the author's thought, which moves consistently within the category of God's twofold action on behalf of his one people. Obermueller rightly believes that the passage requires a double hermeneutic: liturgical and sociological; but this states the problem rather than solving it. The problem is not solved even by appeal

to the context of the entire epistle, with its implied or expressed cosmology; first of all, because the author appears to work with two distinct cosmological schemes (Ellingworth); and secondly, more important, because the present "location" of Christians in any such scheme is by its very nature ambivalent and transitional.[18]

There is more of that to come, but it leaves the matter even muddier.

Some seem to think that a polished writer, which the author of Hebrews certainly is, must be a profound thinker. But over and over the jointures of this Letter will not bear close scrutiny. That will become even clearer when we look at the Letter's doctrine on sacrifice.

NOTES

1. On ritual oversight, see Jacob Milgrom, *Leviticus 1–16* (Doubleday, 1991). He quotes Rabbi Akiva: "The burnt offering expiates, in the main, for neglected performative commandments" (p. 175). And: "The inadvertent offender . . . has contaminated the sanctuary" (p. 256). And: "A good example of this usage is the case of the Nazirite who accidently comes into contact with a corpse" (p. 229).
2. Sir Hugh Lloyd-Jones, "Ritual and Tragedy," in *The Further Academic Papers of Sir Hugh Lloyd-Jones* (Oxford University Press, 2005), pp. 156–57.
3. Milgrom, op. cit., p. 1030.
4. See the plan of the Shrine in Milgrom, op. cit., p. 135.
5. Paul Ellingworth, *The Epistle to the Hebrews* (Eerdmans, 1993), vol. 1, p. 477; David L. Allen, *The New American Commentary: Hebrews* (B&H Publishing Group, 2010), p. 485.
6. Ellingworth, op. cit., p. 477.
7. Harold W. Attridge, *The Epistle to the Hebrews* (Fortress Press, 1989), pp. 262–63. Peter T. O'Brien agrees with Attridge—see his *The Letter to the Hebrews* (Apollos, 2010), pp. 336–37.
8. O'Brien, op. cit., pp. 336–37; Allen, op. cit., pp. 485–86; F. F. Bruce, *The Epistle to the Hebrews*, revised edition (Eerdmans, 1990), pp. 228–29.
9. William L. Lane, *Hebrews 9–13* (Word Books, 1991), p. 247.
10. Myles M. Bourke, "The Epistle to the Hebrews," NJ, p. 938. The Letter, of course, makes no mention of such a division—and, in any case, the earthly purification takes place in the inner Shrine as well as the outer.
11. Luke Timothy Johnson, *Hebrews: A Commentary* (Westminster John Knox Press, 2006), p. 243.
12. Bourke, op. cit., p. 932.

13. Thomas Aquinas, *Commentary on the Letter to Hebrews*, par. 744.

14. Raymond Brown, "The Pater Noster as an Eschatological Prayer," in *New Testament Essays* (Doubleday, 1965), pp. 279–323.

15. Ellingworth, op. cit., p. 709.

16. Hans-Josef Klauck, "Sacrifice, New Testament," translated by Reginald H. Fuller, ABD, vol. 5, p. 890.

17. Bruce, op. cit., pp. 381–82.

18. Ellingworth, op. cit., p. 716.

IV

Jesus as Sacrifice

THIRTEEN

Human Sacrifice

The Greek word for sacrifice (*thysia*) occurs fifteen times in the Letter to Hebrews—more times than in all the rest of the New Testament, where it is mainly used for Jewish sacrifices, not that of Jesus, or for the unbloody offerings of devotion (Rom 12.1, Phil 2.17, 4.18). In only one place, apart from Hebrews, does the New Testament say that Jesus was sacrificed, in the supposedly Pauline Letter to Ephesians (5.2)—which is one of many reasons for thinking that Ephesians was not written by Paul himself. As Joseph Fitzmyer wrote:

> Paul never says that Christ was sacrificed for our sake. That notion enters the later theological tradition, but it is not one that can be traced directly to Paul . . . The notion of Christ's death as a sacrifice is more tributary to Hebrews and to the Deutero-Pauline Ephesians 5.2 than to the uncontested Pauline letters.[1]

And even Ephesians does not expressly compare Jesus to the high priest who offers a blood sacrifice. That idea is found only in the Letter to Hebrews. This alone argues that the change from animal sacrifice to human sacrifice is, in the case of Jesus, an improvement, a "higher sacrifice" of which the Aaronic sacrifices were just inferior "types." Such a claim goes against what most cultural historians have held—that the change from human sacrifice to animal sacrifice was a mark of greater enlightenment, of more settled civilization. Humane leaders were credited with the abolition of human sacrifice. According to ancient sources:

> Human sacrifices have long been abolished by various civilizers, divine and human: Lycurgus at Sparta, Dionysus at Potnieae, Eurypylus at

Patrae, and Diphilus in Cyprus. Gods and heroes have put an end to the practice among non-Greeks also: the descendants of Orestes upon arrival in Tenedos; Aphrodite, who turns the Cypriot Cerastae into bulls for sacrificing humans to Zeus; and Heracles, who, led to the altar as a victim by the Egyptian king Bousiris, kills Bousiris and his followers, thus putting an end to the savage custom. [One can add Artemis at Aulis.][2]

Human sacrifice was "remembered" in Greece as prehistoric. Since it is prehistoric, there is no direct written evidence for it. But as soon as writing comes in, there is little or no trace of it. It does not occur in Homer or Hesiod or the early lyric poets. It becomes a frequent subject, almost an obsessive one, only in fifth-century Attic tragedies, where it is seen as a distant and discredited ancestor of animal offerings. Human sacrifice as a reality gets little support from archeology. In a survey of all the cases brought forward for remains suggesting human sacrifice, Dennis Hughes finds mainly signs of ritual killing, which is different from sacrifice. Ritual killing—for example, sending slaves into a grave with a king or queen—is not an offering to a god but a provision for the king or queen in the afterlife.[3] Ritual cannibalism, if it occurred, is not necessarily a sacrifice, either.[4] The classics scholar Hugh Lloyd-Jones is properly skeptical about human sacrifice occurring in Greek prehistory:

> [Albrecht Henrichs] rightly concludes that the evidence for the practice of human sacrifice during the archaic period, not to mention the classical and Hellenistic periods, is insufficient, and that even for the Bronze Age the evidence that has been brought forward leaves much room for doubt. He is right, also, to point out that the known fact that in historical times a beast was often sacrificed, in theory, as a replacement for a human victim does not by itself suffice to prove that in earlier times a human victim had indeed been sacrificed.[5]

As soon as human sacrifice is remembered (or invented), it is treated with horror as a crime. This is typified by Agamemnon, who—in tragedy, but not in all that Homer has to say of Agamemnon—trades the life of his daughter, Iphigeneia, for favorable winds to carry his fleet. The winds had been obstructed by the goddess Artemis, who demands the sacrifice. She was upset that Agamemnon's men had killed a stag in her sacred garden.[6] Sophocles calls Iphigeneia a "stand-in" (*antistathmos*) for the stag (*Electra* 571). Aeschylus says that Agamemnon, in killing his daughter, was driven by *internal* winds that were "impious, unholy, impure" (*Agamemnon* 219–20). Euripides calls the sacrifice an "unholy slaughter by an unholy father" (*Iphigeneia in Aulis* 1318). Lucretius (1.101) tells the story of Iphigeneia to condemn religion in general:

Tantum religio potuit suadere malorum.
So suasive is religion to our bane.

Given the revulsion which human sacrifice generally inspired, one has to wonder why the Letter to Hebrews praises it so. Even the attempted sacrifice of Isaac by Abraham is often interpreted as a tale of cultural progress, replacing human oblation with an animal. We have seen that Greeks attributed that change to noble human or superhuman intervention. In this case, Yahweh himself overrules himself. He commands Abraham through an angel to offer a ram and not his son (Gen 22.1–18). Christian theologians from the time of the fathers have taken Abraham's willingness to kill his son as a foretype of Jesus' sacrifice to the Father.[7] But the sacrifice of Jesus *reverses* the Old Testament story. In Genesis, a ram is substituted for Isaac. In the Letter, Jesus is substituted for the goats and bulls killed on the Day of Atonement. That seems to be regression, not progress. The god(s) must again have human blood.

To make the problem even darker, we should remember that not only human sacrifice fell into disfavor. Animal sacrifice, too, is no longer practiced or held in any regard by our culture—or by modern Jews, even the most observant, even in Israel. In fact, some think that the notion of human sacrifice was accepted, back when it *was* accepted, to help explain anomalies in animal sacrifice, or to justify it as a more humane successor to some imagined primitive forebear. Certain theorists, it is true, cling to the idea of an original savagery "tamed" in later ritual—Walter Burkert, for instance, and René Girard.[8] But myth could just as well have invented bloodier origins to explain what are not very convincing rationales for animal sacrifice itself.[9]

Even this less "primitive" form of sacrifice was subjected to a withering critique while it was still being carried out. After all, what is the logic of sacrifice? It is that humans offer a god something he or she needs or wants in return for divine forgiveness, favor, protection, or promotion. The god, in other words, is biddable; can be bargained with; will respond in proportion to gifts given. To stress the commercial aspect of this transaction, evaluations were made of the victim's worth—it must be pure, choice, male not female, with no blemishes. In some Greek sacrifices, the monetary value of the victim was expressly established. In the fourth century BCE, on the island of Cos, the price of a bull for sacrifice to Zeus was produced for the priests.[10]

What does the god need or want? At the most primitive level, he or she must be fed, and humans can give them the desired sustenance. Leviticus (1.9) calls burnt offerings "a food-offering of soothing odor to the Lord." But Psalm 50.12 has a crushing answer to that idea, since Yahweh kicks sacrifice away from him:

If I were hungry, I would not tell you,
for the world and all that is in it are mine.

Nonetheless, the Deutero-Pauline Letter to Ephesians (5.2) could still quote Leviticus with approval, saying that Christ "gave himself over for your sake, as an offering and sacrifice with an odor soothing to God." But if the god is powerful enough to grant what the sacrificer is asking for, why is he or she not powerful enough to forage for his or her own food?

Some gods seem to need not food, but flattery. They hold a grudge if they are slighted by humans, and they avenge the slight. Artemis was feeling insulted when she demanded Iphigeneia from Agamemnon. The gods fight for turf and credit among themselves. Hera would save Troy while

Zeus dooms the city. Even if the gods are not feeling assuageably hurt or angry, men seem to feel they should give the gods something to exact favors from them. According to the old saying, "I give that you may give" (*do ut des*). Expressing human need, the sacrificers give up something of value to themselves. The expectation is that the gods will reciprocate with something of value to them. If they cannot do this, if they do not have something of value they can part with, there is no equity in the exchange. That is why Aristotle said that men cannot deal with gods on an equal basis.[11]

But what can men supply that the gods do not have? Honor? Gods should have a sense of their own worth. Woodrow Wilson famously said that some nations are "too proud to fight." Gods, if they are gods, should be too proud to solicit the esteem of inferior beings. Ancient philosophers held that even a virtuous human—far less the "highest and best" gods—would not stoop to the deceit, begging, and rivalries that the Greek gods exhibited. That was felt in Greece as early as the sixth century BCE, when the philosopher Xenophanes (c. 570–c. 475 BCE) said, "Homer and Hesiod attributed to the gods all the worst, most shameful things that could be said of men—that they steal, commit adultery, and lie to each other."[12] Xenophanes' younger contemporary, Heraclitus (c. 535–c. 475 BCE), dismissed the idea of blood sacrifices as purifying: "It is an idle claim to remove the stain of blood guilt with more blood staining, as if one stepping in mud could scrub it away with mud."[13]

Even in the fifth century BCE, when the idea of human sacrifice filled the tragic stage, divine patronage secured by sacrifice looked vain. The gods who could bestow favor often lost their favored ones, and lamented the loss—the woes of Zeus over Sarpedon, of Thetis over Achilles, of the Muse over Rhesus, were typical of divine frustrations. The anomalies of divine patronage accumulated by the time of Euripides. According to Richard Bodéüs:

> With Euripides, the tragic poetry of the fifth century attains a culminating point in the criticism of traditional theology: the true god must be above all reproach and respectful of justice. Otherwise, one must renounce belief in the gods. Criticism of "theology" reaches a

culminating point here, because it is aware of the arguments for athe-
ism. The irrationality of the unjust god can lead us to infer his nonexis-
tence. It is the poet who is aware of this possibility.[14]

By the fourth century, philosophers had hardened their critique of the
traditional gods. In *The Republic* (381), Plato says that a god who can be
altered by anything men say or do, or by anything that they sacrifice, lacks
the perfection that a god must have. In the *Laws* (905–6) he argues that
true gods always do the just thing, so they do not need to be rewarded for
doing it, and they cannot be bribed by human gifts to do something unjust
(like ordering a father—whether Abraham or Agamemnon—to kill his
child).

Aristotle, Plato's pupil, does not defend sacrifice as a way of exacting
something from the gods. He says it is an expression of gratitude for all that
the gods have given mankind. The things the gods gave mankind are specified as existence, nurture, and education.[15] But Richard Bodéüs notes that
Aristotle does not allow for a creator god or a divine providence affecting
individuals. The Aristotelian divine principle, the unmoved mover, does not
effect particular sublunary changes.[16] So even if humans express their gratitude to the gods by sacrifice, this will not make the gods do anything in
return. That removes the basic reason for sacrifice, since, as Jacob Milgrom
says, "A gift to the deity *to induce his aid* seems to be the only purpose that
manifests validity in all sacrificial systems."[17]

Since the idea of sacrifice seemed unworthy even in some polytheistic
societies, one might expect greater uneasiness over its defense in a monotheistic culture. After all, the one God has no need to battle for turf with
rival deities, or to have his hegemony challenged or bolstered by human
acts. In accord with that expectation, both Jewish and Christian apologists
were somewhat embarrassed by the presence of sacrifice in their sacred
writings. Moses Maimonides gave a lengthy report on all the sacrifices
required in the Pentateuch, but added that God did not really want any of
these things—he only allowed them so his people would not surrender to
the allure of other nations' confidence in sacrifice.[18]

Jacob Milgrom notes that later rabbinical writings "betray uneasiness with this institution."[19] Origen said that if he were asked to expound the Bible to a religious beginner, and he had to start with all the victims slaughtered for sacrifice, the newcomer would "vomit such food as indigestible."[20] Animal sacrifice is so far from the acceptable frame of things in the modern world that those attempting it would be convicted of cruelty to animals. And *human* sacrifice is simply unthinkable. Then why did the Letter to Hebrews revert to this concept?

It must be said that putting sacrifice at the center of his thinking led the author of Hebrews to various forms of primitive thinking. An example of this is the passage at 2.14–15:

> Now, since offspring all have the same flesh and blood, he was closely
> fused with both, by his own death to crush death's master (I mean the
> devil) and to free those who had been sentenced, by their very fear of
> death, to a lifetime of slavery.

The scene described here is familiar from the many paintings of the "harrowing of hell," where Christ, fresh from death and carrying his cross as a credential, breaks open the prison where the devil has been keeping the whole human race. The heavy gate of this prison, its huge bars and locks sundered, has crashed down, with the devil crushed under it, so people can walk out across it as a kind of drawbridge, moving toward freedom.

The Letter calls the devil "death's master," literally "one who owns the power [*kratos*] of death." Here the devil is like "this world's ruler" (*ho tou cosmou archōn*) in John's Gospel (12.31, 14.30, 16.11). Paul even calls him "this eon's god" (2 Cor 4.4). This accords with Mark's Gospel (10.45) where Jesus says, "The Son of Man, moreover, came not to be ministered to but to minister, and to give his life as a ransom [*lutron*, 'release'] for many." But Mark does not say to whom the ransom must be paid. The Letter to Hebrews specifies the recipient as the devil—and that is how Christian teachers generally took the passage for the first millennium of their history. But why would Jesus be sacrificed to the devil?

So prevalent was this "ransom theory" of payment to the devil that in 1141 Abelard was condemned as a heretic by the Council of Sens because, among other things, he rejected the devil's-ransom theory.[21] When the Letter refers to "a lifetime of slavery," it is saying that men are the devil's slaves, his lawful possession. People are naturally hesitant to say that God himself made men his slaves, so the only other candidate for master must be the devil. The ransom that Jesus has paid was his blood, which is why he could only come to the imprisoned to "harrow hell" bearing the cross. But if blood was paid to the devil, what made the devil accept it as currency? Why did he accept the payment as sufficient—the trade of one life for millions seems like a bad deal for the devil. Or if, by contrast, the payment was made to God the Father, why did the devil submit to what deprived him of his vassals? The author of the Letter, like his classical forebears, lived in a slave culture, where the master had a right to his property, by legitimate conquest, inheritance, or purchase. "Giving the devil his due" originally meant recognizing such *property* rights.

Some talk as if Jesus substituted himself for the slaves, as if some Sydney Carton had put himself in the position of a slave on condition that the slave be let go. If one frees a slave by taking his place, the slave master has not lost by the trade—he still holds the equivalent of the first slave. So if this was Jesus' deal with the devil, even if he traded one life for millions, this would surrender Jesus himself to ownership by the devil. This and other anomalies in the theory led to its gradual abandonment, beginning in the eleventh century.

The first heavy blow to the concept was delivered by Anselm of Canterbury (1033–1109) in his influential book *Why God-Man?* There Anselm argued that the devil can have no property rights over what God created. He did not have the right of conquest, since he did not take man by force—rather, mankind freely surrendered to him.[22] But men did not own themselves, so they had no right to turn themselves over to the devil. God owned them, as he owned all his Creation—including the devil. Anselm recognized that the quasi-legal case for the devil's "right" to his property was based on poor law. The devil cannot plead a cause before God because he does not have what in modern law is called "standing"—no more than Job can he invoke some grievance against the court itself.[23]

Then why was the devil able to terrorize men? Because God allowed this punishment, as a ruler might turn over the torture of malefactors to a jailor: "Though it was just that man be tortured by the devil, this action did not make the devil just."[24] Anselm also undermined what had been a leading argument for what was thought of as "the devil's bond"—a passage in the Letter to Colossians (2.14), thought then to be by Paul himself though modern scholars call it pseudonymous. The relevant passage is best translated: "The Son has erased our bill of admitted debts [*cheirographon*], with its particulars [*dogmata*] to which we were liable, making it void by nailing it to the cross." A *cheirographon*, something written by one's own hand, was used as a debtor's confession of what he owed.[25] The *dogmata* were requirements under the bill.[26] This was translated in the Latin Bible that came down to Anselm as a "bond of the decree," and it was taken as the devil's certificate of possession, binding men to do the devil's will. Anselm answered that only God can bind man, and what he bound him to was the punishment of the first sin by an inability to resist sin of his own nature, since grace was needed.[27]

Though Anselm had made the case against the devil's possession of mankind by a bond of slavery, the old doctrine continued its hold. As has already been mentioned, Abelard (1079–1142) was condemned for denying the devil his due half a century after Anselm had demolished that claim. It must be admitted, however, that Abelard made his arguments more provocatively. He used the same analogy that Anselm had, of a ruler using a functionary to torture the rebellious.

> What ownership rights had the devil over man but, perhaps, the right to torture by God's allowing it or even handing him over for it . . . how could the torturer rightly object when he had no right to torture but what the Lord had granted him?[28]

He added more legal arguments to those Anselm had brought against any "bond with the devil." The devil, in order to bring about the Fall of man, promised Adam and Eve eternal life if they ate of the evil fruit—but Abelard says the devil had no power to fulfill this promise, so his contract was based on a fraud. It had no legal force.[29] It is true that Abelard began to question God for turning mankind over to a torturer, but that carries us into greater problems with the entire idea of human sacrifice, problems still to be addressed.

NOTES

1. Joseph A. Fitzmyer, *Romans* (Doubleday, 1993), p. 122. On the non-Pauline authorship of Ephesians, see Raymond E. Brown, *An Introduction to the New Testament* (Doubleday, 1997), pp. 626–30.

2. Dennis D. Hughes, *Human Sacrifice in Ancient Greece* (Routledge, 1991), pp. 187–88.

3. Ibid., pp. 43–47. There is evidence for the sacrifice of children in Phoenician Carthage; see Richard Miles, *Carthage Must Be Destroyed* (Viking, 2011), pp. 68–73.

4. Hughes, op. cit., pp. 18–24.

5. Sir Hugh Lloyd-Jones, *Greek Comedy, Hellenistic Literature, Greek Religion, and Miscellanea* (Oxford University Press, 1990), pp. 309–10.

6. Though Aeschylus does not tell the story of the stag's killing, the best editor of the *Agamemnon* believes it was already there in the epic tradition: Aeschylus, *Agamemnon*, edited by Eduard Fraenkel (Oxford University Press, 1950), vol. 2, p. 98. Lloyd-Jones thinks it was Artemis's more general protection of wild animals that caused the sacrifice of the daughter in Aeschylus's play (*Greek Comedy*, "Artemis and Iphigeneia," pp. 306–30).

7. The third surviving Attic tragedian, Euripides, gives us a variant of the Isaac story: Artemis, who first demanded the sacrifice of Iphigeneia, has a change of heart and sacrifices a deer in her place—as Yahweh changes his demand for Isaac and substitutes a ram. See Euripides, *Iphigeneia in Aulis*. To add to the ruminations over animal vs. human sacrifice, Euripides in another play has the surviving Iphigeneia, as a priestess of Artemis, preside over human sacrifices in Tauris. She almost sacrifices her brother, but with the help of Athena she runs away with him from Tauris. But later, as the priestess of Artemis in a new shrine, she again conducts human sacrifices "that the goddess may have her holy honor" (*Iphigeneia in Tauris* 1461). Euripides, as so often, seems to be mocking the rites he "explains." In *Iphigeneia in Aulis* he has the chorus say, "There is something sick in what is called for and in the goddess calling for it" (*to tēs tuckhēs de kai to tēs theou nosei*, 1403).

8. Burkert argued that sacrifice was a way hunters had of ritually apologizing to animals after they had been killed. The classical scholar Hugh Lloyd-Jones said

that this theory imports modern sentiment into ancient cultures, and Burton Mack points out that not all sacrificing societies began with hunters. See *The Further Academic Papers of Sir Hugh Lloyd-Jones* (Oxford University Press, 2005), p. 142. Mack writes in *Violent Origins*, edited by Robert G. Hamerton-Kelly (Stanford University Press, 1987), pp. 29–30:

> The hunting hypothesis is now in serious trouble among paleoanthropologists. There does appear to be evidence for the hunting of mammoths, but it is not at all clear, even in this case, that hunting was a chief source of food. Burkert has emphasized the necessity of the hunt as that activity on which survival depended for the exceedingly long reaches of primitive culture; but the picture painted by current studies in primitive cultural anthropology is that gathering was at least as important as hunting, and perhaps more significant as the normal means of getting food. As for the "noble" hunt, there now appears to be evidence that primitive man was a scavenger much of the time.

Girard maintained that all societies are founded on an act of communal murder that myth conceals by minimizing or condoning it. Mack (op. cit., pp. 19–20) says that the myth is so far from the original murder that one wonders where the urgency for concealment came from:

> As Girard explains the relation of a ritual event to this first collective murder, he must have recourse to the language of memory (though it is partial), repetition (though inexact), and reenactment (though only as "attempts"). This is where the language of mimesis appears to break down (i.e., at the level of social history), and the reader is left wondering how human history, with such a dark, dramatic origin, has been energized for so long by cultivating concealments of it.

9. For the ever-receding claim of actual, historical human sacrifice, see Dirk Obbink, "Dionysus Poured Out: Ancient and Modern Theories of Sacrifice and Cultural Formation," in *The Masks of Dionysus*, edited by Thomas H. Carpenter and Christopher A. Faraone (Cornell University Press, 1993), pp. 65–86, with special note of the feigned deaths in initiation rites.

10. Franciszek Sokolowski, *Lois sacrées des cités Grecques* (E. de Boccard, 1969), p. 151.

11. Aristotle, *Nichomachean Ethics* 1163b. 13–18.

12. Xenophanes, fragment 11, in Hermann Diels, *Die Fragmente der Vorsokratiker*, tenth edition, revised by Walther Kranz (Weidmannsche Verlagsbuchhandlung, 1961), vol. 1, p. 132.

13. Heraclitus, fragment 5, Diels, op. cit., p. 151.

14. Richard Bodéüs, *Aristotle and the Theology of the Living Immortals*, translated by Jan Edward Garrett (State University of New York Press, 2000), p. 189.

15. Aristotle, op. cit., 1162a. 4–10.

16. Bodéüs, op. cit., pp. 141–48.

17. Jacob Milgrom, *Leviticus 1–16* (Doubleday, 1991), p. 441.

18. Moses Maimonides, *Guide for the Perplexed*, cited in Hans-Josef Klauck, "Sacrifice, Old Testament," translated by Reginald H. Fuller, ABD, vol. 5, p. 871.

19. Milgrom, op. cit., p. 440.

20. Origen, Homily on Numbers 27: *tamquam non sibi aptum cibum recusat.*

21. Constant J. Mews, "The Council of Sens (1141): Abelard, Bernard, and the Fear of Social Upheaval," *Speculum: A Journal of Medieval Studies* 77 (April 2002), pp. 342–82. Mews argues: "The Council of Sens needs to be seen as marking a key stage in the institutionalization of the process by which heresy was identified" (p. 345). Bernard of Clairvaux, who manipulated the Council's condemnation of Abelard, listed four heresies he was guilty of, and the third was "that Christ did not come to free humanity from the yoke of the devil" (p. 344). Bernard was following the brief drawn up by his secretary Geoffrey of Auxerre, who claimed that Abelard was "gutting the debt of redemption," *pretium redemptionis evacuans* (p. 369).

22. Anselm, *Cur Deus Homo? Sources Chrétiennes* 91, edited by René Roques (Éditions du Cerf, 1963), book 1, chapter 7 (367 A–B).

23. Ibid., 367 B.

24. Ibid., 367 C.

25. Markus Barth and Helmut Blanke, *Colossians*, translated by Astrid B. Beck (Doubleday, 1994), p. 370: the *cheirographon* was "a legal instrument of default which was drawn up freely by the debtor himself, without involving a notary, and was signed by him in his own hand." On the authorship of Colossians, see ibid., pp. 114–24.

26. Ibid., pp. 329–30.

27. Anselm, op. cit., 368 B–C.

28. Peter Abelard, *Commentaria in Epistolam Pauli ad Romanos*, edited by Eligius M. Buytaert, O.F.M., *Corpus Christianorum Continuatio Mediaevalis* 11 (Brepols, 1969), pp. 114–15.

29. Ibid., p. 115.

FOURTEEN

Who Killed Jesus?

It seems extremely cruel and evil to demand the death of a person without guilt as a form of ransom, or that one could take pleasure in the death of a guiltless one— and even more for God to accept his own Son's death as the means of returning all the world to his esteem.

—Abelard[1]

The tie between animal and human sacrifice is blood. The Letter to Hebrews makes this absolutely central to the salvation of mankind: "Without shed blood there is no freeing from sin" (9.22). Under the first Pact, there were many uses of blood. As the Letter said, "Nearly all purifications under the Law are by blood" (9.22). Blood, however, was used not only for purification but for consecration and for atonement. Indeed, the rite that is repeatedly invoked as a parallel for Christ's sacrifice is the great atonement ceremony enacted only once a year (Yom Kippur). There, blood was splashed around both the outer and the inner Shrines, seven times on the altar of sacrifice in the former, and seven times on and before the altar of atonement in the latter (Lev 16.14, 19). There was so much blood involved that it has been argued that the high priest had to change his vestments at one stage in the ceremony (Lev 16.23–24) because they had been so spattered with blood.

Why was blood so important to the ceremonies of the ancient world? According to Leviticus 17.11: "The life of a creature is the blood, and I appoint it to make expiation on the altar for yourselves: it is the blood, that is the life, that makes expiation." Is the offering of animal blood a vicarious offering of the worshiper's life? Jacob Milgrom points out that the substitution theory, contrary to what Letter to Hebrews says, does not work for the

Day of Atonement, where sacrificial blood "does not substitute for him [the priest] on the altar."[2] The only substitute for sin is the Azazel goat (Lev 16.22), and it is not sacrificed: "The scapegoat, which indeed carries off sin, does not even die or, for that matter, rate as a sacrifice."[3]

It is not clear how the blood of Christ was to be used in terms of the new Pact's atonement service. In the Letter, we are told that the suffering of Christ takes place "outside the camp," as the hides and bones left over from sacrificial animals were burnt outside the camp (13.11). This is an odd—indeed grotesque—parallel for the sacrifice of Christ. The bits of animals taken outside the Holy Places are treated that way because they are unclean, unlike the parts that have been purified and sacrificed inside the Shrine. Now it is true that a crucified man was unclean (Deut 21.22–23), which is why Jesus had to be buried in new and unsanctified ground. But he hardly took unclean things to the Father. All sacrificial victims were supposed to be without stain or flaw. There has, indeed, been controversy over whether Christ takes sins or sinful man—or even the blood that "buys" them—into heaven to complete his offering. On one side, F. F. Bruce writes, "Our author [of Hebrews] deliberately avoids saying that Christ carried his own blood into the heavenly sanctuary."[4] But Ceslas Spicq writes that "Christ enters the sanctuary and reveals himself to the Father, along with his blood, as the sacrificial lamb [of Revelation]" (S 2.268). In fact, Spicq says that Christ's priesthood is not perfected until his exaltation in heaven (S 1.292–300), and how can that be done without displaying the matter of his sacrifice?

Such uncertainty about how Christ's blood is to be treated—how it compares with the manipulations of blood in the high priest's atonement ceremony—shows a vagueness at the very core of Hebrews. The Letter mentions the place of atonement (hilastērion) when describing the Mosaic Holy of Holies (9.5), but never specifies what is this place under the new Pact, in heaven.[5] The blood cannot be lodged anywhere for an extended time, since it is revivified in the body of Christ by the Resurrection. That embodied blood cannot be equated with the exsanguinated residue of animals "outside the camp." Where is the altar of the new Pact, something to be paired and contrasted with the Atonement Place of the old Pact?

The only other New Testament use of *hilastērion* is at Romans 3.24–26. Since the word is used there in conjunction with Christ's blood, this might seem an explanation for what Hebrews is getting at. But the verses in fact are subversive of Hebrews' whole argument.

> All, admittedly, went astray and were deprived of God's splendor, but they are restored [*dikaioumenoi*] gratuitously [*dorean*] by God's favor, through their unshackling [*apolytrōsis*] in Christ. God advanced [*pro-etheto*] him as the nexus of atonement [*hilastērion*] through our trust in his blood. This was a proof of his integrity in ignoring former sins,[6] which God seemed not to notice [*en tēi anokhēi tou theou*], a proof of his integrity at this point of fulfillment [*kairos*], to show his own integrity and his restoration of it for those who are faithful to him.

Here we have some of the things important in Hebrews—the freeing from sin, the blood of Christ, the *hilastērion*. But notice what is missing. There is no priest, no offering of sacrifice, no bargaining with God. The absence of a priest comports with all the New Testament texts except Hebrews. But here the absence is made more glaring, since the mention of the *hilastērion* would call for a priest in the Old Testament. Even more to the point, God is not the *object* of sacrifice in this passage but the *subject* of active and pre-emptive forgiving. God himself takes the initiative to free men, after a period of letting their sins go unpunished but unforgiven. He does it gratuitously, asking nothing. This could not be further from Hebrews, where the Father acts only in response to a sacrifice made to him. Here he reconciles mankind to show his own integrity. Rather than have Christ offer up his blood, acting for men, the Father advanced his Son as the nexus of atonement.

The word I translate as "advanced" is *pro-etheto*, literally "put forward." Fitzmyer says of this word:

> It could mean "God designed him to be" . . . i.e., proposed him to himself, as he planned of old a new mode of human salvation. But if the stress is put on the prefix *pro-*, then it would mean that "God proposed

him," i.e., set him forth or displayed him publicly. Then it would be a reference not so much to the divine plan of salvation as to the crucifixion (cf. Galatians 3.1, "before whose eyes Jesus Christ was publicly displayed [*paregraphe*] as crucified).[7]

This passage stands in dramatic—perhaps shocking—contrast with the "ransom theory" of atonement. It says that sacrifice does not originate from or represent sinners, but that it comes from the Father's side. The truly shocking suggestion is that the Father is responsible for the death of Jesus. He killed his Son—as passages in the Gospels indicate: "The cup the Father has given me, am I not to drink?" (Jn 18.11). But the idea that God killed his own Son was unthinkable—after all, even Abraham was spared that gruesome task. Much of later Christian thought would be a scrambling around for other suspects to have killed the Lord. Different candidates were proposed, and most had a long run as suspect-in-chief.

1. The Devil Killed Jesus

It was earlier noted that this was the prevailing explanation of Christ's death for the first millennium of Christian history. Anselm fought it down, saying that the idea of the devil having any right to own part of God's Creation was absurd. Then why did the devil have any power over humankind? Anselm says that God gave him that power, as a ruler might commission a torturer to punish a rebel. Abelard repeated that explanation, but hinted that it was unsatisfactory, since it made God "hand Christ over" for torture. Surely the person commissioning the act is more responsible for it than his mere agent. That would make God the torturer-in-chief—a conclusion which Abelard (as we shall see) could not accept.

2. The Jews Killed Jesus

This, too, was a popular belief. Anselm first repeated it, before going on to a larger consideration of the matter.[8] It is true that some of the Jewish priests connived with Pontius Pilate to compass Christ's execution. But that does not mean that all Jews were guilty. And the "explanation" is no more final than the torturer hypothesis. In both cases, the supposed killer did not have the power to inflict his will unless God allowed it. Why would the Father put up with the actions of a minor part of his Creation against his Son, his equal in the Trinity? The onus returns to the Father.

3. Sinners Killed Jesus

Since he dies for our sins, were not all of us responsible for Jesus' death? This takes the scapegoat theory to a new level—the sins are loaded onto a surrogate, who is killed in our stead. The problem is that the Azazel goat of Leviticus was not killed, and it was not a conscious recipient of people's subjective guilt. Abelard took seriously the idea that we are the killers of Jesus, but rejected it because we did not consciously do this, no matter what our sins. Jesus, in fact, says from the cross about those killing him, "Father, spare them, they do not realize what they are doing" (Lk 23.34). If mankind killed Jesus, Abelard said, that would be a greater crime than Adam's sin in the garden.[9] Heraclitus had rejected the idea that blood can wipe out blood (like mud scrubbing mud). This would be a case of a crime canceling a crime.

Since the preceding solutions to the crime of Jesus' death had definite flaws, Anselm took a new look at the problem, with unparalleled boldness. He seemed to succeeding generations to have solved the crime definitively. With only a little exaggeration, Anthony Bartlett wrote in 2001:

> Anselm's *Cur Deus Homo* is unquestionably the major single document in Western atonement doctrine. It occupies a commanding position, guarding the route back to the older popular consensus about the meaning of Christ's death, and pointing the way forward decisively to what was to become the subsequent common, reflex model. The intellectual concentration of its argument produces the appearance of seamless and irresistible logic . . . To study *Cur Deus Homo* is to be

confronted with a reasoning that gives the impression of being cast in stone, of being a force almost of nature . . . Thus, although frequently contested and even more frequently unread, it maintains a privileged, even sacred status in the Western theological canon . . . Anselm took considerable pains over its composition and the immense scope of its influence is testimony in part to the care and rigor with which he approached his task.[10]

Anselm faced a problem no one had summoned the nerve to deal with before in any thorough way—the idea that God killed God. But he found a way to make God guiltless of the murder that he, nonetheless, committed. God did it, Anselm tells us, because he *had* to, because there was no other way to save mankind—thereby saving his whole plan for the Creation of the universe. The obligation God fell under had several layers, giving us confluent divine motives for the death of Jesus.

4. Justice Killed Jesus

To face the fact that the Father killed Jesus, Anselm had to differentiate this from all the forms of sacrifice that diminished gods—the idea that the gods were needy, or angry, or vengeful; that they could be bribed, bargained with, or assuaged by human gifts. God had to plead necessity—that he was obliged, unlike Abraham, to kill his own Son. Though the idea that God could be compelled was unusual, if not shocking, Anselm argued that God was compelled only by his own nature. There are, in fact, some things God *cannot* do (like lying). Because he is by nature goodness and truth, he cannot deceive or be complicit in deception. In the same way, because he is justice itself, he cannot commit an injustice *or tolerate injustice*. That was the key point—God seems to be caught between two impossible tasks, either to tolerate the huge injustice of sin or to commit the apparent injustice of killing his Son. But what if the latter course were the only way he could avoid the first one, complicity in the injustice of sin? Even one sin challenges the divinity itself. What of the whole course of evil loosed on the universe by the successor generations of men inheriting the legacy of Adam's first disobedience? Anselm declares:

> To permit sin means not to punish it. There is no way to correct unredressed sin but punishment. If it is not punished, it is incorrectly dismissed . . . So it does not suit God's worth to let sin go unpunished . . . If divine wisdom did not fit punishment to crime when depravity tries to subvert the proper order of the universe, there would be a wrenching of that universe from its ordained course of beauty, which God is bound to maintain.[11]

Sin tries to undo God's Creation. It is a negation of being itself. Being itself must respond to such a challenge. God could not tolerate such a vast collapse of his created order and still claim to be a just God. But mere punishment would not be sufficient to restore the original good order of things. Punishing a finite being will not undo the attempt to undo the Infinite. Sin has the limitless scope of the God it offends. Humans are incapable of repairing what they have done. They are too tainted by their action to offer a proper apology to God:

> When man does not will what is right, he dishonors God so far as he is affected by that honor, since he does not submit his will to God's plan, to the orderly beauty of the universe; rather, inasmuch as he can, he wrecks it . . . The entirety of humankind is so rotten and seething [*fermentata*] in sin that it cannot reconstitute its place in heaven . . . It is completely unable, since one sinner cannot restore another sinner's integrity.[12]

Even if there were one sinless man left to speak for all the others, he could at most save himself. And, of course, there is no such man. Then could an angel take on the task, or some new kind of person created by God? No, says Anselm, since the line of Adam did the sinning, anyone redressing the wrong must also be sprung from Adam.[13] The redress must come from one who can supply an infinite righting of an infinite wrong—which means that God's own Son must take on human nature in the line of Adam. He and he alone can bring abundance of redress to deal not only with the original wrong but with what in modern law would be called "damages," the insult added to injury—the infinite interest on the infinite debt.

To allow the Father a loophole through which to avoid the charge of murdering his own Son, Anselm stresses over and over that Jesus was a knowing and voluntary victim (unlike, say, Isaac, who did not know that Abraham was planning to kill him). It is true that Scripture says Jesus was obeying the Father's command; but his will and the Father's are in perfect accord, so Jesus willed his own death to accomplish the Father's purpose, bringing mankind back into compliance with a just order in the universe.

> God the Father did not treat him as you [Anselm's interlocutor] think he did, giving over an innocent man to die for the guilty. He did not force him against his will to die, or let him be murdered, but Christ himself voluntarily experienced death, in order to rescue men.[14]

The Anselmian argument throws a grotesque new light on the doctrine of the Trinity. Jesus is made a man so he can be made a "stand-in" for human sinners—as Iphigeneia was a stand-in (*antistathmos*) for Artemis's stag in the Sophocles play. But Jesus is also the Son of God. If he is being punished as the substitute for sinners, thus securing the justice and honor of his Father, this introduces a punitive note into the relationship of the divine Persons, where only perfect love should exist. The old idea of an angry God is hardly made more bearable if the Father is angry at the Son.

The argument that justice killed Jesus raises many problems, beginning with the idea that finite man has an infinite power of evil if he disobeys God. There is also the problem of necessity and the obligation imposed on God. Why must he punish sin by such a drastic remedy as the death of his Son? In order to understand why Anselm came up with this novel argument, we should place him in his historical, social, and philosophical context. He and his landed monastery were embedded in a deeply feudal society. And he was the inheritor of a Platonic view of ideal reality and its perfection. Put those together with the idea of priestly sacrifice derived from the Letter to Hebrews, and the product was bound to be strange. It meant, in effect, that honor and perfection, along with justice, would kill Jesus.

5. Honor Killed Jesus

The earlier belief in a devil's bond took shape in a slave-holding culture. Anselm's argument arose in a feudal culture, where fealty to overlords was the necessary glue of society. That is why sin is so destructive in the eyes of Anselm. When he rejects the idea that an angel or a specially deputed agent could have saved men, it is not only because he thinks the savior must be a descendant of Adam. If someone else had saved men, they would owe their allegiance to that immediate overlord, which would be a challenge to God's supremacy.

> Can you not see that if someone else, of any sort, should recover man from eternal death, then man would rightly be a serf [servus] with allegiance to his rescuer? In that case, he would not have recovered the dignity due him had he not sinned, since he, who would formerly not have been the serf of anyone but God, just like the angels, would now be the serf of someone who was not God, and who had no angels as his serfs.[15]

What is more, though Anselm had rejected the idea that the devil owned men, he brought that old argument back in by a side door, when he said that the devil had overcome men, had conquered them, and the credit for reversing that conquest should not go to a lower being than God himself. The honor of victory was at stake.[16] Also, if man were absolved of his fealty to his liege Lord, it would place him beyond good and evil, with a freedom that mocks the freedom of God. It is blasphemous for "injustice to mimic God."[17] Anselm's feudal sense of social order went along with his belief that this social order set a high ideal—an ideal also causing Jesus' death.

6. *Perfection Killed Jesus*

Among other necessities incumbent upon God, in Anselm's view, was the necessity that a perfect God must take the most perfect of all options for action. Thus God could only redress infinite sin by the action of an infinite actor:

> This cannot occur unless there be one who can render unto God for human sin something greater than everything that exists apart from God . . . And one capable of giving to God something greater than all that is below God must himself be higher than anything that is not God.[18]

It will be seen that this has an affinity with the famous "ontological argument" in Anselm's *Proslogion*. To put the ontological argument simply: God, properly understood, is perfect; but if he lacked existence, that would be an imperfection; so he must exist. Some philosophical followers of Anselm would say this is putting the matter not only simply but crudely.[19] But Thomas Aquinas dismissed Anselm in one short paragraph (ST 1.2 a2), saying that forming a concept of the perfect God *in intellectu* does not make him exist *in re*. Thus calling the death of Jesus an intellectually elegant solution to the problem of human sin does not necessarily make it an actual one.

A word that is used everywhere in Anselm's book is *conveniens*. That is not anything so flabby or weak as our "convenient." In accord with its etymology (*con-veniens*, "coming together") it means "fitting." Befitting. Appropriate. What is befitting a perfect God? Perfect acts, with perfect outcomes. That is the largest context for Anselm's argument, so large that it includes everything, even the population of heaven. One of the longest sections in the book is devoted to the need for a perfect number of persons in heaven. He asks whether this means the number before certain angels fell from heaven. Or does it mean that number filled out by the blessed human souls, who have equal citizenship with the angels? Perhaps God fixed the perfect number by taking into account his foreknowledge of the number of angels who would fall out of heaven. Does that mean that the number of humans saved would be the same as the number of rebelling angels? No, that would not bring about a perfect result, since the humans would rejoice in the defection of angels that made room for them—and such lowly feelings would not be perfect in a perfect heaven.

God therefore arranged that there would be more substituting humans than defecting angels, with no one knowing who filled whose space. And that means, of course, that he foreknew and fore-ordained the heaven-minus-angels and the heaven-plus-extra-humans to equal the perfect total at the End Time. All this long argument—it fills three chapters, including the extended chapter 18 of book 1—is based on the prior certitude that there must be, finally, a perfect number of citizens in the City of God.

Anselm leaves us with the impression that God loves symmetry, as part of his duty of being perfect. He calls this "the beauty of logic."[20] Hans Urs von Balthasar took many points from Anselm in creating what he called a "theological aesthetics."[21] Here are some of Anselm's symmetries:

> It was helpful that, just as death invaded the human race by reason of human disobedience, so life should be regained through a man's obedience. And as the sin that caused our damnation was derived from a woman, so the founder of our restoration should be born of woman. And as the devil conquered by soliciting man with the fruit of a tree, so he should be conquered by a man whose suffering on a tree he executed. And there are many other things that, studied with care, demonstrate the unspeakable beauty of a rescue wrought in this way.[22]

Anselm did not make things easy for himself. He would not say what was the perfect way of saving man until he had considered and dismissed alternative ways. For instance, how was it best to make God incarnate? There are four ways to create a man:

1. From man and woman interacting—normal birth.
2. From neither man nor woman—Adam.
3. From man without woman—Eve.

That leaves only a fourth way, from woman without man—Jesus. This was fitting, because it restored women's hope, since they now had a different legacy from that of the deceiving Eve.[23]

In the same way, Anselm sifts through the Persons of the Trinity to determine the proper division of labor for saving mankind, by incarnating one of the Persons in human flesh. Should it be the Father or the Spirit, rather than the Son? No, because there would then be *two* sons of God, the Second Person (Logos) as one, with either the Father or the Spirit, whichever took flesh from the Virgin Mary, as the second son of God. Besides, the Holy Spirit impregnated Mary by descending on her, which would make it unfitting for him to be his own son. And the Father, as a son of Mary, would be his own grandson.

> If the Father were to take flesh, there would be two grandsons in the Trinity, since by becoming a man, he would be the grandson of Mary's parents, and the Word, without taking on humanity in any way, would be the Son of her son [the incarnate Father]. All such possibilities are unfitting [*inconvenientia*], and do not occur if it is the Word who becomes man.[24]

The claim of Anthony Bartlett, quoted earlier, that Anselm's theory of atonement commanded the field after him is borne out by the fact that the most influential theologian after him, Thomas Aquinas, accepted an argument that was "basically Anselmian" two centuries after the time of Anselm.[25] This is true despite the fact, noted earlier, that Aquinas did not accept Anselm's ontological argument for God's existence, and despite the fact that he introduced several hedging maneuvers to Anselm's treatment of atonement. He said, for instance, that atonement by the sacrifice of Jesus was not strictly necessary, just the "most fitting" (*convenientissimum*) course of action (ST 3.46 a3r). He says that God was not obliged to choose this course, if one meant by necessity a constraint from some outside force, but he obliged himself because "No proper judge can neglect sin and its punishment, so long as justice is to be maintained" (ST 3.4 a2 ad3). Thus "Christ will have been bound [*debuerit*, future perfect] to die on the cross" (ST 3.46 a4r). Anselm would accept such minor trimmings to protect his basic point. Thomas steered clear of the larger contexts that Anselm worked from— God's feudal honor, for instance, or a perfect number for the inhabitants of heaven. By his very avoidance of such excrescences to the argument, he strengthened its hold on the minds of later generations.

It is not surprising that Thomas propped up Anselm's argument. He could not have done otherwise than accept it, after he accepted the Letter to Hebrews position, that Christ offers a sacrifice to allay the Father's wrath. He professed, along with the Letter, that Christ was a priest in the line of Melchizedek (ST 3.22 a6). But he added to the Letter the notion that other priests are also in that line, and that they offer a sacrifice like that of the Jewish high priest. Thomas, like most believers in the Christian Mass, does not identify an equivalent for the Jewish rites' *destruction* of the sacrificial victim. Would transubstantiation be this form of destruction, since the substance of bread and wine is swept out of existence? But, no, Thomas denied this "annihilationist" theory of the Eucharist. Do we destroy the victim by eating it? That is the worst kind of cannibalism. And anyway, by that hypothesis, Jesus would not be sacrificing himself to the Father but to those consuming him. Despite Thomas's intellectual prowess, he is trapped in absurdities—as when he had to dispose of insects in the chalice—so long as he follows the Letter to Hebrews, as supplemented by Anselm, on the question: Who killed Jesus?

NOTES

1. Peter Abelard, *Commentaria in Epistolam Pauli ad Romanos*, edited by Eligius M. Buytaert, O.F.M., *Corpus Christianorum Continuatio Mediaevalis* 11 (Brepols, 1969), book 2, par. 117.
2. Jacob Milgrom, *Leviticus 1–16* (Doubleday, 1991), p. 441.
3. Ibid. Sending the goat to Azazel, a name for an obsolete demon, is sending sins down what Orwell would call a "memory hole" (ibid., pp. 1020–21). This

resembles the advice of Ira Gershwin in his brother's song "Clap Yo' Hands" from the Broadway show *Oh, Kay!* in 1926: "'Trouble must be treated / Just like a rebel / Send him to the devil."

4. F. F. Bruce, *The Epistle to the Hebrews*, revised edition (Eerdmans, 1990), p. 213.

5. *Hilastērion* is the Greek translation of the Hebrew *kapporet*, "the solid gold slab atop the Ark" (Milgrom, op. cit., p. 1014). Though it is often translated into English as "mercy seat," or "cover," Milgrom says that "the verb kipper never implies mercy or cover." Since it is "the focal point of the purgation rite (*kipper*), perhaps it took its name from its function on the Day of Purgation" (ibid.). For the New Testament sense, the derivation of *hilastērion* from the verb *hilaskesthai* ("to propitiate") makes it mean "atoning" (if an adjective), or "nexus of atonement" (if a noun); see Joseph A. Fitzmyer, *Romans* (Doubleday, 1993), pp. 349–50. See also Gordon D. Fee, "Paul and the Metaphors for Salvation," in *The Redemption*, edited by Stephen T. Davis et al. (Oxford University Press, 2004), pp. 55–62.

6. "Ignoring former sins" translates *paresis*, not (as used to be the case) as coming from *par-hienai*, "to forgive," but from *par-ienai*, "pass over." It means that there was no accountability for sins until God's final erasure of them. Until then God's not-noticing (*enokhē*, literally "holding up" in the sense of "delay") was a marking of time until the fulfilling time (*kairos*) came. See Fitzmyer, op. cit., pp. 351–52.

7. Ibid., p. 349.

8. Anselm, *Cur Deus Homo? Sources Chrétiennes* 91, edited by René Roques (Éditions du Cerf, 1963), book 1, chapter 9 (370 C): "Why did the Jews persecute him all the way to his death?"

9. Abelard, op. cit., book 2, par. 116.

10. Anthony W. Bartlett, *Cross Purposes: The Violent Grammar of Christian Atonement* (Trinity Press, 2001), pp. 76–77.

11. Anselm, op. cit., book 1, chapters 12 (377 A–B) and 15 (381 A).

12. Ibid., book 1, chapters 15 (380 B) and 23 (396 A–B).

13. Ibid., book 2, chapter 8 (405 C–406 A).

14. Ibid., book 1, chapter 8 (370 A).

15. Ibid., book 1, chapter 5 (365 C–D). Compare book 2, chapter 8 (405 B–C, 406 A).

16. Ibid., book 2, chapter 11 (412 A).

17. Ibid., book 1, chapter 12 (377 C).

18. Ibid., book 2, chapter 7 (403 D).

19. See, for instance, Charles Hartshorne, *Anselm's Discovery* (Open Court, 1965).

20. Anselm, op. cit., book 1, chapter 1 (361 C), *pulchritudo rationis*.

21. Hans Urs von Balthasar, *The Glory of the Lord: A Theological Aesthetics*, translated by Erasmo Leiva-Merikakis et al., second edition (Ignatius Press, 2009).

22. Anselm, op. cit., book 1, chapter 3 (364 C).

23. Ibid., book 2, chapter 8 (406 B–C, 407 A).

24. Ibid., book 2, chapter 9 (407 C). Anselm, who liked this argument, had made it at even greater length in his *De Incarnatione Verbi*, chapter 10. People my age may irreverently remember the 1947 Latham-Jaffe song, "I'm My Own Grandpa."

25. Robert J. Daly, *Sacrifice Unveiled: The True Meaning of Christian Sacrifice* (T & T Clark, 2009), p. 114.

V

Jesus as Rescuer

FIFTEEN

The Saving Trinity

Anselm, as we saw in the last chapter, bound God himself in the chains of necessity. The Father *had* to save man by the sacrifice of his Son, since that was the just and honorable and perfect way of acting—so how could God do other? Even more audaciously he bound members of the Trinity, one by one, in the straitjacket of his argument: the Father *could not* become incarnate, as the Spirit *could not* become Mary's son—so the Second Person, the Logos, *had* to perform the task. This not only imposed a division of labor within the Trinity but introduced discord there. As the advocate of sinners, the Son had to placate the anger of the Father. It has been left to recent theologians to point out that the rescue of humankind was the work of the Trinity as a whole, not of a single Person of it.[1]

These thinkers not only do not restrict salvation to the work of a single divine Person; they do not restrict redemption to a single act of that incarnated Person, his death. They point out that the Incarnation is the great mystery, and that Jesus was sent by the Father and guided by the Spirit in his whole saving life, from his birth through his ministry and miracles to his death and Resurrection. Those making this argument were preceded by Augustine, who also saw the entire Trinity working in the life of Jesus. The Father sent the Son, which in all cases other than the Trinity would mean that the Father was the prime agent. But in the Trinity, all agency is united.[2] And the Spirit was infused in all aspects of the Incarnation of Jesus:

So it was said of John the Baptist, "He will be filled with the Holy Spirit from the moment he is in the womb" (Lk 1.15), and his father Zachary was seen to be full of the Spirit when he spoke those words of his son. And Mary was filled with the Holy Spirit to proclaim the wonder of the Lord she was bearing in her womb, and Simeon and Anna were filled with the Spirit to acknowledge the majesty of the baby Christ.[3]

Augustine rejected Anselm's argument seven centuries before it was made.

Can one really say that, because God the Father was angry at us, he looked on at his Son's death, and that made him accept us again? Does that mean that the Son already accepted us to the extent of dying for us, while the Father remained so angry that he would not have accepted us if the Son had not died for us? If so, what are we to make of these words from the teacher of the Gentiles [Paul]: "How shall we consider our situation? Since God is with us, who can oppose us? He did not exempt his own Son, but surrendered him for our sake—and is that not to give us everything?" (Rom 8.13). How could the Father deny exemption for his own Son, but surrender him for us, if he had not already accepted us? This text refutes an earlier one. There the Son first dies for us, and only then does the Father accept us because of that death. But here the Father is, as it were, the first to act from love, and because of that did not exempt his Son but surrendered him for our sake. The Father's love takes precedence, since he loved us not only before his Son died for us but before he created the universe. As the same Apostle said, "He chose us to be his even before the initiation of the universe" (Eph 1.4). And when it is said that the Father did not exempt his Son, that does not mean that the Son did not volunteer his death, since it is written, "He loved me [Paul] and volunteered himself for me" (Gal 2.20). Everything, therefore, was done at once and equally and interactively [*concorditer*] by the Father, the Son, and, proceeding from them both, the Spirit.[4]

Augustine was always less interested in the Passion than in the Incarnation, which is why his sermons made more of Christmas than of Good Friday. For him, the great saving mystery was the fact that God became man. He lowered himself to raise us: "When he took on flesh in time, in order to share our temporal life, he did not lose eternity in the flesh but honored flesh with eternity."[5] Dealing with the holy patriarchs who were saved before Jesus lived (or died), Augustine says that they had a prophetic sense, not by the Passion and death, but by the Incarnation:

> Christ the Lord is the Beginning [*Principium*], by whose Incarnation we are cleansed . . . Thus the Beginning, by receiving its own flesh and blood, purified both flesh and blood . . . We, fleshly, weak, vulnerable to sin, cloaked in dark error, could not recognize the Beginning till we were purified and made whole by it, because of what we were and what we were not—we were men, but not innocent, whereas he was by his Incarnation both man and innocent, without sin. Mediating thus, he reached his hand out to us in our fallen state . . . It was by believing in this sacred bond that the men of old were purified and returned to innocence by living virtuously.[6]

Augustine presents the Incarnation as a second (and better) Creation, by which God not only restores fallen man but exalts him to a higher state by incorporation of the whole body of believers into the Son.

> God wants to make you God, not merely by his own only begotten, but by a free adoption. Just as he, in becoming man, shared in your death, so he makes you, by his exaltation, share in his deathlessness . . . Thus man, thoroughly deified, will be united to the endless and changeless truth.[7]

Being at one with Christ is a higher state than being at one with Adam in his original condition: "Don't be Adam any more."[8] The Incarnation is God's way of harmonizing the universe. Augustine searches for a way to describe Christ's union with his believers, rejecting noun after noun as inadequate until he comes up with a new noun:

> This joining together [*congruentia*]—or say the fitting together [*convenientia*], or the adjusting together [*concinentia*], or sounding together

[*consonantia*]—or, to put it better where notes in octave are concerned, this joining is essential in whatever is held together [*compaginatio*], or, to be even more precise, whatever is tuned together [*coaptatio*].[9]

He goes on to discuss *coaptatio* in musical terms, as the notes sounded at "one and two" (i.e., when a lyre string is one length or two), what we can modernize as "at the octave." He says that Jesus sounded his one death (of the body) in accord with our two deaths (of the soul and of the body): "Our present task is to learn, with God's help, how the single death of our Lord and Savior fits our double death and somehow accords with [*congruat*] our rescue."[10] The harmony results not simply from Christ's dying but from *his becoming man*.

Christ lowered himself in humility to lift us in dignity, meeting us halfway, as it were, entering our time to bring us to his eternity.[11]

Since we were not fitted to appreciate the eternals, so mired were we in the muck of sin—so stuck in our affection for the temporals, naturally coated with the consequences of our death—that we needed to be cleansed. But if our cleansing were to be suited for eternals, it had to be through temporals, like those that suited our captivity. Health, it is true, is the opposite of sickness, but cure mediates between the two—if it did not engage the sick, it could not draw him toward the healthy. Malignant temporals frustrate the sick, but benignant temporals revive those being cured and strengthen them toward the eternals . . . So the Son of God came to us to be the Son of Man, so he could attach our faith to him, by which he would draw us on to his truth, adopting our mortality without losing his immortality. For the Beginning is to eternity as truth is to faith. Thus we had to be cleansed by the one who began here while remaining eternal, so he could be the same in our faith as he is in truth. Our Beginning could not take us to eternals unless he became our partner in passing toward his eternity. That is how our faith goes along with the one we believe in, as he rose up. After he began among us, he died, he was raised, he was vindicated. Of those four things we have experienced two, since we know how men begin here and die. Of the last two, being raised and being vindicated, we rightly hope for that for us because we believe in that for him. As he goes from his earthly beginning to eternity, we hope to pass over from our beginning to eternity, our faith attaining his truth.[12]

Compare Sermon 190.2:

This Christmas we celebrate not only the birth of a divinity but the birth of a man, by which he is attuned [*contemperatus*] to us that, by his invisible self made visible, we may travel through his visibles to his invisibles.[13]

Augustine explains the Incarnation in his commentary on the passage of John's Gospel (9.1–7) where Jesus takes earth, spits on it, and cures a blind man's eyes with it. The flesh Jesus takes is a medicine for the blindness of humanity. In his *Interpretations of John's Gospel*, Augustine says that Jesus took flesh to cure humanity's lack of faith: "He spat on the dirt, and from his spittle he made a paste—that is, the Word was made flesh."[14] In Genesis (2.7) it is said that God made man "from the dust of the ground." The scriptural passage that Augustine used most often in his Christmas sermons was Psalm 85.12, which read in his Latin Bible *Veritas de terra orta est*, "Truth takes its rise from dirt."[15] Though dirt was unclean in Jewish thought, Augustine argues that the dirt from which Jesus rose up—"that is, the flesh of the Virgin"—was not unclean, because she preserved an aboriginal innocence (*integritas*).[16]

Mary was like the uncontaminated earth from which Adam was made. But Jesus, the Truth, the Logos, the Origin, does not simply repeat the "clean" first birth of Adam. He is far superior to the merely natural man. But he, too, springs from dirt. So, in the healing of the blind man, he takes dirt and sanctifies it by his saliva. This is another case of the "halfway" attuning of man to God—the flesh of Jesus is dirt but it is holy, like the paste he plasters over the blind man's eyes.

Though Augustine speaks of the general "attuning" of God to man throughout the whole life of Jesus, he must face the general emphasis on one aspect of that life, its ending—the Crucifixion. He does not treat this as a sacrifice meant to placate the Father. For one thing, he remains enough of a Neoplatonist to believe that God is changeless. Thus his emphasis is always on the effect of Jesus' action on the believer, not on God himself. He says that even the atonement, the "justification" of other theories, does not effect a change in the Godhead:

> We believe, accordingly, that God does not require the sacrifice of a bull, or of anything else on earth and corruptible, or even of man's justi-fication [*justitia*], since every proper homage to God is meant for the benefit of man, not of God. One does not, after all, oblige a fountain by drinking from it, or oblige light by seeing it.[17]

God cannot change in order to grant something in return for a sacrifice. Even prayer cannot make him grant favors. The true aim of prayer is to make the believer acknowledge that the will of God is better than one's own will—he knows better than I do what is good for me: "For when I pray for the recovery of a sick person, my motive is not at all for a magic cure, but that I may submit willingly to whatever You will" (C 10.56). In a famous part of the *City of God* (book 10), Augustine renounced all previous notions of sacrifice. He said that the only true sacrifice is a sacrifice of one's own will to God's. For this sacrifice the proper altar is man's heart, the proper incense his affections, the proper fire his love.[18]

We cannot deflect what God has timelessly willed for the universe. God created time, but he did not create it *in* time—Creation was an eternal will-ing that time would be (C 11.14). Developments within time correspond in general to the *seminales rationes* ("provisions in their origin")—that is, to what is sometimes called natural law.[19] God can depart from his own natu-ral provisions if he wills it, as when working miracles, but even these "depar-tures" were foreseen and fore-ordained. Man's ability to sin is a freedom to defy the will of God, but that does not change or defeat the will of God. Jesus by the Incarnation came to attune man's will, through his will, to a restored harmony with God.

Augustine repeats the prophetic protests that God does not need anything we can give him in sacrifice. But he goes further. He says that the realm of sacrifice is that of the devil: "That liar, who had been a diplomat [*mediator*] of death to man, blocked the way to life by promising to cleanse man from sin by rites and irreligious sacrifices, by which the self-sufficient were taken in."[20] Here he means, principally, the heathen sacrifices to pagan gods. But even the sacrifices of the Jews, he says, were only symbols of true sacrifice, that of the heart, not true sacrifices in themselves.[21]

How, then, can the Crucifixion be considered a sacrifice? Augustine says that true sacrifice, submission of one's will to God, is supremely effected when Jesus incorporates the wills of all his believers in his Mystical Body and brings them into accord with the Father's will:

> Four things count in any sacrifice—the one it is being offered to, the one offering it, what is being offered, and for whom it is being offered. In this case the one offering is our truest Mediator, uniting us to God in the peace that is being offered, while he is united with the one to whom the offering is made, and is himself the offerer and the offered.[22]

But Augustine also speaks of the Crucifixion as breaking the hold of the devil upon men's hearts, as when he tempts them to sin. Christ broke this hold, not by paying the devil a ransom (the old theory) or by outbidding the devil with a priceless gift to the Father (Anselm's theory). No, *he tricked the devil*. He lured him into a trap, so the devil was *non ditatus sed ligatus*, not paid but betrayed—lured by a bait into the trap that held him tight.[23]

The devil celebrated when Christ died. But by that very death the devil was done in. He took the bait, as in a mousetrap. He was happy at this death, since he was the herald [*praepositus*] of death. But what delighted

him, ensnared him. The mousetrap for the devil was the Lord's cross.
The bait that lured him was the Lord's death. But just look! The Lord
Jesus Christ was resurrected! What has happened to that death on the
cross?[24]

To follow Augustine's thought here we must see it as the working out of
his "harmonizing" theory of the Incarnation. He said that there was a
two-to-one harmony between the two deaths of man (spiritual and physical) and the one death of Jesus (physical). There was also a two-to-one relation of the devil to man's two deaths and the devil's spiritual deadness. But
the devil, who caused human death when he lured him into the Fall, cannot
join man in a physical death. He foolishly thinks that Jesus, by dying, has
entered his own realm of death; but Jesus has a spiritual life even in physical
death. By Resurrection, he breaks free from death and takes his Followers
with him to the Father. Jesus rescues us by joining us as what Augustine
calls "our comrade in the fellowship of death" (*in consortio mortis amicus*),
from which the devil is excluded.[25] The Latin *amicitia* was a stronger term
than our "friendship," as anyone knows who has read Cicero's treatise *De
Amicitia*. It signifies "other-self-hood," or camaraderie.[26]

The Incarnation gave Jesus an intimacy with man that the devil cannot
equal:

Thus that liar, who had been a diplomat [*mediator*] of death to man,
blocked the way to life by promising to cleanse man from sin by rites
and irreligious sacrifices, by which the self-sufficient were taken in,
since he could not share our [physical] death, nor have a resurrection
from his [spiritual] death. He had, it is true, one death to match our
two, but he could not achieve the one resurrection which is the mystery
of our individual rescue and the pattern for a general raising of the dead
at the end of time. By contrast, Christ, the true diplomat [*mediator*] of
life to man, expelled from the souls of those who believe in him that
dead spirit who conducted men to death, so the devil would no longer
have an internal claim on man, but only an external hostility that could
not overthrow him. The true conductor even let himself be tested, so

that for resisting our tests he would offer us not only his help but also his company.[27]

Jesus did not so much get mankind out of the devil's possession as he called in the "pawn tickets" (*nexa*) the devil held for claiming man:

For our rescue the blood of Christ was a kind of payment, but when the devil took it he was not paid but betrayed, since we were quit of his pawn tickets [*nexibus*] and he could no longer draw a man in a net of sins toward a second and lasting [spiritual] death, once the man had been freed from any obligation, by the blood Christ was not obliged to shed [in a physical death].[28]

Jesus came to earth to join us, just as the father of the Prodigal Son went to him:

His father saw him returning, while he was still far off, and emotion racked him [*esplangkhnisthē*], so he ran out, threw his arm around his neck, and hugged him. (Lk 15.20)

He also came to seek as the shepherd hunts for his lost sheep:

Which of you, having a hundred sheep but losing one, would not leave the ninety-nine safe and go exploring for the lost one, till he found it? Having found it, he lifts it onto his shoulders out of pure joy, to carry it home, where he invites family and friends, telling them, "Be just as happy as I am, since I have found the sheep that was lost to me." (Lk 15.4–6)

God initiates the salvation of man to express the Father's love, not a punitive deflecting of the Father's anger.

He ran to meet us at the end of our journey, our death, but not by the way we had journeyed. We traveled to death along our path of sin, but his path was toward what is right. Our death is what we deserved for sin, while his is a remedy-offering for that sin.[29]

Again it should be said that "He held it right to become our comrade in the fellowship of death" (*in consortio mortis amicus*).[30] He traveled to death, to meet us there:

> The mind of our Conductor made this clear—that he did not accept death in the flesh as a punishment for sin, since he did not give up his life of necessity but because he willed it, when he willed it, how he willed it. Since he was at one with the Word of God, he could say: "I have the authority to give up my life, and I have the authority to take it back. No one takes it from me, but I give it up and I take it back." (Jn 10.17–18)[31]

Jesus directly achieves this harmonization of mankind with himself. One does nothing but disrupt this harmony by interjecting superfluous intermediaries between Jesus and his body of believers. When these "representatives" of Jesus to us, and of us to Jesus, take the feudal forms of hierarchy and monarchy, of priests and papacy, they affront the camaraderie of Jesus with his brothers.

NOTES

1. On salvation as the work of the Trinity, see especially Edward J. Kilmartin, *Christian Liturgy: Theology and Practice* (Sheed and Ward, 1988), and *The Eucharist in the West: History and Theology* (Liturgical Press, 2004), as well as Robert J. Daly, *Sacrifice Unveiled: The True Meaning of Christian Sacrifice* (T & T Clark, 2009). Daly draws on or praises a range of theologians who share Kilmartin's and his approach: Raymund Schwager, *Jesus of Nazareth: How He Understood His Life*, translated by James Williams (Crossroad Publishing Company, 1998), and *Banished from Eden: Original Sin and Evolutionary Theory in the Drama of Salvation* (Gracewing, 2006); Anthony W. Bartlett, *Cross Purposes: The Violent Grammar of Christian Atonement* (Trinity Press, 2001); Hans Boersma, *Violence, Hospitality and the Cross: Reappropriating the Atonement Tradition* (Baker Academic, 2004); Stephen Finlan, *Problems with Atonement: The*

Origins of the Controversy About the Atonement Doctrine (Liturgical Press, 2005); S. Mark Heim, *Saved from Sacrifice: A Theology of the Cross* (Eerdmans, 2006); Gregory Anderson Love, *Love, Violence, and the Cross: How the Nonviolent God Saves Us Through the Cross of Christ* (Cascade Books, 2010).

2. Augustine, *De Trinitate* 4.29 (Jacques-Paul Migne, *Patrologia Latina* 42, column 908).

3. Ibid. (columns 908–9).

4. Ibid., 13.17 (Migne 42, column 1025).

5. Augustine, Sermon 187.4 (Migne 38, column 1002).

6. Augustine, *De Civitate Dei*, edited by Bernard Dombart and Alphonse Kalb, fifth edition (Teubner, 1981), 10.24–25, pp. 438–39.

7. Augustine, Sermon 166.4–5 (Migne 38, column 309).

8. Ibid.

9. Augustine, *De Trinitate* 4.4.

10. Ibid., 4.5.

11. Ibid., 4.13.

12. Ibid., 4.24.

13. Augustine, Sermon 190.2 (Migne 38, column 1007).

14. Augustine, *In Joannem Tractatus* 44.2.

15. Augustine, Sermons 184.1, 185.2, 189.2, 191.1, 192.1.

16. Augustine, Sermon 191.2.

17. Augustine, *De Civitate* 10.5, p. 408.

18. Ibid., 10.3, p. 406.

19. Augustine, *De Genesi ad Litteram* 9.32.

20. Augustine, *De Trinitate* 4.17 (Migne 42, column 899).

21. Augustine, *De Civitate* 10.5, pp. 408–10.

22. Augustine, *De Trinitate* 4.19 (Migne 38, column 901).

23. Ibid., 13.19 (Migne 42, column 1029).

24. Augustine, Sermon 263 (Migne 38, column 1210).

25. Augustine, *De Trinitate* 4.17 (Migne 42, column 900).

26. The Latin concept of *amicitia* was taken from extensive Greek writings on *philia*. *Philos* meant "one's own," a tie so close that Homer could talk of one's own heart (*philon ētor*, Iliad 3.31) or one's own knees (*phila gounata*, Iliad 9.610). Linguists connect *philos* with reflexive uses of the pronoun *spheis*, intensifying the sense of "one's own." See Hjalmar Frisk, *Griechisches etymologisches Wörterbuch* (Carl Winter Universitätsverlag, 1969), p. 1020.

27. Augustine, *De Trinitate* 4.17 (Migne 42, column 899).

28. Ibid., 13.19 (Migne 42, column 1029). For the meaning of *nexum*, see Marcel Mauss, who discusses "one of the most controversial questions of legal history, the theory of the *nexum*." He concludes that a *nexum* is the token of a pledge. It does not seal a bargain or conclude a purchase, but gives a claim on later fulfillment of the pledge; see Mauss, *The Gift: Forms and Functions of Exchange in*

Archaic Societies, translated by Ian Cunnison, with an introduction by E. E. Evans-Pritchard (W. W. Norton, 1967), pp. 47–48.

29.	Augustine, *De Trinitate* 4.15 (Migne 38, column 898).
30.	Ibid., 4.17 (Migne 42, column 900).
31.	Ibid., 4.16 (Migne 41, column 898).

SIXTEEN

Christ as Comrade

Those who agree with Anselm on the meaning of atonement are bound to think the Augustinian views expounded in my last chapter "soft" and subjective. The first view gives us the sacrifice of Christ as acting "objectively," *ex opere operato.* The official position of Anselmian theologians may be thought of as the Great Buying Off of God. The second, or Augustinian, position is that Jesus came to heal mankind, to make humans attuned to God, to win faith and affection. Acting in this way, he did not effect some change in the Godhead itself but a change in those sharing the brotherhood of Jesus. For Anselm, Jesus paid the price, the Father accepted, and the bargain was concluded. For Augustine, Jesus took his Followers with him into the inner life of the Trinity.

These differences over the atonement retrace, in a different arena, the argument between Thomists and Augustinians on the Eucharist. The believers in transubstantiation looked to objective facts, to substantial change wrought in inert matter. By contrast, people like Ratramnus, Berengar, and Guibert were merely "subjective"—they reduced the Eucharistic miracle to the faith of its recipients. These latter thinkers were so condemned that they had almost disappeared from the controversy until Henri de Lubac brought them forth again (cautiously, fearing condemnation from Rome, which eventually descended on him).

In both cases, that of the Eucharist and of the atonement, Augustine was too big a figure to be surrendered to the "dissidents," so his original views were neglected, soft-peddled, or distorted, to bring them into conformity with "orthodoxy." But his followers, or simply those who agreed with him, were dismissed as heterodox. For the Eucharist, as we have seen, this was the fate of all the "lost" thinkers refound by de Lubac. For the atonement, figures as early as Irenaeus (second century) and as late as Abelard (twelfth century) were considered "sports" outside the theological consensus—the former as a mere "recapitulationist," the latter as a mere "exemplarist." Irenaeus, it was said, claimed that Jesus saved man simply by "redoing Adam's life" as if Adam had never fallen.[1] Abelard—so ran the charge—thought that Jesus saved man simply by leading an exemplary life himself. Both cut down the Incarnation to a series of enacted "life lessons" to be learned from the Savior. Man could save himself, in other words, just by asking What Would Jesus Do?

Both men were caricatured by this treatment of them. It is true that Irenaeus thought that Jesus had to fulfill the highest expectations of human life at each of its stages—so he argued that Jesus had to live till at least fifty, to show the right conduct of a mature teacher.[2] But recapitulation was a capacious concept with him, one that drew on deep scriptural sources and on the thought of fellow Christians like Justin Martyr, Theodosius, Clement of Alexandria, and Tertullian.[3] Eric Osborn says that there are eleven different meanings of "recapitulation" in Irenaeus, and all eleven are in constant play.[4]

The word normally translated as "recapitulation," the Greek *anakephalaiōsis*, with its verb *anakephalaioō*, was originally a grammatical or rhetorical term. It meant "arrangement [or to arrange] *according to headings*." The ancients did not have tables of contents for their books, but if they had, this would have been the perfect word to describe such a thing. Aristotle used the word for the "summing up" of an argument. That is often how Paul is translated at Romans 13.9, where he says that all commandments are summed up or contained (*anakephalaioutai*) in the command to love one's neighbor. This is the completion (*plērōma*) of them all.

But the richer use of the Greek word is at the Deutero-Pauline Letter to Ephesians 1.10, which says that God's plan was "for all things to be re-ordered [*anakephalaiōsasthai*] in Christ—in the heavens, upon earth, all in him."[5] This obviously extends God's plan over more than the repeating of Adam's life. It embraces the entire cosmic plan of God, and includes man "in

Christ" along with *everything* in heaven or on earth. That is how Irenaeus uses the term in his most expansive passages.

According to Irenaeus, Jesus achieves what Augustine would call the harmonization of God, man, and universe.

> He united man with God, and brought about a communion of God and man, we being unable in any other wise to have part in incorruptibility, had it not been for his coming to us. For incorruptibility, being invisible and imperceptible, would not touch us; so he became visible, that we might be brought into full oneness with incorruptibility . . . so he came to join battle on behalf of his forefathers.[6]

The idea in that last sentence is that the incarnate Jesus had human ancestors. As Irenaeus said, in *Against Heresies:* "As man he was a fighter for his forebears" (*Erat enim homo pro patribus certans*).

> He was in the strife, and he prevailed. As a man he was a fighter for his forebears, since he recruited the strong, upheld the weak, and restored his own handiwork, proving that he is a most loyal and compassionate Lord, in love with humankind.[7]

If the Word had not taken flesh himself, he would not have been ordering *all* things in himself, saving man in his totality.

> Mankind that was perishing was made of blood and flesh, since God had taken up dirt to fashion him; and this was the humankind for which the Incarnation was ordained—so the Son too had flesh and blood, not of a different kind from the stuff that the Father had made, so that all things could be reordered in him [*in se recapitulans*] as he sought out the perishing.[8]

It is typical of Irenaeus that he sees the cross less as an instrument for punishment than as God's pattern for reordering ("anacephalizing") the cosmos:

And because he is himself the word of God Almighty, who in his invisible form pervades the whole world—encompassing all its length and breadth and height and depth (since by God's word everything is arranged and kept in order)—the son of God was likewise crucified in all of these, imprinting the form of the cross on the universe; for he had necessarily, in becoming visible, to bring to light the universality of his cross, in order to show openly through his visible form what his action is—that it is he who illumines the height (what is in heaven) and contains the depth (what is in the bowels of the earth), and by his reach extends the length of east and west, containing also the northern parts and the sweep of the south, to bring everything dispersed everywhere into acknowledgement of the Father.[9]

If Irenaeus anticipated much that Augustine would write about the Incarnation, as a harmonization of all elements in God's cosmos, Abelard echoed such thoughts in a later time. It has already been mentioned that Abelard was denigrated for offering Jesus simply as a guide to proper behavior, an *exemplum*, whose effect was merely subjective, merely acting upon those wishing to imitate him. The passage that has repeatedly been cited and fought over is in Abelard's commentary on the Letter to Romans 3.21–26:

It seems to me, nonetheless, that we are completed [*justificati*] in Christ's blood and reunited with God since, by the singular favor shown us, his Son took on our human nature, and in that nature—enlightening us both by word and action [*exemplum*]—he bore up even to the point of death, to clasp us even closer to his side in love, so that, aflame with such assistance from divine favor, our love would not balk at doing anything for his sake. This was the assistance, we can be sure, that enflamed with love the Old Testament heroes, in anticipation of fidelity, just as it enflames us in fulfillment of that fidelity—for it was written of them: "Those coming before, like those coming after, were crying out, Hosannah to the son of David." But we are more completed than they, after Christ has suffered, because we love God more, since an assistance bestowed enflames with more love than one just promised.

Our rescue [*redemptio*], in other words, is the supreme love shown in his suffering, which not only lifts from us the bondage of sin but gives us true liberty as sons of God, that we may expand all our capacities [*cuncta impleamus*] with love instead of fear. For no greater favor could be shown us, as he himself assured us: "No greater love exists," he says, "than giving up one's life for one's friends." This is the kind of love he described elsewhere: "I have come to cast fire on the land, and what can I want but that it enflame?" This is his warrant to true freedom, the love he came to spread among us. Duly attendant on this the Apostle said in his writings, "The love of God permeates our hearts, by the Holy Spirit infused in us." (Rom 5.5)[10]

It was mainly on the basis of this passage that Abelard was condemned as an "exemplarist." Jesus, in this view, set a loving example for us to imitate, and our imitation of him is the only atonement we need for our sins. So God's justice, it was claimed, does not take effect in Abelard's writings.

Some modern scholars acquit Abelard of "pure exemplism," and they adduce other parts of his writing that are more like official atonement doctrine.[11] But we must be careful not to bring him into line with Anselm. We saw in an earlier chapter how much he disdained that kind of theology— how he mocked the idea of God buying off God, holding his Son hostage to his own anger, and thinking that human sacrifice is the only way to unite man and God. Besides, those who claim to derive exemplarism from Abelard treat him as a dolt. How can it be true that human beings are supposed to pattern themselves after Jesus' life? He offers no paradigm for married people or parents, since he was celibate and childless. Was he a "family values" model when he left his parents without telling them and went off for days while they searched in anguish for him (Lk 2.48), or when he refused to admit his mother when she asked to come into his company (Mk 3.31–33)? Should his Followers order a man not to attend his father's funeral (Mt 8.22), or tell other people to hate their families (Lk 14.26)? Should they whip people who sell items in a church precinct (Jn 2.15–16)? Or destroy a whole herd of pigs not belonging to them (Mk 5.13)? When people ask themselves, What Would Jesus Do?, this is not what they have in mind. But unless one is prepared to work miracles and make claims to Godhead, it is better not to claim what Jesus did as an excuse for one's actions.

But the main thing no Christian can do, though Christ did, is put aside Godhead and become a man. No man can become something above humanity and then assume humanity. In that sense, the main miracle worked by Jesus is his Incarnation, and Augustine was right to treat it as more astonishing than anything else Christ did once he had taken on flesh. Other humans can die a grisly death, as Jesus did. They cannot be born, as he was, as God incarnate.

Abelard knew this. In the passage given above he says that the assistance (*beneficium*) God gave us was based on the fact that "his Son took on our human nature." He came to lift us into a human life above that which Adam had been granted in Eden, and only he could do this in order "to clasp us even closer to him in love" (*ut nos sibi amplius per amorem adstrixit*). But why did he have to die? It would not be truly joining us, taking us up in our entirety into his higher human reality, if he just dropped into time to share some aspects of our life and then leave before undergoing the greatest trial of our existence. Irenaeus said that *all* of human life had to be gathered into him.

I am reminded of Norman Mailer's claim that an "existential" God would have to suffer. In G. K. Chesterton's metaphysical whodunnit *The Man Who Was Thursday*, a group of secret agents is sent out by their mysterious boss to adventures that make them struggle, without knowing it, against themselves, misunderstanding each other, thwarting each other, not knowing that they were all on the same side. When they finally realize what they have been doing and confront their secretive master, "Sunday," they feel that the person sending them out must have been amused at their misadventures. But Sunday says that he saw in them "Iliad on Iliad."[12] After they complained that they all had suffered in their endeavors, one of them turns angrily on Sunday and asks, "Have you ever suffered?"

As he gazed, the great face [of Sunday] grew to an awful size, grew larger than the colossal mask of Memnon, which had made him scream as a child. It grew larger and larger, filling the whole sky; then everything went black. Only in the blackness before it entirely destroyed his brain he seemed to hear a distant voice saying a commonplace text that he had heard somewhere, "Can ye drink of the cup that I drink of?"[13]

Chesterton developed the same concept more fully in a play that was found in his papers after he died—*The Surprise*.[14] A holy Franciscan friar journeying through the Pyrenees comes across a caravan with life-size puppets, whose playwright-creator asks the friar to hear his confession. When the friar agrees, the author says his play is his confession—and he puts it on. The play is a wittily playful melodrama. A poor wandering poet helps a princess deceive a king who has been promised her hand in marriage. The king and the princess's loyal friend are in love, but political factors keep them apart. By benign trickery, the poet and the princess work things out. End of play. The friar has noticed that there is no villain in the play, and the author admits he wrote it on a bet with a fellow author that a play could not be interesting without a villain.

But what is the confession? The author admits that he is sad because the puppets are just emanations of his mind. He wants to cast them outside his mind, so he can react to them as living people, not just as reciters of his own words. He wants the friar to work a miracle. The friar says he cannot and will not do such a thing, but that sometimes God gives a sign. Even as they speak, the puppets begin to stir on their own. They rise up and redo the same play. But this time little things going wrong accumulate and make the plot swerve. The poet is not only carefree but somewhat dissolute; the princess cares for her subjects in a hectoring way; the king's sense of honor verges on pride. As misunderstandings entangle each other, the poet and the king are swept into conflict, and are trying to kill each other in a duel, when the author's head emerges from an upper part of the scenery and he cries: "Stop! I am coming down."

That is Chesterton's parable of the Incarnation. Some might hesitate to take instruction on such a deep mystery from a popular journalist like Chesterton. But how does his message of an author trying to save his creations differ from Augustine's statement that Christ came to be "our comrade in the fellowship of death"? Or from Irenaeus's claim that the Word took on human forebears to be a fighter (*certans*) for them? Or from Abelard's claim that Jesus came to "clasp us even closer to his side"? All these make atonement "subjective"—that is, they measure it in changes wrought in the human soul, not in the Father's sense of justice. Love itself is just "subjective." All the authors just cited talk of mending mankind, not of changing an angry God. Since God knew how to make us, he knows how to mend us. And to do that, he comes into the fray with us.

If man is saved by being inspired to love, as Abelard says, that is admittedly a subjective view of salvation. But faith is just as subjective a response, and Paul says that faith is what rescues us:

> Moses, remember, writes of our making-right [*dikaiosynē*] according to the Law: "Anyone observing its provisions will find life in them." But the making-right according to faith admonishes: "Do not ask in your heart, 'Who will mount into heaven, to bring Messiah down,' or 'Who will descend into the abyss, to bring Messiah up from the dead.'" Its message is, rather, "What you want to hear is at hand, on your lips and in your heart." This is what the word you want to believe is announcing. If you profess with your lips that Jesus is the ruler and if you believe in your heart that God raised him from the dead, you will be rescued. Such faith, held in the heart, brings about the making-right. Such profession, voiced on the lips, leads to rescue. For Scripture says, "The believer in him will not be disappointed." (Rom 10.5–11)

The Incarnation means that no matter how we suffer, how deep we go into the abyss, how fearfully we die, God has been there, he is with us. "Even though I walk through a valley dark as death I fear no evil, for thou art with me" (Ps 23.4).

Why has this view of the atonement not prevailed through most of Christian history? Why did the legalistic and punitive theory of Anselm hold sway for so long? This is not so surprising when we consider that the

Letter to Hebrews brought back into Christianity the centrality of animal sacrifice in the worship of God. Indeed, the Letter made things worse by revalidating *human* sacrifice as pleasing to God. Anselm's theory was just a spelling out of the consequences of the Letter to Hebrews. In combination, they turned a religion that was originally priestless into one that requires priests at every stage of one's life (at least in the Catholic and Orthodox branches of that religion), from birth to death, from baptism to last rites, with penance and Eucharist dispensed along the way. It was this concatenation of concepts that condemned as merely subjective the view that the Eucharist is a celebration of the people of God and that atonement is achieved through faith and love, and not by buying off God's wrath.

It was noted earlier that Henri de Lubac brought out of the shadows a line of thought developing Augustine's claim that the Eucharist is the body of Christ as fulfilled in his members, the church. The "heretical" views of atonement have been revived or re-created, not by one man at the outset, but by a whole school of modern thinkers, including the ones listed at note 1 of chapter 15. Many of these people have been influenced by René Girard, who challenged the Hebrews-Anselmian thesis that Christ is a sacrifice:

> There is nothing in the Gospels to suggest that the death of Jesus is a sacrifice, whatever definition (expiation, substitution, etc.) we may give for that sacrifice. At no point in the Gospels is the death of Jesus defined as a sacrifice. The passages that are invoked to justify a sacrificial conception of the Passion both can and should be interpreted with no reference to sacrifice in any of the accepted meanings.[15]

God is a God of non-violence. The Father could not demand violence, and the Son would not submit to violence from the Father. Even the violence of men did not offer Jesus as a sacrifice—his murderers were not trying to placate God. He could not be a scapegoat on whom sins were laden, since he is the opposite of sin. When the Letter to Hebrews quotes Psalm 40 as substituting Jesus for sacrificial animals, Girard says, it "interprets this text as if it were a sacrificial dialogue between God and Christ."[16] He criticizes the Letter for its "failure to see anything but irrational structural analogies among the whole range of sacrifices, including the one attributed to Christ."[17]

The same criticism is made even more pointedly against medieval theologians like Anselm, who carry the sacrificial reading of Hebrews even further. They reverse the tendency of the fathers to read the New Testament in the light of Old Testament prophecies. They read the Old Testament in the light of the New, in a regression to sacrificial concepts debunked by Jesus.[18] As one of Girard's followers put it: "Instead of God throwing a wrench into the gears of human sacrifice, Anselm's God has endorsed that machinery, borrowing it to perform the biggest and most effective sacrifice of all."[19] By perpetuating the sacredness of violence, Girard says, "historical Christianity took on a persecutory character."[20]

Girard's claim was all the more striking since he thought most other societies and religions were based on violence, on coalescence around a "founding murder," and that Christianity, with its prefigurations in the Old Testament, is the only body of belief to escape the need for violence.[21] One need not accept his general view of society to see how exceptional he makes Christianity. One does not need, either, to accept his explanation of social cohesion, though some of those cited earlier do so.[22] What is promising is that a new body of Christian thinkers is somehow escaping the imported cult of human sacrifice initiated by the Letter to Hebrews and defended by Anselm with his prolonged success. But the questions these theologians are raising have not disturbed much of the superstructure built upon the idea of a sacrificing priest at the center of Christian religion. That supernatural and sacramental superstructure remains to be examined.

NOTES

1. For recapitulation as "Christ redoing Adam's life (some things done, some avoided) with such planned perfection that all humankind should be subjected to him," see Eric Osborn, quoting the nineteenth-century theologian G. Molwitz; Osborn, *Irenaeus of Lyons* (Cambridge University Press, 2001), p. 97.

2. Irenaeus, *Adversus Haereses* 2.2, Latin text of book 2 in Norbert Brox, *Gegen die Häresien* II (Herder, 1993), p. 190. The mirroring of Adam and Christ works both ways for Irenaeus. Since Jesus had an infancy, Adam was created as an infant, so all ages would be represented in both: Irenaeus, *Proof of the Apostolic Preaching* 12, translated by Joseph P. Smith (Paulist Press, 1952). The lost original Greek work was called by Irenaeus the *Epideixis* (Exposition). It survives only in an Armenian version, which Smith translates into English.

3. Smith, *Proof,* pp. 37–39; Osborn, op. cit., p. 97.

4. Osborn, op. cit., pp. 97–98. He gives the eleven meanings of the noun as unification, repetition, redemption, perfection, inauguration, consummation, totality, the triumph of Christus Victor, ontology, epistemology, and ethics. He thinks all these should be at play in every use of the word (p. 115).

5. The same thought is put at Eph 1.22–23: "He subordinated everything to him, and made him the head [*kephalē*] of all things in his believers, who are his body, completed by him who completes everything."

6. Irenaeus, *Proof* 31 (Smith, pp. 67–68).

7. Irenaeus, *Adversus* 3.18.6 (Brox edition, vol. 3, 1995, p. 232).

8. Ibid., 5.14.2 (Brox edition, vol. 5, 2001, p. 118).

9. Irenaeus, *Proof* 34 (Smith, pp. 75–76).

10. Peter Abelard, *Commentaria in Epistolam Pauli ad Romanos,* edited by Eligius M. Buytaert, O.F.M., *Corpus Christianorum Continuatio Mediaevalis* 11 (Brepols, 1969), pp. 117–18.

11. See, for instance, John Marenbon, *The Philosophy of Peter Abelard* (Cambridge University Press, 1997), pp. 321–23; Thomas Williams, "Sin, Grace, and Redemption," in *The Cambridge Companion to Abelard,* edited by Jeffrey E. Brower and Kevin Guilfoy (Cambridge University Press, 2004), pp. 274–76.

12. G. K. Chesterton, *The Man Who Was Thursday* (Sheed and Ward, 1975), p. 194.

13. Ibid., p. 198.

14. G. K. Chesterton, *Collected Works 11: Plays,* edited by Denis J. Conlon (Ignatius Press, 1989), pp. 297–340.

15. René Girard, *Things Hidden Since the Foundation of the World* (Stanford University Press, 1987), p. 180.

16. Ibid., p. 229.

17. Ibid.

18. Ibid., p. 227.

19. S. Mark Heim, *Saved from Sacrifice: A Theology of the Cross* (Eerdmans, 2006), p. 300.

20. Girard, *Things Hidden,* p. 225. Fifteen years after making these charges against the Letter to Hebrews, Girard vaguely withdrew them, saying, "There is no serious problem. But in *Things Hidden,* I ask Hebrews to use the same vocabulary I do, which is just plain ridiculous." Girard, interviewed by Rebecca Adams, in *Journal of Religion and Literature* 25, no. 2 (Notre Dame, 1993), p. 28. Perhaps,

as an adult convert to Catholicism, Girard hesitated to condemn a putatively inspired part of the New Testament. His interviewer had asked if he was "slaying the father" in the form of "the authority of Scripture, the closed canon, and so forth." It is interesting that Girard's followers, who have been more open in their criticism of Hebrews, are, many of them, priests (including Jesuits and Franciscans) teaching in theological faculties of Catholic schools—men whose faith might be less challengeable than Girard's.

21. "Everything in my research leads to this special revelation which defines the uniqueness of Christianity" (Girard in *Journal of Religion and Literature* 25, p. 31).

22. Girard's most basic concept, in all his literary criticism (where he began), is that of mimetic desire, of which he has said, "It is everything" (*Journal of Religion and Literature* 25, p. 24). In effect, he reduces the seven deadly sins to one—*invidia*. Lust is simply the rivalrous resemblance of people desiring sex with the same (or a similar) person. Why the first desirer acted before competition could begin is never explained. This reminds me of Calvin Trillin's wonderment that his mother could always serve him "leftovers" though he never found the original meal from which they were left over. It is a variant on Plato's "third man" problem.

VI

Monopoly on the Sacred

SEVENTEEN

Priestly Imperialism

The regulation of Christian spirituality, in its Catholic and Orthodox branches, is achieved through the seven sacraments, which span the whole of mortal life. The seven are baptism, confirmation, Eucharist, penance, ordination, marriage, and extreme unction. With the partial exception of baptism, all sacraments must be administered by priests (sometimes by priest-bishops). The number seven is as sacred in Christianity as in Judaism, but it took centuries for that number to be fixed for the tally of sacraments.[1] In the twelfth century, Peter Lombard sifted through various traditions, pronouncements, and practices, and compiled them in his *Sentences*, which became the source of all later treatments of the seven sacraments.[2] Because each sacrament had to be validated as coming directly from God, and the scriptural basis for that claim is very shaky for most of them, there was for a long time no certainty on what should be included in the list.

Since, for instance, there were no priests in the early church, ordination, which makes a man a priest, could not have existed then. It is held that Jesus instituted the priesthood, but it took time for the church to understand what Peter and Paul never did. Also, when the Last Days were thought to be imminent, there was no provision for forgiveness after the great sin-canceling ablution of baptism. Marriage, as Jesus affirmed it at Cana, was a Jewish institution, not one he changed to a Christian service when he helped the Cana couple feast their guests. Jesus anointed no one with oil, as is required in four sacraments. On the other hand, he did drive out devils, though exorcism is not one of the sacraments, only a "sacramental" (ST 3.67 a3 ad2).

The sacraments, indeed, are distinguished from sacramentals. The latter term refers to blessings, the use of holy water, the wearing of blessed emblems, making the sign of the cross, saying the rosary, going on pilgrimage, and similar "pious works." These practices are instituted or condoned by the church (C 1667–79), but God must directly institute a sacrament (ST 64.2). Some of the sacraments (but none of the sacramentals) are necessary for salvation, and all of them are necessary to fulfill the church's mission. Though baptism is the precondition for all other sacraments, as making the recipient a saved Christian, Aquinas says that all sacraments are based on (*ordinantur ad*) the Eucharist, which is the "most powerful and completing" (*potissimum et perfectivum*) act of the church (ST 3.65 a3).

What sets the sacraments apart, according to Aquinas, is that they bestow justifying grace, as opposed to lesser graces given for good works, prayer, blessings, and blessed objects. The word for grace in the New Testament is *charis*, widely and often used there to mean "favor." Paul and his imitators usually invoke God's "favor and peace" on recipients of their letters.[3] A sign of God's favor is *charisma*, usually translated "gift," as in the powers bestowed by the Spirit on one with the gift of wise speech, one with deep knowledge, or with healing power, or with prophecy, or with speech in different languages, or with their interpretation (1 Cor 12.8–10). Aquinas grants that these are graces, in a first sense of *gratia*—what is given "gratuitously" (*gratia gratis data*). It is notable, in Paul's list of ministries, that priesthood is not included, though Aquinas counts priesthood greater than prophecy or healing or speaking in tongues.

Sacraments bestow a different kind of grace, what Aquinas calls *gratia faciens gratum*, favor making man "acceptable" (ST 1.2 a110 ad1r), making him "worthy of God's love," *dignus Dei amore* (ST 1.2 a112 ad5c). Some people have thought that God loves even the unworthy, the prodigal son, the lost sheep. But Anselm does not allow God to do that. In his system God is allowed to love only those who have satisfied his justice, assuaged his dignity, and met his standard of perfection. Since man cannot do any of those things on his own, only the sacrifice of Jesus can make him worthy of the Father's love. That is why, Thomas says, every sacrament is derived from the Passion of Christ (ST 3.62 a5). Only the grace won by that death can make man *dignus* again, "justified." The *justificatus* is one able to stand before the bar of justice. He is "right with the court again"—not innocent, in the case of humankind, since it was guilty of original sin and actual sins, but with a guilt covered over by the innocence of the sacrificial victim, Jesus. This exempts one from the consequence of sin. It is a pardon. It "imputes" to man the sinlessness of Jesus.

The idea that only Christ's sacrifice saves men was vividly presented in many pictures of the Last Judgment. Christ, in meting out just rewards and punishments, presents his credentials for this task—the instruments of his Passion: the cross, the crown of thorns, the pillar where he was whipped, the spear that drove into him, even (in Michelangelo's *Last Judgment*) the dice that soldiers threw for his cloak. But for these signs of his accomplishment, even he would have no right to let the sinners off who had offended God's justice, and dignity, and perfection.

And since Jesus was the priest as well as the victim offering the saving sacrifice, only priests can channel the result of that sacrifice through the sacraments (with the formal, rarely exercised, exception of baptism). The priest acts *in figura Christi.* That is why he says "*I* baptize you," or "*I* absolve you," or "This is *My* body." Once the priest was made the sole person able to trigger the miracle of transubstantiation, he pushed out imperially to conduct all the other sacramental transactions of the church. It used to be said that "Outside the church, there is no salvation." By the church was meant the Catholic Church. As Lenny Bruce said of Catholicism, "It is the only *the* church." Though the claim to have a monopoly on salvation is less heard from Catholics in our more ecumenical age, the sacramental system makes the same pretension more indirectly.

First, no one can be saved but the baptized. Since any believer can, if necessary, baptize a new believer, people baptized by a Protestant minister are arguably saved. After the spiritual death of Adam's sin, spiritual life is

restored by the grace of baptism. But if such a baptized Protestant later
commits a mortal sin, spiritual life dies in him, and it cannot be restored by
any Protestant minister, since only a priest can say "I absolve you" in the
sacrament of penance. Even Anglican priests cannot perform any of the
sacraments, except baptism, according to the Vatican, since they have not
been validly ordained in the succession of bishops from Peter. And the spiritual life cannot be sustained without the help of priests. Aquinas treats the
spiritual life as parallel to physical well-being. As the human body comes
into being by birth, and is strengthened by growth, and is nourished by
meals, and is healed by medicine, so baptism gives one spiritual birth, confirmation strengthens the struggling life, the Eucharist maintains the nourishment needed for sustenance, and extreme unction cures spiritual failures.
All these elements are necessary to the full life of the Christian in Aquinas's eyes, and all of them are miraculous, and only priests can work the
miracles.

Just as Aquinas gave the Eucharist a rational-seeming explanation in
terms of substance and accidents, so he gives sacraments an Aristotelian
gloss in terms of matter and form (ST 3.60 a6). Every sacrament is explained
in these terms. Baptism's matter, for instance, is water, and it is given the
form of baptism by the act of ablution and the words "I baptize you in the
name of the Father, the Son, and the Holy Spirit." The result is an invisible
mark (*character*) on the soul, which makes one a Christian forever. Even if
one sins, and refuses to repent, and goes to hell, one goes there as a Christian. (Mark Twain rightly answered Andrew Carnegie's boast that America
is a Christian country by saying that "so is hell.")

Like Aquinas's use of substance and accidents to "explain" the Eucharist, his use of matter and form is a distortion of Aristotle, not an applica-
tion of him. Water has its own form, which is not displaced by the "miracle"
of baptism—unlike the bread that turns to Christ's body, it remains water.
You do not need to dispose of the water as if it were a different substance, as
you must with a Host. Water has its own form in Aristotle—and, since it is
one of his four basic substances, its matter is "pre-eminent [formless] mat-

ter," *kyrios hylē*, which Aquinas calls *materia prima*. This is the formlessness that underlies all changes of forms. When a table is broken up into its components, it does not become formless; it takes on the new form of lumber. The change takes place through an intermediate lack (*sterēsis*), but that is a temporary condition. The continuous element throughout all changes of form is formless matter. As Aristotle says:

> "Matter" is primarily and preeminently [*malista kai kyrios*] to be taken as the substratum for generation and obliteration. But it can, in a secondary sense, be taken as the continuum in other changes of one thing into another [as from a table to lumber].[4]

Thomas admits that his supernatural action, producing a permanent mark (*character*) on the soul, is a layer of change placed on and over the natural process of change. So the Aristotelian terminology is a distraction, like the shells over the pea in prestidigitation.

The language of matter and form is strained throughout. In some cases, the "matter" is material—water, bread and wine, sacred oil, a chalice. But in others the matter is a mere inner disposition—in penance, the desire for forgiveness; in marriage, the desire for a spouse. These wants are more like the *sterēsis* of Aristotle than like his *hylē*. The matter for confirmation and extreme unction is oil blessed by a bishop, and the form is given this matter by rubbing it onto the believer and saying, in the first case, "I seal you with the sign of the cross and confirm you with the chrism of salvation, in the name of the Father, the Son, and the Holy Spirit" or in the second case, "Through this holy anointing may the Lord in his love and mercy help you with the grace of the Holy Spirit" (C 1513). In Aquinas's system, a priest who comes across an accident victim cannot give him the sacrament of extreme unction if he fails to have blessed oil with him.

The divine institution of the sacraments takes some imaginative construing of the New Testament.

Baptism

This is the one thing, later called a sacrament, that is clearly in the New Testament. Jesus was baptized by John—but that was not a sacrament, according to the church, since only John and no one else was authorized to administer it to Jesus (ST 3.38 a2). Jesus did not baptize anyone in the Synoptic Gospels, though in the Gospel of John (3.22–23) he is said to be baptizing at the same time as John. The same Gospel amends this when a later hand says (at 4.2) that Jesus himself did not baptize, though his disciples did.[5] Since the later church derived the saving aspect of baptism from the Passion, it considered the tale of Jesus' baptizing during his life a retrojection from that event. The clear command to baptize is at Matthew 28.19: "Traveling off, make followers of all peoples, baptizing them into [eis] the name of the Father, the Son, and the Holy Spirit." Since there are no priests in the New Testament, laypeople were the first baptizers—a role reluctantly granted them in later times.

In the first centuries, baptism was given to adults only after long indoctrination in the truths of Christianity, with multiple bodily examinations, cleansings, and exorcisms.[6] But after Augustine's doctrine of original sin took hold in the church, thoughts on the fate of unbaptized children led to two developments—first, infant baptism, and then the invention of limbo ("margin"). Augustine had taught that unbaptized babies go to hell; but that was too cruel a teaching to endure, so it was softened by saying that the babies could not be saved (since the fruits of Christ's Passion were not applied to them by baptism), but they would be spared the pains of hell, as well as the joys of heaven, in an intermediate state of permanent pleasantness without ecstasy (ST 3.69 a6c). To this limbo of unbaptized babies was annexed by Saint Thomas a limbo of the unbaptized patriarchs—they were virtuous enough not to deserve hell, though without baptism they could not enjoy the promises made to them (ST 3.68 a6).[7]

This limbo was the "bosom of Abraham" in which Old Testament heroes were said to rest (ST 31.68 a4).[8] The afterlife was therefore sorted out into four eternal places (loca)—heaven, the limbo of the patriarchs, the limbo of the babies, hell—and one temporary staging area, purgatory, for the baptized with venial sins to be punished (ST 3a.69 a7). Baptism is a passport that never expires.

Confirmation

Aquinas makes the institution of this sacrament Christ's promise at John 16.7 to send the Spirit after his departure (ST 3.72 a1 ad2), a promise kept when the Spirit descended on the disciples at Pentecost. But there was no holy oil or bishop in the "upper room" at Pentecost. It is hard to define this coming of the Spirit in a way that distinguishes it from baptism, and in fact down to the fourth century the "sealing with the Spirit" was simply a part of baptism.[9] But after infant baptism became common, Christians reached maturity without ever having to affirm their faith sacramentally. Thus, lacking one of the rites of passage common to many cultures when adulthood is reached, the church repeated one of the earlier baptismal practices (the seal of the Spirit).

This could not be treated as a delayed part of baptism, since that would grant that baptism had not given one the full spiritual life. So a separate sacrament was invented. Some Scholastics carried over from Ambrose's baptismal ceremony the idea that confirmation bestows the seven gifts of the Spirit indicated at Isaiah 11.2.[10] The derivation from baptism is clear in the use of a sponsor for confirmation (C 1311). Early baptism had required someone to testify to the past behavior of applicants. When infant baptism came in, that role was reassigned to "godparents," attesting to the future behavior of baptizands.[11] If those being confirmed have reached maturity, there is no need for someone else to speak for them; but the trappings of baptism remained.

Penance

Forgiveness of sins is a power normally traced to Christ's words at Matthew 16.19: "I will give you heaven's keys: Whatever you lock out on earth will have been locked out [*dedemenon*, future perfect passive] of heaven; whatever you let in will have been let in [*lelymenon*] to heaven." Literally *dein* and *luein* in this passage mean "tie up" and "untie." But they have to be read as explaining the image of heaven's keys in the first part of the sentence. Church membership, withheld or affirmed, is an image of heavenly exclusion or inclusion. Jewish rabbinical teaching similarly used language of binding and loosing "for imposing and releasing from a ban of exclusion from the community."[12] This was the earliest understanding of the power, as we shall see, and it is the point still being affirmed in the modern Catholic catechism (C 1445):

> The words *bind and loose* mean: whomever you exclude from your communion, will be excluded from communion with God; whomever you receive anew into your communion, God will welcome back in his.

The two powers mentioned there divided the early church. The power to exclude was early seen as necessary. The power to accept back, if ever and under what circumstances, would be contested for many years.

The power to exclude was not necessarily perspicuous. Believers were made members of the body of Christ by baptism. Who could, as it were, amputate a person from that source of life? But apostasies did occur, and the church would recognize that as a choice made by the one departing. Leaving the community of the saved was a personal rejection of the Holy Spirit—which is why some saw it as the "unforgivable sin" of Mark 3.28–29:

> Solemnly I tell you: Men will be forgiven all sins and whatever insults [*blasphēmiai*] they may utter; but the one who insults the Holy Spirit will not find forgiveness, ever.

A similar warning is given at Matthew 12.30–32:

> Who is not for me is against me, and whoever does not bring in [flocks] with me, scatters them off. That is why I tell you: Every sin and insult

will be forgiven men, but an insult to the Spirit will not be forgiven. Even if one voices a word against the Son of Man, forgiveness will be his. But should one speak against the Holy Spirit, there is no forgiveness for him, in this age or any other.

This explains the ferocity with which the Letter to Hebrews judged apostasy:

> Let us keep one another in mind, an inspiration to love and good works, not neglecting the assembly as some do, but strengthening one another, the more since we see what day is coming.
>
> But if we sin again on purpose, after seeing the truth, no sacrifice remains for our sins, only a terrifying judgment to come, and a wild fire voracious of recalcitrants. Anyone rejecting the Law of Moses dies without pity if two or three testify. What worse punishment will he earn who has trampled on the Son of God, disregarding the blood of the Pact in which he was cleansed, and mocking the favors of the Spirit? We know, of course, who says, "Punishment is mine, I shall exact it," and "The Lord will judge his people." Fearful is it to fall into the hands of the living God. (10.24–31)

In the passage already quoted on "heaven's keys," Jesus was speaking to Peter, as a symbol of the church. Since there were no priests or popes in the New Testament, later in the same Gospel Jesus gives the power to exclude or include to the whole body of believers (Mt 18.18). Thus, in the first example of excommunication we are given, Paul urges the community to expel notorious sinners.

> There is an uncontradicted report of sexual offense among you, and such offense as does not prevail even among the Gentiles—that is, a man wedding his own father's wife. Can you still preen as a proud community? Should you not rather have shown your grief by expelling him? . . . I wrote in a former letter that you should not have in your company sexual offenders—but I did not mean sexual offenders of the secular world [kosmos], any more than I meant the wealth-besotted, or robbers, or idolators in general. To avoid them you would have to stop

living. No, I have written that you should not keep in your company *as a Christian* the sexual offender, the wealth-besotted, the robber, the idolator, the abuser, the drunkard. Do not have him at table with you. This has nothing to do with my judging outsiders. But is it not your task to judge insiders? God will judge outsiders; but you are the ones to banish them from your company. (1 Cor 5.1–2, 9–13)

So there was power in the first communities to lock out. Was there a power to let back in? The Letter to Hebrews said no. But Paul seems to leave room for that in his Second Letter to Corinthians. There Paul asked the community to lift a punishment he first asked for (in a lost letter).[13] But whether we are speaking of church punishment in Hebrews, 1 Corinthians, or 2 Corinthians, the common elements are that the offense must be a public and scandalous one, and the agent for acting on this was the whole community, demonstrating an "entirely democratic handling of the case."[14] But even those who favored readmission to the straying said that it could be done only once. It was not a repeatable indulgence. "As there is only one baptism," wrote Ambrose, "there is only one penance."[15]

This may seem at odds with the Jesus who dined with the disreputable, welcomed sinners, and told the Pharisees that "tax gatherers and prostitutes will precede you into the reign of heaven" (Mt 21.31). But the early church felt it needed what military thinkers call unit integrity. Under the threat of persecution or misunderstanding, it wanted to distinguish itself from other Eastern religions in the Roman Empire (like the Mithras cult), from fellow Jewish offshoots (like the Essenes), and from its own dissidents (Gnostics, Docetists, Arians, etc.). This led to what looks like an obsession with heresies and rigorism. When persecution led to defections, Christians like the Donatists felt there was no way to readmit the traitors but by a new baptism. (Augustine's opposition to this set the mold of thinking about some sacraments as unrepeatable, having made a permanent mark on the soul—not only baptism, but confirmation, ordination, and marriage.)

The discipline that formed in the second and third centuries called for communal solidarity, group expulsion of the sinner, public penance assigned and performed, and then a ceremony of readmission to the church. Tertullian (c. 160–c. 220 CE) set the terms of acceptance for the sinner: he must wear sackcloth, be scattered with ashes, and undergo a long period of life on the edge of the community while its members prayed for him.[16] Ambrose of Milan, though a strong bishop, made it clear that the community was in charge of such "binding and loosing": "[The sinner] is purified by the good works of the whole congregation, he is washed from sin by their tears, he is reclaimed by their words and mourning, and he is inwardly restored."[17] This was a kind of second baptism by humiliation. Ambrose had an opportunity to show in action what he wrote about when, in the name of the Milanese community, he demanded that the Emperor Theodosius strip off his regal garments and publicly repent his massacre of rioters in Thessalonica.[18]

There was one problem with this program for the restoration of sinners. It was such an ordeal that people began putting it off until the end of their life, just as baptism had been postponed to be inclusive of all previous sins. But the church had invested its credit so heavily in this practice—the only recognized way of coping with post-baptismal sins—that it was hard to back off from it. Rescue came from Ireland, where, remote from more heavily populated parts of Europe, missionaries could not rely on public scandal in scattered villages or on the marshaling of communal consensus, so priests there began receiving sinners back after *private* confession. Also, since monasteries were the one Christian community that was integral, the monks began hearing each other's confessions. In the words of Michael Driscoll:

> Penitents sought out a confessor or a director of conscience in these monasteries, corresponding to the *amnchara,* or soul friend—a name indicating the importance of this person in the spiritual development of the one being directed. Considering, therefore, both the penitential manuals and the very detailed and exhaustive nature of the Celtic

prayers, penance should be considered more a way of life than merely a confession of sin.[19]

It was in this intimate and individualized setting that a seal of secrecy became the accepted norm of penance.[20] When the Irish began forming monasteries in England and on the Continent, in the early Middle Ages, these became famous for their penitential practices, recorded in the "Celtic Penitentials."[21] Bishops and priests began adopting some of the Irish practices to keep up with competition among the faithful.[22] Thus, slowly, the public penance was replaced with a private one. And confession was in time applied not only to public and infamous sins, but to venial ones—though even in the thirteenth century Aquinas said that only mortal sins called for the sacrament that deals with spiritual life-or-death grace (ST 3.87 a2). Venial sins could be taken care of by private repenting and the use of sacramentals like holy water and blessings (ST 3.87 a3).

But history was on the side of the Irish, who had changed the emphasis from communal reunion to individual introspection. When I was growing up, Catholics were encouraged to go to confession often, even if they had no serious sins to report. Examining one's conscience was praised as a beneficial exercise, and, sins or no sins, one would get the grace of the sacrament. Saint Thomas would not have recognized this practice. Enough of the original healing for excommunication survived in his time for him to say that any grace that does not restore from spiritual death is merely "sacramental," not a sacrament. This reduces confession, for those not in need of it because of grave sin, to the same level as crossing oneself with holy water. The public penance disappeared entirely. In fact, the order of penance-and-pardon was reversed. The original practice was to assign a long and public penance, and only after that to grant pardon. Now the priest in a confessional pardons, and only afterward is the penance (usually trivial, a few Hail Marys or Our Fathers) performed, on the honor system, in private.

Matrimony

Marriage, Aquinas admits, is an institution in the natural law of God (ST 3.61 a1). God in Genesis said that man and woman should "be fruitful and increase" (1.28) and that man and wife become "one flesh" (2.24). How does sacramental marriage differ from that in Mosaic Law? Aquinas says that it cannot be simply because marriage "in the church" is indissoluble, since that was true of marriage in the natural law, according to the Gospel of Mark 10.6–9, where Jesus reaffirms the words of Genesis 2.24:

> From the very origin of what he made, he created male and female, which is why a person will leave his father and mother and be fused [*proskollethesetai*] with his wife, and the two shall become one flesh. So they can no longer be two, but only one in flesh. Consequently, what God has yoked together should not be uncoupled.

From the church's early days, people struggled to reconcile this passage with Matthew 5.32 and 19.9, which allow a man (only a man, not a woman) to leave his wife if she is unfaithful.[23] Given such uncertainties and the general agreement on marriage as a natural right, it is not surprising that there are no recorded early formulae for a specifically Christian matrimony. "Before the eleventh century there was no such thing as a Christian wedding ceremony in the Latin church, and throughout the Middle Ages there was no single church ritual for solemnizing marriage between Christians."[24] In fact, one of the earliest papal pronouncements on marriage came near the end of the fourth century, when Pope Siricius said that all clerics had to have their marriages solemnized by a priest: "Around the year 400, then, the only Latin Christians who had to receive an ecclesiastical blessing on their marriage were priests and deacons."[25]

An inhibition to serious thought about marriage came from the fact that, in many church circles, marriage was a definitely second-class institution, less "holy" than virginity, than lives in monasteries or convents, or than the priestly calling—so how could it be a sacrament? In the thirteenth century, even as Aquinas was granting that marriage is a sacrament, he wrote: "Those in holy orders handle the sacred vessels and the sacrament itself, and therefore it is proper [*decens*] that they preserve by abstinence a body undefiled [*munditia corporalis*]" (ST 3a.53 a3r). For centuries, married couples were advised that they should have intercourse only for the begetting of children.

Still, as the Western Roman Empire collapsed, and northern tribes with different marriage customs came into "Christendom," church authorities began to impose some uniform rules. They began to think that priests must bless a marriage—though Aquinas stated that such blessings, considered alone, are just sacramentals, not a sacrament (ST 3.42 a1). The consent of the couple is the efficient cause of marriage (ST 3.45 a1), but that does not make consent a sacrament. For that, sanctifying grace must be bestowed through the action of a priest, channeling the love shown in the Passion of Christ into conjugal love when the priest pronounces them man and wife (ST 3.42 a1 ad1). The church would in time decide that if the marriage was not a sacrament, it was not a marriage—which is why Catholics can divorce non-Catholics who did not receive the sacrament's grace, and therefore were not married.

The aim of marriage was often stated in a favorite formula of Augustine: it exists for *fides, proles, sacramentum* ("fidelity, offspring, and reverence").[26] *Sacramentum*, here, did not mean "sacrament" in the later sense. As Frederik van der Meer wrote: "Every reader will notice that Augustine calls all kinds of things *sacramenta* . . . It is clear that for him the word *sacramentum* is still something very imprecise."[27] The Latin *sacramentum* was generally used to translate the Greek *mystērion* in the New Testament (often meaning "secret"). It also had the secular meaning of a "pledge," either military or monetary. In Augustine's phrase, it probably recalled both contexts. It cannot mean simply the pledge of the spouses to each other—that is covered in *fides* ("fidelity"). It must mean a pledge to God, raising the union to a higher level. As the Deutero-Pauline Letter to Ephesians put it: "Husbands, love your wives, just as Christ loved the Gathering, and gave himself up for her"

(Eph 5.25). But Paul was speaking of marriage before any sacramental service existed, or any priests to administer it.

Most of Aquinas's treatment of marriage has to do with the validity of
unions, impediments to it (impotence, for example, or slavery, or consan-
guinity), and conditions for dissolving it. These problems, as adjudicated by
church authorities, entered into high politics and everyday life. Kings seeking male heirs put pressure on Rome to give them annulments—a practice
not unknown to lesser celebrities even today. Marriage annulments are
notoriously easy to get in America (75 percent of them are granted here) if
one has money and influence. Among Catholic politicians, John Kerry,
Rudy Giuliani, and Joseph P. Kennedy II had first marriages of long dura-
tion annulled in Rome. Since annulment proceedings are secret and confi-
dential, the wife of Joseph Kennedy did not even know her marriage was
being declared invalid until after the fact.[28]

These marital uncertainties affect even ordinary people. My own parents were wed in a civil ceremony. But my Catholic mother wanted a later
church wedding, though my father was not a Catholic. They were wed by a
priest, but in the sacristy, not the body of the church; and my father had to
promise to raise his children as Catholics. Did my mother receive the sacrament? How could she, when the consent of two believing people in a state of
grace is required for a sacrament to give justifying grace?

My father kept his promise—my sister and I were raised as Catholics.
But what could my mother have done if he did not keep it? Divorce him?
Church authority forbade that, as her priest emphatically told her when she
wanted to divorce him for multiple infidelities. She divorced him anyway,
and the priests told her she was still married "in the church's eyes," and she
could not remarry. She adhered to that prohibition. When, after an intervening second marriage, my father returned to her and became a Catholic,
they finally received the sacrament from a new parish priest. But the church
was not finished regulating my family's life. When I was brought to the
church to be baptized, the priest said I could not be christened because I
had no Christian name. My birth certificate gave my middle name as Lee.
The priest said that if that were changed to Leo, I could be made a

Christian—though I am sure that my parents had no idea who Pope Saint Leo the Great was, and I doubt that I will be excluded from heaven if I fail to respond when the name Leo is called out.

The power of priests is asserted in many small ways as they supervise weddings, forbid divorces, or recommend annulments to Rome. When my wife and I were planning to be married, the priest made it a condition of his administering the sacrament that we each attend a "Cana Conference," meetings held by an organization meant to promote "the true meaning of marriage." The whole Cana concept was based on the myth that the wedding at Cana was a Christian sacrament, not a Jewish event, not a non-sacramental marriage under the natural law understanding of Genesis. And as Raymond Brown wrote,

> Neither the external nor the internal evidence for a symbolic reference to matrimony [at Cana] is strong. The wedding is only the backdrop and occasion for the story, and the joining of the man and woman does not have any direct role in the narrative.[29]

Nonetheless my wife-to-be and I were told that we must attend talks at the conference or we would not be married in the church. Men and women met together at first, and then separately to be addressed by a devout and trained married man or woman. The veteran instructor on the male side advised prospective grooms that they should not expect an early orgasm from their brides, or perhaps any at all, since "women are not built that way." Reception of the sacrament depended on mandatory attendance at such a silly event. What could be more trivializing of the great teachings of Genesis and Ephesians on the innate nobility of marriage? And what could better illustrate the way priestly control can spread to all facets of Christian living?

Ordination

Aquinas calls the priesthood an *ordo* ("rank") and the process of appointment to it *ordinatio* ("ranking"). The history of both the *ordo* and the *ordina-*

tio is as murky and circuitous as that for other sacraments. Jesus is supposed to have founded the priesthood when he chose his disciples (C 1575), but they were expressly and repeatedly forbidden to rank themselves above others (Mt 18.4–5, 23.8–10, Mk 9.35, Lk 14.11). Thus there are no priests in the New Testament, and no Christian sacrifices, outside the Letter to Hebrews. Paul, in the earliest Christian writings, does not call himself a priest or rank himself above his "co-workers" and "brothers" and "sisters." The various ministries he names are charismatic, given by the Spirit, not appointed by any authority or hierarchy.

Naturally, as the Christian community spread outside its original home churches, some organizers were needed. This process is presented typically at Acts 6.2 and 6.4 where The Twelve in the Jerusalem church ask for separate functionaries to manage the community food (*diakonein trapezais*), while The Twelve continue to serve the Gospel. This is how Luke introduces "deacons" (*diakonoi*) into the church. By the end of the first century, the leading figures in the church are the Elders (*presbyteroi*)—the fictive "Peter" in 1 Peter 5.1 describes himself as a fellow Elder (*sympresbyteros*). By about 110 CE, the time of Ignatius of Antioch, "over-seers," *episkopoi*, are the leading figures—from them, by way of Old English *biscop* we get the word "bishop." Ignatius recognizes single bishops for the cities of Asia Minor (though not for Rome). The *Didachē*, however, from about the same time, has several bishops (and several deacons) for each place.[30]

The earliest reported rite for ordaining a bishop or a deacon (not a priest) came, it used to be thought, in *The Apostolic Tradition*, attributed to Hippolytus of Rome, (170–235 CE), but that is now considered a compilation of texts from varying times and places.[31] The document makes the imposition of hands the ordaining act. In fact, "to ordain" was simply *kheirotonein*, "to stretch hand over" someone.[32] The same verb was used for a community *electing* bishops and deacons in *Didachē* 15.1–2: "You [plural] stretch hands *for yourselves* [*en heautois*] over bishops and deacons."[33] That is still the ordaining action in the Roman church (C 1573), though Thomas thought this was a gesture too generally used to be reserved for the sacrament of *Ordo*. He made the proffering (*porrectio*) of a full chalice, along with the words empowering the new priest to consecrate it, the *forma* of ordination:

> The conferring of power happens when something is given [to the ordinands] that expresses the specific exercise of that power. Since the pre-eminent action of a priest is the consecration of the body and blood of Christ, the mere fact of bestowing the chalice on him, along with the proper form of words, imprints the sacramental character . . . By taking the chalice, he receives the power. That is when the character is imprinted within him. (ST 3.37 a4 ad3 and a5c)

A deacon was ordained with the proffer of an empty chalice, to show he had care of the sacred vessels. A subdeacon was given a cruet full of water, to show he cares for the provisions of the materials for consecration. An acolyte was given an empty cruet, to show he brings the offerings of the people (ST 3a.37 a4 ad6).[34]

The verb to-stretch-hand-over was used in the *Didachē* for local elections: "You [plural] stretch-hand-over bishops and deacons to serve you." This, as the *forma* of the sacrament, had to act on its *materia*, on a man with the potency for this act—that is, a male (with no doubts about his gender, like a lack of genitals), one baptized, in the state of grace, not a slave, physically able to perform his duties, with no repugnant features, and (in the Western rite) unmarried (ST 3.39). The qualifications show that men were still thinking in terms of the Jewish priesthood, as the Letter to Hebrews had taught them to do.

> Physical impairments disqualified a priest under the Old Law [Leviticus 1.17], so they should be a far greater [*multo fortius*] disqualification under the New Law . . . Those with impaired bodies are barred from receiving the sacrament if their impairment entails a noticeable flaw, by which personal comeliness [*claritas personae*] is blunted [like the lack of a nose]. (ST 3.39 a6)

This shows how far the Letter to Hebrews could carry men away from the Jesus of the Gospels, who embraced the lame and lepers.

Extreme Unction

Unction means "anointing," and it is to be done with olive oil, which was held to have medical properties in antiquity. In fact, Aquinas calls the oil a *medicatio* (ST 3a.30 a2r). The sacrament is supposed by some to be derived from Christ's healing of the sick (C 1503), but he never used oil. The only material thing he used in these cures was his own saliva (Mk 7.33, 8.23, Jn 9.6), and no one tried to replicate this procedure. For the use of a healing oil, many have referred to the Letter of James (C 1526):

> Is someone in pain? Let him pray. Is he well? Let him sing. If one of you is frail, let him call in the Elders of the gathering so they may pray for him, anointing him with oil in the name of the Lord. And prayer made in faith will cure the sick one, and the Lord will restore him. Even if one has committed sins, it will be forgiven him. So confess your sins openly *to one another* [italics added], and pray for each other, so you may be healed. The petition of a just man is powerful. Elias was a man in a condition like yours. In prayer, he prayed against rain, and no rain fell on the earth for three years and six months. And he made a contrary prayer, and heaven sent rain, and the earth was fertile with its harvest. (5.13–18)

Four things should be noted about using this passage as a basis for extreme unction: (1) No priest is involved. (2) There is no mention of impending death, just "frailness." (3) The pardoning of sin by using unction conflicts with the widely attested procedure of expulsion from and reintegration into the community. (4) There is no mention of Christ, just of prayer in general and specifically of prayer in the Old Testament (by Elias "in a condition like yours").

It is hard to make that the basis for extreme unction. Various healing ceremonies with oil were engaged in by Christian communities over the years, anointing the part of the body that was causing pain, but "the first known *ecclesiastical* rite for anointing sick Christians dates from the ninth century."[35] It is true that in 416 Pope Innocent I wrote to a bishop that the procedure in the Letter of James should be used to cure *spiritual* ailments, but it was only in the Frankish churches of the ninth century that a liturgical ceremony took root. It took place in church, for those who seemed terminally ill, and it involved three or more priests. Now the oil was put not on the part of the body causing pain, but on the eyes, mouth, hands, and feet, as organs that might have been used in *sinful* practices.[36]

People still found it difficult to decide whether the ceremony was for physical illness or sins; whether it should be used in all cases of sickness or only for the terminally ill; and, if it involved forgiveness of sins, how it was to be distinguished from the sacrament of penance. On this latter point, Franciscans and Dominicans disagreed. Franciscans followed the example of their own saint, Bonaventure, who said that venial sins or forgotten sins not reported in the confessional were forgiven by a "last anointing."[37] Dominicans followed their saint, Thomas, who said that the debilitating aftereffects of sin were wiped away (ST 3.30 a1r). In 1438, the Council of Florence adopted both effects, and based both on the Letter of James.[38] Aquinas argued that the principal effect of the sacrament was not physical healing, but it could occur where the body was showing the effects of sin (ST 3.30 a2).

According to Thomas, Christ instituted the sacrament when he gave the disciples the power to heal with oil at Mark 6.13 (ST 3.29 a3 ad1). But that was a *physical* healing, which Thomas says is not the primary effect of extreme unction (ST 3.30 a2 ad1). A certain contradiction is built into the history of this sacrament. It is part baptism, part penance, part medication. And if it is meant in any way to heal, why put it off till the end of life is near, when it is least likely to have that effect?

This, like most of the sacraments, is more an institution for the priestly controlling of life than a reflection of Jesus in the Gospels. When it was decreed that Catholics must receive the Eucharist at least once a year, a corollary of that was an injunction to go to confession at least once a year if one had committed any mortal sin since one's last communion. The sacramental system makes all its parts interconnect. And the central node of the whole system is the one sacrament left to be considered, what Aquinas called "the sacrament of sacraments," the Eucharist, which was supposedly instituted by Christ at the Last Supper. I consider that last.

NOTES

1. The number seven was holy not only in the Jewish and Christian religions but in pagan antiquity, at least from the time of Pythagoras. Cicero gave classic expression to this view in his "Dream of Scipio" (*De Re Publica* 6.18). He says the music of the spheres produces seven sounds from the moving spheres under the motionless *primum mobile*.

   The eight [moving] spheres, two of which maintain the same speed, produce seven sounds of different pitch, and that number is what holds together, as it were, the whole universe [*rerum omnium fere nodus est*]. Talented men, by imitating these sounds with stringed instruments or the voice, have gone back up among the spheres, and the very wisest of them have become attentive to divinity in their humanity.

2. Joseph Martos, *Doors to the Sacred: A Historical Introduction to Sacraments in the Catholic Church*, revised and updated edition (Liguori Publications, 2001), pp. 47–51.

3. 1 Cor 1.3, 2 Cor 1.2, Gal 1.3, Phm 1.3, Phil 1.2, Thess 1.1, Eph 1.2, 1 Tim 1.2, Titus 1.4.

4. Aristotle, *De Generatione et Corruptione* 320a. It should be noted that some Aristotelian scholars now doubt that he believed in "prime matter" (despite the *kyrios hylē* of the *De Generatione* passage). But Aquinas did. He thought of prime matter as pure potency, just as God is pure act—see, for instance, ST 1.66 a2.

5. Raymond E. Brown, *The Gospel According to John*, vol. 1 (Doubleday, 1966), p. 164: "[4.2] is clearly an attempt to modify 3.22, where it is said that Jesus did baptize, and serves as almost indisputable evidence of the presence of several hands in the composition of John."

6. The course of fourth-century preparation for baptism is fully described by Ambrose in *De Sacramentis* and *De Mysteriis*.

7. Dante added to the limbo of the children and the limbo of the Jewish patriarchs a "painless limbo" (*Inferno* 4.25–42) of noble pagans. It is from there that Virgil comes to guide Dante (*Purgatorio* 7.28–42).

8. Some medieval thinkers had abolished the bosom of Abraham, in order to explain the article of the Creed that says Jesus "descended into hell" after his death. They thought he had gone there to apply the merits of his death to the patriarchs, saving them retrospectively. See Jacques Le Goff, *The Birth of Purgatory*, translated by Arthur Goldhammer (University of Chicago Press, 1984), pp. 157–59.

9. Ambrose, *De Sacramentis* and *De Mysteriis*.

10. Martos, op. cit., p. 197.

11. Ibid., pp. 158–59.

12. John Nolland, *The Gospel of Matthew: A Commentary on the Greek Text* (Eerdmans, 2005), p. 678. The power to exclude from community was also marked at Qumran. See Victor Paul Furnish, *II Corinthians* (Doubleday, 1984), p. 161.

13. Furnish, op. cit., pp. 159–68.

14. Ibid., p. 165.

15. Ambrose, *De Paenitentia* 2.10.

16. Tertullian, *De Paenitentia* 9.

17. Ambrose, *De Paenitentia* 1.9.

18. Neil B. McLynn, *Ambrose of Milan* (University of California Press, 1994), pp. 323–30.

19. Michael S. Driscoll, "The Conversion of the Nations," in *The Oxford History of Christian Worship*, edited by Geoffrey Wainwright and Karen B. Westerfield Tucker (Oxford University Press, 2006), p. 191.

20. John T. McNeill and Helena M. Gamer, *Medieval Handbooks of Penance* (Columbia University Press, 1938), p. 28.

21. Ibid., pp. 21 ff.

22. Martos, op. cit., pp. 291–93.

23. The latter passages echo the concern of many legal systems with inheritable property. If the wife is unfaithful, how is the husband to know his child is his biological heir? The church had to cope as well with the so-called Pauline privilege based on 1 Cor 7.15: "If a non-believing spouse wants to separate [from a marriage], let him separate; neither man nor wife is bound in this case. God has called you to be at peace with one another."

24. Martos, op. cit., p. 351.

25. Ibid., p. 364.

26. The formula is used, among other places, at *De Genesi ad Litteram* 9.12.

27. Frederik van der Meer, *Augustine the Bishop*, translated by Brian Battershaw and G. R. Lamb (Sheed and Ward, 1961), p. 280.

28. The wife, Sheila Rauch Kennedy, wrote a famous book critical of Rome's annulment procedures, *Shattered Faith* (Pantheon, 1997). In 2005, the Kennedy annulment was reversed, and again she did not hear of it till after the fact.

29. Raymond E. Brown, "The Johannine Sacramentary," in *New Testament Essays* (Doubleday, 1965), pp. 105–6.

30. *Didachē* 15.1–2. Kurt Niederwimmer, in *The Didache*, translated by Linda M. Maloney (Fortress Press, 1998, pp. 200–202), argues that locally chosen bishops and deacons are being promoted to the same level as the itinerant charismatic prophets and teachers that Paul recognized in Corinth.

31. Paul F. Bradshaw, Maxwell E. Johnson, and L. Edward Phillips, *The Apostolic Tradition*, edited by Harold W. Attridge (Fortress Press, 2002), pp. 13–15; Paul F. Bradshaw, *The Search for the Origins of Christian Worship* (Oxford University Press, 2002), pp. 80–83; Maxwell E. Johnson, "The Apostolic Tradition," in *The Oxford History of Christian Worship*, edited by Geoffrey Wainwright and Karen B. Westerfield Tucker (Oxford University Press, 2006), pp. 32–75. Johnson concludes (pp. 31–35):

> The emerging scholarly view is that this *Apostolic Tradition* probably was not authored by Hippolytus, not even necessarily Roman in its content, and probably not early third century in date, at least not as it exists in the various extant manuscripts in which it has come down to us . . . all medieval or later in date. Hence the "tradition" of this so-called *Apostolic Tradition* may well reflect a synthesis or composite text of various and diverse liturgical patterns and practices, some quite early and others not added until the time of its final redaction . . . The so-called *Apostolic Tradition*, therefore, must be used with great caution in attempting to discern the patterns, theology, and ritual practices of early Christianity. In other words, while the *Apostolic Tradition* may certainly be seen as a "tradition," this document, which has exercised considerable influence on twentieth-century ritual revision in the Roman Catholic Church [e.g., C 1568] and beyond, can no longer so confidently be claimed as either Roman, Hippolytan, or early third century.

32. Bradshaw, Johnson, and Phillips, op. cit., pp. 24, 60.

33. Niederwimmer, op. cit., p. 200.

34. Aquinas considered three offices as adjuncts to the priest's sacred act—deacon, subdeacon, and acolyte. Three other offices were caretakers at the outworks of that sacred circle—porter (excluding non-believers), lector (instructing catechumens), and exorcist (making sure the recipients of the sacrament were worthy) (ST 3.37 a2r).

35. Martos, op. cit., p. 325.

36. Ibid., pp. 334–35.

37. Ibid., pp. 337–38. This teaching would have had serious effects if it had been widely accepted. Wiping away venial sins could have spared believers from a term in purgatory. Buying "indulgences" to reduce that sentence was a vital source of income for the papacy, which therefore had a stake in Thomas's alternate explanation of the last anointing.

38. Ibid., pp. 338–39.

EIGHTEEN

The Lord's Supper(s)

Pagans in the Roman Empire did not recognize Christianity as a religion, since every religion they recognized (including the Jewish one) had at its center a sacrificial ritual—most of them public, though mystery religions like the Mithras cult held their sacrifices in private. But the Christians had no sacrifice (*thysia*), public or private. According to Pliny the Younger, writing to the Emperor Trajan, who had forbidden guild meetings, Christians claimed they only met in the mornings to pray and at night to eat a meal of "various and healthful food."[1] The fact that a meal was mentioned, not a sacrifice, is not surprising, since much of the ministry and message of Jesus was carried on at and about meals. According to the Gospel of John, his disciples began to believe in him after the marriage feast at Cana.

Jesus did not speak of any spiritual meaning in marriage at Cana. He just supplied the feast with one of its necessities—more wine when the party ran out of it. Why was this, as John 2.11 says, "the first sign and revelation of his splendor, so that his followers believed in him?" What made this sign so powerful? Jesus did not just change water to wine. He worked the miracle in six huge stone vessels, the kind Jews had on hand for their many ablutions (Jn 2.6). Since each jar held "two or three measures," and a measure was about eight gallons, that made for sixteen to twenty-four gallons per vessel, measuring at least ninety-six gallons in all—more than any party, however large, could consume.[2] Filling the jars of water kept for Jewish ritual purpose was a sign of Christ's bringing the new wine of the revelation. As the manager of the feast (*arkhitriklinos*) says, "You have kept the best wine for this moment" (*arti*).

The sheer quantity of the wine was an eschatological sign. Spectacular abundance showed God breaking into human life with excess that can cause

ecstasy—as when Moses struck the rock and "water gushed out in abundance and they all drank" in the desert (Num 20.11), or when bread fell
from heaven and each person had "as much as he can eat" (Ex 16.16). This is
the abundance that Jesus provides in the feeding of the four thousand or
five thousand: from five loaves and two fishes, "all of them ate all they
wanted, yet the leftovers filled twelve baskets" (Mk 6.42–43).

That is how Scripture regularly describes the working of God—in terms
of a land flowing with milk and honey (Ex 3.8), or a river flowing with honey
and curds (Job 20.17), or trees bearing every kind of fruit (Ez 47.12), or of
an overflowing cup (Ps 23.5). This is how the end of history is described by
Isaiah:

> On this mountain the Lord of Hosts will prepare
>   a banquet of rich fare for all the peoples,
>   a banquet of wines well-matured and richest fare,
>   well-matured wines strained clear.
> On this mountain the Lord will swallow up
>   that veil that shrouds all the peoples,
>   the pall thrown over all the nations;
>   he will swallow up death forever.
> Then the Lord God will wipe away the tears
>   from every face. (25.6–8)

Jesus, too, will describe the rewards for his Followers as "ample recompense of crammed-in, sifted-down, overtoppling good showered into your
lap" (Lk 6.38). As he told the Samaritan woman at the well: "Anyone drinking from this well will be thirsty again; but anyone drinking from the water
I shall give him will not thirst ever again. The water I shall give will be an
inner fountain bursting forth into eternal life" (Jn 4.13–14). As he later tells
the crowd following him, "I am the very bread of life. No one who comes to
me shall hunger again, and no one who believes in me shall be thirsty again"
(Jn 6.35). When Jesus ate and drank with sinners (Mk 2.15–17, Mt 11.19,
Lk 15.2), he was declaring that the old purity codes of the Jews were now
transcended. It was what Maxwell Johnson calls "a celebration of the

in-breaking of the eschatological 'reign' or 'kingdom of God,'" and Joachim Jeremias called "a pledge of a share in the meal of the consummation."[3] In these meals he was saying, as in the discourse on the bread of life, "come to me" (Jn 6.35). There were many "Lord's Suppers." They cannot be reduced to the one, last, supper.

It is in this tradition of Jesus' "table fellowship" that we should consider the Last Supper, which is one of many eschatological suppers he had with his Followers. Jesus says there, "With yearning I have yearned to eat this paschal lamb with you, since I assure you I shall not eat in any way (*ou mē*) until its fulfillment in the reign of God" (Lk 22.15–16). Jeremias notes that this is a vow, like that of the Nazirites, and it means that Jesus is abstaining from the meal, even as he assures the others that they should eat and drink.[4] Earlier, when the disciples asked Jesus why he was not eating, he said, "I have food to eat of which you are unaware . . . My food is to do what the one who sent me desires and to carry out his order" (Jn 4.32, 34). He is going to an ordeal they cannot comprehend: "Where I am going, you cannot come" (Jn 13.33). That is why he tells them to repeat their table fellowship "in a memory of me"—they are to keep it in mind so that, after his incomprehensible death, the Spirit can lead them to understand why they are still united with him (Jn 16.7–13).

That, after all, is the message of the Last Supper in the longest explication of it, the Gospel of John, *where the words "This is my body" do not occur.* John's is a Last Supper without a first communion. Why does John alone omit this? Jeremias makes the weak suggestion that John is preserving the *disciplina arcani,* the code of secrecy about the church's most sacred rite.[5] But it is universally held that John is later than the Synoptics, which all have the words taken as what is called the "consecration formula" ("This is my body . . ."). Raymond Brown holds that the Last Discourse is a late layer of John's Gospel, which means it came out after the Letter to Hebrews.[6] That Letter approximated Christ's death to the Temple sacrifices of the Jews. John says rather that Jesus and his Followers are spiritually united, offering a spiritual sacrifice to the Lord. He does not offer them "the fruit of the vine," but says they are part of the vine (i.e., himself). This is what the

Augustinians said, down through the ages, of the Eucharist—that it means the body of Christ, the believers with him as their head: "I am the vine, you the branches. The one remaining in me, as I remain in him, is rich in grapes, though severed from me you can bear none" (Jn 15.5).

Some think that the Eucharistic discourse, embedded in the Last Supper by the Synoptics, was displaced by John to an earlier chapter, as part of the "bread of life" discourse. But that follows on the eschatological feeding of the five thousand, and when he says there that people must eat his flesh (Jn 6.56), it is clear that this is a *spiritual* absorption. John has made sure that no one will take him to mean a chewing of God (an idea that Augustine derided). As he says in the earlier discourse, "Whoever feeds on my flesh and drinks my blood *remains in me as I in him*" (the same words used of the vine and the branches remaining in each other). It is not a question of the believer ingesting God into oneself, but of one's being absorbed, above oneself, into God. Justin Martyr says: "It is our teaching that the Eucharistic nourishment feeds our flesh and blood by changing us into the flesh [*sarka*] and blood of the flesh-assuming [*sarkopoiēthentos*] Jesus."[7]

These considerations have led Robert Daly and other liturgical historians to conclude that the Last Supper is not a sacrifice, in the mode of the Letter to Hebrews, but an eschatological meal like the other meals and feedings of the Gospels.[8] The early Christian document known as the *Didachē* ("Teaching"), from about 110 CE, gives us what Kurt Niederwimmer calls "the oldest formula for the Christian Eucharistic liturgy."[9] The most striking thing to notice about this text is "that the words of institution are absent."[10] No "This is my body." The meal is called a *eukharistia*, a "thanksgiving," after its principal prayer, "We give thanks" (*eukharistoumen*), and this is clearly an eschatological meal:

> For the thanksgiving, give thanks this way:
>   First, for the cup:
>   We thank you, our Father,
> for the sacred vine of David your son [*pais*],

whose meaning you made clear to us
through your son [*pais*] Jesus,
yours ever be the splendor.

And for the [bread] fragment:
We thank you, our Father,
for the life and wisdom
   whose meaning you made clear to us
   through your son Jesus,
   yours ever be the splendor.

As this fragment was scattered [*dieskorpismenon*] high on hills,
   but by gathering was united into one,
so let your people [*ekklēsiae*] from earth's ends
   be united into your single reign,
   for yours are splendor and might
      through Jesus Christ down the ages. (Did 9:1–4)[11]

This prayer calls for the in-gathering of all peoples on the day of salvation, fulfilling the vision of Isaiah already quoted above. The passive of verbs for "scattering," *diaskorpizein* and *diaspeirein,* is a regular part of these eschatological calls for the final reunion. Examples of the call are:

He will . . . gather together those driven out of Israel;
he will assemble Judah's scattered [*diesparmenous*] people
from the four corners of the earth. (Is 11.12)

I will collect them from all over earth
Where I have scattered them [*diespeira*],
And I will bring them back to this place. (Jer 39.37, Septuagint)

I will gather them from among the nations
and assemble them from the countries

over which I have scattered [*diespeira*] them,
and I will give them the soil of Israel. (Ez 11.17)

From the four winds of heaven
I shall gather you, says the Lord. (Zec 2.10, Septuagint)

This gathering of many peoples into one resembles Augustine's theology of the Eucharist, where the gathering of many grains into bread is a symbol of the union of many members in the body of Christ:

> If you want to know what is the body of Christ, hear what the Apostle [Paul] tells believers: "You are Christ's body and his members" [1 Cor 12.27]. If, then, you are Christ's body and his members, it is your symbol that lies on the Lord's altar—what you receive is a symbol of yourself. When you say "Amen" to what you are, your saying it affirms it. You hear, "The body of Christ," and you answer "Amen," and you must be the body of Christ to make that "Amen" take effect. And why are you bread? Hear the Apostle again, speaking of this very symbol: "We, though many, are one bread, one body" [1 Cor 10.17].[12]

Augustine is quoting Paul's First Letter to Corinthians, occasioned by the fights that had occurred over the Lord's Supper. Different classes brought different food to the dinner and did not share it. Though this letter is the first to narrate in this setting the Lord's words, "This is my body . . . ," Paul does not say the Corinthians have been sacrilegious toward transubstantiated elements, but that they have destroyed the meaning of the union of Christ's body by their separation from each other (1 Cor 11.17–34). He does not appeal to some priest or other official in Corinth to heal these wounds. He just addresses the people as a whole—that is, as Christ.

If we look to other early records of the Lord's Supper, we find several in Justin Martyr, in his *Dialogue with Trypho* and his *First Apology*, both from the first half of the second century. Here there is no priest, but only a presider, *proestos* (literally, a "stander-in-front"). There is no sacrifice, only a thanksgiving prayer. There is no consecration formula in this prayer, but an improvised recounting of God's gifts. This prayer is an inclusive treatment of God's dealings with his people, from the Creation to the Incarnation to the Resurrection—much like the scriptural exposition the risen Jesus gave before the first supper of his resurrected life (Lk 24.25–27), a possible image of the earliest liturgy.[13] Here is the passage from Justin's *First Apology* (65.3):

> Then bread and a cup of water and of mixed wine is brought to the one standing in front of the brothers. Taking these, he praises and glorifies the Father of the universe in the names of his Son and the Holy Spirit, and gives extended [*epi polu*] thanksgiving for all the things we were granted. At the completion of the prayers and thanksgiving, the whole body voices its Amen, which is Hebrew for "Let it be effected."[14]

The task being accomplished is giving thanks, and the people as a whole effect it. The improvising role of the presider is again emphasized at 67.4. After a lector has read from the Scripture and the Prophets, "the man standing in front, considering well [*nouthesian echōn*], encourages us to act in accord with these wonderful revelations."[15]

The priest who told me that the Protestant Lord's Supper was just a sermon, not a sacrifice, might without knowing it have been describing the second-century service of Justin Martyr. Justin's *Dialogue with Trypho*, describing the supper ceremony, contrasts Christian with Jewish sacrifices, and concludes: "I aver that only those prayers and thanksgivings offered by acceptable men are complete ones and win the favor of God."[16] These texts are not describing a Mass.

Nor is the second account in the *Didachē* describing a Mass. After giving the account quoted above in chapter 9, the *Didachē* gives another account of the Lord's Supper in chapter 10. For a long time, these were thought to describe two different kinds of meal—a "thanksgiving," where consecration and communion occurred, and a meal of love (agape), where a normal meal was consumed. But in fact those terms are used of both meals.[17] The meal Paul described at Corinth was one where much was consumed yet the body of Christ could be desecrated by community divisions. Recent scholarship denies that there were two different kinds of meals being described in the *Didachē* or elsewhere:

> Whatever conclusions may be drawn about Eucharistic origins, our earliest documents (1 Cor 11 and Didache 9 and 10) do confirm that the Eucharist was initially a literal meal, held most likely in the evening within a domestic "house church" setting, with the contents of the meal provided by members of the assembly.[18]

The great liturgical scholar Paul Bradshaw says of the two-service hypothesis:

> There is no actual evidence at all that Eucharist and meal were ever distinguished in this way in primitive Christianity. On the contrary, it seems to be a pure product of the minds of modern scholars who find it impossible to imagine that early Christians might have viewed the whole meal as sacred.[19]

Later, as the priesthood developed—along with the concept of the Eucharist as less a meal than a sacrifice—the community was reduced from participation to spectatorship, and parallels with Jewish Temple procedures were adopted from the Letter to Hebrews. This went against the whole tradition of Jesus' table fellowship, of all the Lord's suppers that had preceded the Last Supper.

> This meal was first seen as "eating with Christ" recognized as present through faith, as shown by the testimony of the disciples at Emmaus. An evolution occurred in the direction of "eating Christ" according to the concept of Jewish sacrifices and pagan sacred meals, in which oblations offered to the deity and accepted by it were regarded as bearers of its presence (see what is said of the food offered to idols in 1 Cor 8–10).[20]

Or, as Jeremias put it: "The meals of the Early Church were not originally repetitions of the last meal which Jesus celebrated with his disciples, but of the daily table fellowship of the disciples with him."[21]

That development also went against the eschatological emphasis, the idea of the heavenly banquet that was being anticipated, in early liturgies. This emphasis is found just as much in *Didachē* chapter 10 as it was in chapter 9. This alone is enough to prove that these are simply different versions of the same service collected in the *Didachē*. The second version is in *Didachē* 10.1–7:

After being filled, give thanks this way:
We thank you, holy Father,
for the sake of your holy name,
which you have lodged in our hearts,
and for the wisdom and belief and deathlessness
whose meaning you made clear to us
through your son Jesus,
yours be the splendor through the ages.

You, all powerful Lord, made all things
to exalt your name,
and you gave men food and drink
for them to savor
and give you thanks.
Favor us in the same way with spiritual food and drink
and deathlessness through your son Jesus.
Above all we thank you
because you are mighty,
yours be the splendor through the ages.

Keep the memory [*mnestheti*], Lord,
of your congregation [*ekklēsian*]

to deliver it from every evil
and to complete them in your love.
And unite them from the four winds
into your reign.
For might and splendor are yours down the ages.
May favor arrive, and this world pass away.
If one is pure, let him advance.
If not, let him be changed.
Maranatha! Amen!
(As for the prophets, allow them to give thanks however lengthily they
like.)[22]

There are three things of special interest in that prayer. First, it is
another in the line of eschatological meals. Again we have the final in-
gathering of the peoples "from the four winds," the coming of the heavenly
reign, the prayer for the world to pass away, and (the early Christian call for
the Parousia) the Aramaic *Marana Tha* ("Come, Lord"). In the light of all
these eschatological formulae we must read the line "If one is pure, let him
advance." That has been taken, by those trying to approximate this to later
Eucharistic liturgies, to mean "Let him take communion." But the clear
meaning in eschatological terms is: "Let him advance to greet the Parousia."
The next line, "let him be changed," would mean that the laggard in faith
will be changed by the arriving Lord.

The second thing of great importance is a resounding confirmation
of the prayer's eschatological features. The Lord's Prayer (LP) is echoed
throughout:

Didachē	[We thank you] for the sake of your holy name
	hyper tou hagiou onomatos sou
LP	Be your name kept holy
	Hagiasthētō to onoma sou

| *Didachē* | [Remember your congregation] to deliver it from every evil |
| | *rhusasthai autēn apo pantos ponērou* |

| LP | deliver us from evil |
| | *rhusai hēmas apo tou ponērou* |

Didachē	[Unite it] into your reign
	is tēn sēn basileian
LP	Your reign arrive
	Elthatō hē basileia sou

Didachē	For might and splendor are yours down the ages
LP (Mt)	*Hoti sou estin hē dynamis kai hē doxa eis tous*
	* ainōnas*

Admittedly, some scholars think this last clause was copied into late manuscripts of Matthew's Gospel from the *Didachē* or from a common source for the two passages.[23] But it is appropriate in both places, because both are eschatological texts. Raymond Brown demonstrates that Matthew's version of the Lord's Prayer is eschatological throughout.[24] It is liturgical (p. 283), communal (p. 287), asking for the kingdom's arrival (pp. 297–300), fusing heaven and earth (pp. 300–304), clearing all debts from the past (pp. 311–16), asking to be spared the Tribulation (pp. 317–23). Above all, it anticipates the heavenly feast at Matthew 6.11 (pp. 304–10): "Even today give us the coming food." *Epiousios*, translated as *existing* (daily) bread (from *ep-einai*), is more properly the *arriving* bread (from *ep-ienai*). This matches all the language of the heavenly feast which we have been seeing as the proper meaning of the Lord's Supper. Many Old Testament passages have already been cited. But Jesus himself kept returning to this image.

"I dispose my reign for you as my Father has disposed it for me, that you may eat and drink at my table." (Lk 22.29–30)

"I promise you that many will come from the East and from the West to take their places at table with Abraham, Isaac, and Jacob in heaven's reign." (Mt 8.11)

That last passage is like the references to peoples gathered in the *Didachē* and from "high on the hills," or "from the ends of the earth," or "from the four winds." All these passages remind us that the Lord's Supper is an anticipation of the final banquet with the Father.

I am more cautious in dealing with a third aspect of *Didachē* 10. I am referring to 10.5: "Keep the memory, Lord, of your congregation." That leads me to reconsider an argument by Jeremias that I did not agree with when I first encountered it. He says that wanting to be remembered in the Scripture mainly means wanting to be remembered *by God*.[25] That made him pay close attention to Paul's words, after quoting Jesus.

> "Do this, whenever you drink, to keep my memory." Therefore when you eat this food or drink this cup you are celebrating the Lord's death until he comes. (1 Cor 11.25–26)

When Christ instructs his followers to eat and drink "to keep my memory" (*eis tēn emēn anamnesin*), is he asking his disciples not to forget him? That seems trivial to Jeremias. He notes that asking *God* to remember one, as the *Didachē* prayer does, is more normal. He cites Acts 10.14–15, where God uses the Gentile Cornelius to show Peter that he can eat "unclean" food in a non-Jew's home. Cornelius has given alms to Jews, and an angel appears to him saying his good acts have risen before God "in memory" (*eis mnēmosynēn*). This means as something God will remember. And, sure enough, at verse 31 the angel comes back and tells Cornelius his acts have been remembered (*emnēsthēsan*) before God. Peter is then told to go and feast with Cornelius.

Does this mean, as Jeremias argued, that Jesus is saying, "Do this that my memory will be with the Father"? That seems a stretch. After all, the Acts passages both specified that the memory was "before God" (*emprosthen tou theou*), and "in God's presence" (*enōpion tou theou*). No such specification of who is to remember occurs in Paul. But Jeremias may be pointing in the right direction when he notes that at Passover prayers God is asked to "remember Messiah"—that is, to remember the promises to him. Thus Jesus' words in Corinthians could mean not simply "remember me when I was with you and what I did this night," but "remember me as the promised Messiah" and therefore "remember that I will be coming at the Parousia."

This accords with what Paul immediately appends to Christ's words: "Therefore [*gar*] when you eat this food or drink this cup you are celebrating the Lord's death *until he comes*."[26] He looks forward, as all the eschatological meals do. The old understanding of this passage was backward looking—do this to remember what happened in the past, at one room, at one of the many Lord's Suppers with his own. The entire orientation of the Gospel meals and early liturgies is toward the Parousia. That is why Paul celebrates Christ's death as a signal that he comes. In the same way he had made of the cross a boast (Gal 6.14), a folly to the lost, but power (*dynamis*) to the saved (1 Cor 1.18). This fits better with everything else we know about the repeated emphasis of the New Testament on Jesus' table fellowship, on Jesus' assurance to his Followers that they will share with him the promised banquet of the Last Days.

A torrent of evidence on the meaning of the "thanksgiving" prayer in early Christian worship therefore warrants the scholar Paul Bradshaw's answer, quiet but emphatic, to his own question, "Did Jesus institute the Eucharist at the Last Supper?"[27] The answer, No.

NOTES

1. Pliny, *Epistulae* 10.96. The Christians Pliny questioned said that their meal was of "various and healthful food" (*cibus promiscuus et innoxius*) to forestall charges of magic or stealthy acts like witchcraft. Pliny nonetheless banned the meals, invoking the emperor's law against guilds (*hetairiae*). Trajan had earlier disbanded a guild of firefighters, since they met outside the controlled environments of official politics or religion (ibid., 10.34).

2. Raymond E. Brown, *The Gospel According to John*, vol. 1 (Doubleday, 1966), p. 100.

3. Maxwell E. Johnson, "The Apostolic Tradition," in *The Oxford History of Christian Worship*, edited by Geoffrey Wainwright and Karen B. Westerfield Tucker (Oxford University Press, 2006), p. 45; Joachim Jeremias, *The Eucharistic Words of Jesus*, third edition with revisions, translated by Norman Perrin (SCM Press, 1966), p. 205.

4. Some translations add "again" to "I shall not eat," in order to preserve the fact that Jesus is eating and drinking at the meal. But he sees himself as the paschal

lamb, and eating it makes no more sense than eating and drinking the bread and wine he calls his flesh and blood; Jeremias, op. cit., pp. 207–25. Aquinas argued that Jesus did "take communion" of himself from himself (ST 3.81 a81). His proof is that the Gospels describe Jesus as "taking the bread" (Mk 14.22, Mt 26.26, Lk 22.19). But they go on to say that "taking it, he broke it, and gave it." He could hardly have eaten the bread before he broke it. "Taking" here just means he took it *up*. The bread-breaking (*klasis*) was a shorthand for the Eucharist before "thanksgiving" (*eukharistia*) became the common term.

5.　Jeremias, op. cit., pp. 125–37.

6.　Raymond E. Brown, *The Gospel According to John*, vol. 2 (Doubleday, 1970), p. 603.

7.　Justin, *Apology* 1.66.2, in *Apologie pour les Chrétiens*, Greek text edited by Charles Munier (Éditions du Cerf, 2006), p. 304.

8.　Robert J. Daly, *The Origins of the Christian Doctrine of Sacrifice* (Fortress Press, 1978); Gordon W. Lathrop, *Holy Things: A Liturgical Theology* (Fortress Press, 1998), pp. 139–58; Johnson, op. cit., pp. 58–59.

9.　Kurt Niederwimmer, *The Didache*, translated by Linda M. Maloney (Fortress Press, 1998), p. 139.

10.　Ibid., p. 140.

11.　Ibid., pp. 144 ff. I translate the Greek text given there.

12.　Augustine, Sermon 272 (Migne 38, column 1101).

13.　Paul Bradshaw notes that the Passion is given no more emphasis in this account of God's great works than are the Creation and the Incarnation; Bradshaw, *Eucharistic Origins* (SPCK, 2004), p. 90.

14.　Justin, *First Apology* 65.3, p. 304.

15.　Ibid., p. 308.

16.　Justin, *Dialogue avec Tryphon*, Greek text edited by Philippe Bobichon (Academic Press Fribourg, 2003), vol. 1, p. 496.

17.　Niederwimmer argues that there were two different kinds of meals, but one followed without interruption on the other. To claim this, he must say that *eukharistia* in the agape meal does not mean a sacramental *eukharistia*, though it means that in the other (p. 143). There is no evidence that the word meant anything but "thanksgiving" by the time of the *Didachē*.

18.　Johnson, op. cit., p. 49.

19.　Bradshaw, *Eucharistic Origins*, p. 64. Bradshaw plausibly surmises that the full meal began to be reduced to the symbolic bread and cup when Christian communities outgrew their original home churches. They would not want to use earlier spaces like pagan basilicas and temples, so they began to build their own basilicas in the third century, where meals for large congregations would be impracticable (ibid., pp. 66–67).

20.　Marcel Metzger, *History of the Liturgy: The Major Stages*, translated by Madeleine Beaumont (Liturgical Press, 1997), p. 41.

21.　Jeremias, op. cit., p. 66.

22. Niederwimmer, op. cit., pp. 155 ff. The Didachist tries to reconcile the charismatic work of the old itinerant missionaries with the recent appointees of local bishops and deacons; cf. *Didachē* 15.1: "Stretch hands, for yourselves over bishops and deacons worthy of the Lord, gentle men, not addicted to money, truthful and respected, for they too act for the community, as do prophets and teachers." In other words: Be loyal to the local practice unless a prophet shows up to conduct services in another way.

23. The *Didachē* itself prints the doxology with the Lord's Prayer in chapter 8.

24. Raymond E. Brown, "The Pater Noster as an Eschatological Prayer," in *New Testament Essays* (Doubleday, 1965), pp. 279–323.

25. Jeremias, op. cit., pp. 249–56.

26. Most translations say "you proclaim the Lord's death," which is adequate but does not catch the added note of *kata. Angellein* means to announce. *Kat-angellein* means to announce in a definite, public, emphatic, or defiant way. With the same verb one can spread the Gospel or one's fame (Rom 1.8), define the truth (1 Cor 2.1), promise the future (Ac 26.23), assure one of forgiveness (Ac 13.38), confirm that Jesus is Messiah (Ac 17.23), or celebrate Jesus (Phil 1.18, Col 1.28).

27. Paul F. Bradshaw, *Reconstructing Early Christian Worship* (Liturgical Press, 2010), pp. 3–19.

Envoi

I repeat what I said at the start. I feel no personal animosity toward priests. The fact that I can get along without them very well does not mean that I expect them to disappear, or even that I advocate that. I just want to assure my fellow Catholics that, as priests shrink in numbers—in some cases dashing from parish to parish, to put in brief appearances for the supposedly "necessary" things no one else can do (administering the sacraments, saying Mass, hearing confessions, presiding at baptisms or weddings or funerals)—congregations do not have to feel they have lost all connection with the sacred just because the role of priests in their lives is contracting. If Peter and Paul had no need of priests to love and serve God, neither do we. If we need fellowship in belief—and we do—we have each other. If we need instruction in the Scriptures, or counsel, or support, we can get those in the same places that Protestants do.

But if I do not believe in popes and priests and sacraments, how can I call myself a Catholic? What *do* I believe? I get that question all the time. Well, I will tell you what I believe. The things I believe are not incidental or peripheral, but central and essential. They are:

God.
The Creation (which does not preclude evolution).
The Trinity.
Divine Providence.
Prayer.
The Incarnation.
The Resurrection.
The Gospels.

The Creed.

Baptism.

The Mystical Body of Christ (which is the real meaning of the
    Eucharist).

The Eucharist.

The Second Coming.

The Afterlife.

The Communion of Saints.

That seems a fair amount to believe. But it is not enough for those who would impose all the things I *must* believe to be a "real Catholic." Some look with equanimity on the hollowing out of these sacred truths so long as one preserves certain thin external shells around them—the papacy, the prerogatives of the priesthood, the authority of church officials, officially canonized saints, and even more disposable items, like guardian angels, holy water, or Our Lady of Fatima. None of these—including priests and popes—is in the Creed. Yet some act as if disbelieving in the papacy is worse than disbelieving in the Trinity. They can put up with disbelief in the Creed so long as one retains a piety toward miraculous visions of the Madonna.

But how can I believe in all these things the Creed says, or even some of them, without a pope or priests to tell me to believe in them? And if that is "all you believe," as some people put it, why do I stay in the Catholic Church? Other Christians believe in those things, or in many of them. Why do I hang around where in fact there are popes and priests telling me what to believe? Well, I am content to share in the life of other churches. But that does not mean that accepting them requires a rejection of my fellow Catholics. No believing Christians should be read out of the Mystical Body of Christ, not even papists. It will hardly advance the desirable union of all believers if I begin by excluding those closest to me.

The words that should guide us in our attitude toward fellow Christians come from the Gospel of Luke. The disciples have just come back, elated, from the first mission Jesus sent them on. They are bubbling and full of themselves.

John said, "Leader [*epistata*], we found a man casting out devils in your name, and we stopped him, since he was not working with us." But Jesus said, "Why did you stop him? You see [*gar*], whoever is not against us is with us." (Lk 9.49–50)

All those acting in the name of Jesus are our brothers and sisters. How dare we excommunicate them, tell them they have no right to that name, set our own rules for honoring it? One cannot call out to fellow believers while cultivating a general disapproval of different believers. The great scandal of Christians is the way they have persecuted fellow Christians, driving out heretics, shunning them, burning their books, burning *them*. Mary Tudor of England burnt at the stake hundreds of Protestants. Elizabeth I of England had Jesuits physically chopped to pieces. Inquisitions executed all kinds of heretics. Popes preached crusades against Albigensians. New England Calvinists hanged Quakers. American Protestants burnt convents.

Pope after pope starved his fellow Catholics, spiritually, by interdicts that deprived them of all religious services. And I must say, in line with the thesis of this book, that much of this condemnatory, accusatory, persecuting impulse came from the jealousy of prerogative, the pride in exclusivity, the desire to define one's own Jesus as the only Jesus, that the priesthood fostered through the centuries. It was a way of fortifying the monopoly on sacred things. But, having said that, I surmise that some Catholics, simply by defending many of the non-essentials of belief—the outworks, as it were, of the citadel—may have kept certain treasures in that citadel better than they have been preserved elsewhere. Article by article, parts of the Creed are fading in some churches. That is, of course, no reason to reject such churches; it just means they should be called back to their own better days.

So there is much to be said for my brothers and sisters in Christ of the Roman persuasion. For one thing, devotion to the mother of Jesus seems to me a natural corollary of worshiping her son. She, after all, gave him flesh of her flesh to make the Incarnation possible. As Augustine said in wonder, the Maker of the Milky Way sucked milk from her breast. If we are all members of his Mystical Body, she is the most materially mystical part of it.

That is why I find it useful to contemplate the Gospel episodes by saying the rosary that honors her. (There are no priests or popes in the Scripture passages arranged in the rosary.)

Devotion to saints also seems natural to me, though attempt to monitor their entrance into heaven by papal canonization is a laughable example of curial bureaucracy. I do not want to get along without the head of Augustine or the heart of Francis of Assisi to help me. I have not lived almost eighty years in the Catholic Church without having deep memories for which I am grateful.

But so far I have been speaking of fellow Christians, my brothers and sisters. That does not mean we can forget our foreparents, the Jews. They, after all, gave us the one God they taught us to worship. The flesh of the risen Jesus is a flesh circumcised according to the Law. Nor do I count out monotheistic believers of other sorts. Though they do not accept our Creed, they are also children of the same one God (there are not two), who cares about them in ways we may not comprehend. All believers in God set off on broken and blind adventures into mystery. None of us gets all the way to the inner heart of that reality. As Augustine said in a sermon (117.5):

We are, remember, speaking of God when the text says, "God was the Word." And if we are speaking of God, why be surprised if you do not understand? If you could understand, it would not be God. Devoutly confessing that you do not know is better than prematurely claiming that you do.

In that spirit, let me say simply this: There is one God, and Jesus is one of his prophets, and I am one of his millions of followers.

Acknowledgments

My deepest thanks go to Carolyn Carlson, the editor of my sequence of religious books; to Andrew Wylie, the great literary agent; to my wife, Natalie, fellow on my journey; and to the Catholic community I have belonged to for the last third of a century, Sheil Center.

Translating Hebrews

The Letter to Hebrews is a formidable exercise in persuasion, presenting an entirely new set of concepts—Christ's priesthood, an obscure person named Melchizedek who is neither born nor dies, human sacrifice, the Son placating an angry Father. It slides through or leaps over fallacies. It is sometimes devoutly eloquent, sometimes borderline silly (the Melchizedek priesthood is superior to the Levite because Aaron paid tithes to it through his grandfather's loins). To follow its often sinuous presentation, one has to be alert to Greek particles that lubricate its turns and shift its colors. The store of such words is vast—*ara, oun, hothen, toinun, kaitoi, mentoi, toigaroun,* and so on.

But the most useful particle is the simple monosyllable *gar,* used over seventy times in the Letter. This is a broadly inferential tone-setter, normally translated in English with an initial "because" or "for." But it has a wide range of possible meanings, and the Letter exploits them all, linking assertions with a nudge that says something like, "Of course this means that . . ." In its various contexts, *gar* can thus be translated as "in fact," "indeed," "naturally," "obviously," "surely," "accordingly," "actually," or "inasmuch as." Since *gar* is never used to begin a sentence, but is placed after the first word or word-cluster, it is often best translated by English parenthetical words or phrases like: "after all," "however," "you know," "consider," "it is admitted." I adjust my translation to follow these continual nudges of insinuation.

The Letter also uses more unusual or exotic words than any other part of the New Testament. These can pose a challenge to the translator. Let me give just one example. At 4.13, we are told that "Nothing he made escapes his gaze, all is naked and *tetrakelismena* for his inspection." The participle means, literally, "neck-twisted." How are we all "neck-twisted" toward God?

The word is not used in Christian literature, but in non-Christian contexts it normally has one of two meanings, "neck-thrown" (of wrestlers) or "neck-upturned" (of animals under a sacrificial knife). Most editors and translators go with the second sense, and translate "exposed"—as if humankind were universally exposed to God's knife.

But "naked" (*gymna*) has already expressed the element of exposure. It is a strong word—Spicq (S2.90) says this is the New Testament's only use of it in a metaphorical sense. What could "neck-twisted" add to that? We have just been told that God's gaze can penetrate to the inmost physical and spiritual realities of a person—not only to the jointures of a bone but to its inward marrow, not only to the mind but to its intention (4.12). The stress is on *looking*. The intense inspection suggested is not that of a foe throwing a man (or bull) but of a physician diagnosing a man to cure him. The date of the Letter comes in a period when Greek medicine was reaching its apogee in Galen. I suggest then that the basic idea of "wrenching around" means "turned about," to see the other side of the patient.

Spicq sensed the medical tenor of the passage, and suggested in an early article that the two-edged *makhaira* of 4.12 is a scalpel (*bistouri*).[1] That may be a stretch; but the idea of God wielding a two-edged sword, however common elsewhere, occurs when he is slaying error or enemies, not reading the interior of a person. The normal word for sword is *ksiphos* or *rhomphaia*, and *makhaira* can be something shorter, a dirk or dagger or knife. Seeing it as an instrument of inspecting may well explain the end of verse 13, which says "to [or before] him is the *logos* for us," where the universal interpretation is that *logos* has the common meaning of "account." Then the "for us" is taken actively, as if it were a subject—it is *we* who must give an account for our actions. But God has been the agent throughout this paragraph, *his* word is alive and gives vitality, it penetrates to our inmost selves, it is discriminating (*kritikos*). If we are to let the *logos* still be his, it becomes *his* account, or estimate, based on his reading of our inmost self—in effect, his diagnosis. I think the meaning is, "On him rests our diagnosis."

This shows how a difficult or unusual word can make us give its surrounding passage a closer look, to see new meanings in it. But a more common problem than unfamiliar words is that we glide too easily over deceptively familiar ones, which have accumulated anachronistic meanings. I replace standard versions of such words, to bring us back to an earlier, more basic sense. I have explained such choices in the text of the book, but I list a few of the leading ones here:

Diathēkē. "Pact." Literally, *dia-thēkē* means "dis-position." This was often used for the distribution of goods from a last will and testament. Thus "testament" is used to translate *Kainē Diathēkē* as "the New Testament." But this is misleading, since God has not died and left his goods to his Followers. The New Testament is called that to pair it with the misnamed Old Testament (Jewish Scripture). This compares or contrasts the Mosaic and the Christian dispensations. Each defines a relationship with God. The God of Moses made a treaty with his people—he would be their God if they would meet certain conditions. The Ten Commandments are the provisions of that treaty. The Jesus of Hebrews is renegotiating the terms of that treaty. The usual translation of treaty in this context has been "covenant," from *con-vene* ("come together"). That is etymologically too weak, and in usage too stilted and archaic, for *Diathēkē* in the Letter. Those rethinking the term come up with better equivalents. Ceslas Spicq, for instance, gives us the French "Alliance." Jacob Milgrom uses the word "Pact." I follow Milgrom. Jesus is the guarantor of the new Pact.

Hilastērion. "Purgation Site." This was the sacred spot in the Shrine where atonement was accomplished by the sprinkling of blood. Hebrews says it is between the wings of the hovering angel statues, and over the Ark. Thus it has been translated as some kind of "cover" for the Ark, or as the "mercy seat" for winning forgiveness. But Jacob Milgrom argues:

> Either on etymological or on semantic grounds, the verb *kipper* never served an expiatory or covering function . . . As the *kapporet* (rather than the cherubim or the ark) is the focal point of the purgation rite (*kipper*), perhaps it took its name from its function on the Day of Purgation.[2]

So I translate it as "the Purgation Site."

Homoiotēs. "Commonality." This word is used in the Letter for the bond between Melchizedek and Jesus. It comes from one thing (or person) being "like" (*homoios*) another. The word *homoios* would become a site of combat during the Arian dispute on whether Jesus has a likeness-in-being (*homoi-ousia*) with the Father or a sameness-of-being (*homo-ousia*). In that dispute, the orthodox concern was to say that Jesus is *not just like* the Father. When comparing Jesus with Melchizedek, on the contrary, the fathers hastened to assure their readers that Jesus was *no more than like* the human priest. On a different matter, the Letter claims that Jesus is like Melchizedek. How like? The author mentions only two points of comparison—that both were priests, and both priesthoods were "forever." That last point was stretched by heretics to say that Melchizedek was equal to (or, in some hands, even superior to) Jesus. There is no reason to think the Letter was trying to claim that. They simply had some commonality, and so I translate it.

Kharis. "Favor." The word has a wide range of meanings—"free gift," "free thanks," "generosity," "ingratiation," "favor." It has mainly been translated as "grace." But that term now includes the accumulations of theological debate that had not, yet, occurred in the time of Hebrews. Augustinian, Thomistic, Lutheran, and Calvinist doctrines sharpened it for polemical dispute. To use the term anachronistically might seem to raise or settle such disputes. In most cases, I choose the most inclusive and neutral sense, "favor."

Mesitēs. Literally, a "goer-between," so normally translated as "mediator." Jesus is called the *mesitēs* of the new Pact between man and God (8.6, 9.15, 12.24). But he is far more than a mediator, since he offers himself as the pledge for the Pact. The proper term, in this case, is guarantor. He is the guarantor of the Pact.

Pistis. "Fidelity." Normally translated "faith," as if describing a duty to believe. The point of the famous praise of *pistis* in Hebrews 11.1–40 is established by what immediately precedes it. The author has just said that those who have deserted their profession (*homologia*) will not have a second chance. God will not side with the backsliders (10.38–39). The last verse

before the praise of *pistis* contrasts backsliding (*hypostolē*) with *pistis*, where
the word clearly means "fidelity." Thus those joined in the community by
close ties of *pistis* are showing their fidelity to each other and to their profession (10.39). Then we have the list of those who stayed true to the promise
of God. There is a similar use of the adjectival form of the word, *pistos*.
Moses was *pistos* to his house (lineage), which does not mean that he
believed in it but that he was faithful to it, that he stood by it (3.5). Even
Jesus is *pistos* to his promises, not as believing in them but as faithful to
them, showing his fidelity (10.23).

Skēnē. "Shrine." The "Tent," carried through the desert to shelter the
Ark, was not a stable place of sacrifice, like the later Temple. It has conventionally been given the dignified term "Tabernacle." But that now suggests a
more settled and grand affair (as in "Mormon Tabernacle") than the tent
that had to be disassembled and reassembled by the Levites as the people of
God moved toward their Promised Land. The Letter keeps the language of
tents so accurately that God's tent is said to be "pitched" in heaven (8.2).
Our word for a more transient or subsidiary place of worship is shrine, so I
use that.

Sōtēria. "Rescue." Normally translated "salvation." Like "grace," this
word comes with later theological overlays, calling up embattled terms like
"atonement" or "justification." The basic meaning is that of rescue from
danger or captivity or deprivation.

Syneidēsis. "Inner self." Greek *syn-eidēsis* ("with-knowing") is etymologically the same as Latin *con-scientia*. This has come to mean a judicial inspection of what we are doing by "conscience." That is how some translate it in
the Letter. But here the word is used to contrast deep, or inner, *cleansing*
from external purifications under Mosaic Law (9.14, 10.22). This is not a
subjective matter (knowing oneself cleansed) but objective, what Jesus
accomplishes in his rescuing act. Admittedly, 10.22 is subjective in that
those practicing the old purification rites still had an "awareness of sin," but
that is precisely because their inner self has *not* been purified. Thus the
author asks the Letter's recipients to pray for us *inasmuch as* (*gar*) we have a

syneidēsis kalē ("honorable inner self") and want to perform honorable actions (13.18). Versions like that of the New English Bible make this sound more like a boast than a request: "Pray for us; for we are convinced that our conscience is clear; our one desire is always to do what is right." Who is the "we" in this sentence, and how can the one writing it be so sure that the others have, in fact, clear consciences? A subjective awareness cannot be of some *other* subject's conscience. The rest of the Letter suggests the real meaning. The recipients of God's rescue are convinced that this purifies the inner self, and that will show itself in their outer actions—so the author asks his fellows, who are not backsliders, to pray for him as he is still true to his inner purification from Christ, which keeps him from backsliding.

Taxis. "In common with." Jesus is said to be "along the *taxis*" (*kata tēn taxin*) of Melchizedek (5.6, 10, 6.20, 7.11, 17). The word means "rank" or "order." But Jesus should not be *subordinate* to one establishing the ranks or files of a group. Since this group has only two people in it, and their connection lies in just two points they have in common (priesthood and eternity), there should be no suggestion of subordination, as inevitably occurs if one says that Jesus is "in the line of Melchizedek" or "in the order of Melchizedek." The implication of subordination lured heretics into making Melchizedek a being higher than Jesus, or at least as high as he is. The author is not claiming that, and the best way to make his point is to say that Jesus had something "in common with Melchizedek."

In the following translation, I add headings to mark the lines of argument, and print the hortatory sections in italics, to suggest the rhythm maintained between teachings and urgings.

NOTES

1. Ceslas Spicq, "Alexandrismes dans l'épître aux Hébreux," *Revue biblique* 58 (1951), pp. 481–502. He gives Hippocratic parallels on p. 483. He did

not use this interpretation in his 1953 book on Hebrews, probably because he spoke in the article of a scalpel as used in *dissection*—which would not make for a description of the *"living* word of the Lord" penetrating human persons. But the instrument's use in surgery or surgical diagnosis would continue to make sense.

2. Jacob Milgrom, *Leviticus 1–16* (Doubleday, 1991), p. 1014.

Letter to Hebrews

I. Superiority of the New Pact (1.1–14)

Formerly God spoke fragmentarily and figuratively to the fathers through the features of prophecy, but in these final days he has spoken to us through his Son, whom he made the inheritor of all things, and through whom he initiated every era, and

> being a radiation from his splendor
>> and the seal on his existence,
> upholding all by the power of his word,
>> cleansing away sin,

he has taken his seat on high at the right hand of Majesty, greater than angels as the name he inherited is greater. For to what angel did he ever say

> You are my Son,
> this day have I brought you forth?

and also

> I shall be his Father,
> and he will be my Son?

Moreover, introducing his firstborn into the Creation, he says,

> All angels of God, kneel to him.

And he tells the angels,

> He is making his angels be winds,
>   and his attendants be a burst of flame.

But to his Son,

> Your throne, God, is from era to era,
>   and the scepter of justice
>   is the scepter of your reign.
> You have loved the right way and hated lawlessness,
>   For this God, your God, anointed you
>   with the oil of joy, beyond your fellows.

And more:

> You from the origin, Lord, founded earth,
>   and heavens you wrought with your hands.
> They will pass away
>   while you abide,
> they will wear out like old clothes,
>   you will discard them like a garment—
> like a garment they will be changed,
>   while you are the same,
> and years do not pass for you.

And to what angel did he ever say,

> Sit at my right hand,
>   till I make your enemies your footstool?

Are not all angels [merely] helping spirits, to attend those who will inherit the rescue?

Exhortation (2.1–4)

More urgently, then, must we heed what we have heard, not to drift off from it. If the teaching voiced by angels was binding, and to break or ignore it earned punishment, what refuge have we if we neglect the great rescue, the one first proclaimed by the Lord and then confirmed by those who heard it from him, with God's added testimony in the form of signs and portents and every kind of miracle, along with different gifts the Spirit bestowed as he wished?

II. A Mediator Who Shares Our Humanity (2.5–18)

The angels, you see, were not put in charge of history's coming order—as was made clear by a certain solemn testimony:

> What is man, for you to have him in mind,
>   or the son of man, for you to look after him?
> You have placed him a little below angels,
>   with splendor and dignity you have crowned him,
>   ordering all things beneath his feet.

Obviously, in ordering all things beneath his feet he left nothing unordered by him; yet now we see that all things are not so ordered. We do see, however, someone "a little below angels"—Jesus, crowned with splendor and dignity because of the death he suffered, that he might by God's favor taste of death for everyone. It was right that the God for whom and through whom all things exist should perfect through suffering the captain of the rescue that leads many sons to splendor. For, clearly, the one sanctifying and those sanctified have all one origin—good reason for the sanctifier's pride in calling them brothers. He says himself:

> I shall exalt your name before my brothers,
>   Make it a song inside their gathering.

Moreover:

> He will be all my trust.

Moreover:

Here am I, with the children God gave me.

Now, since offspring all have the same flesh and blood, he was closely fused with both, by his own death to crush death's master (I mean the devil) and to free those who had been sentenced, by their very fear of death, to a lifetime of slavery. He does not, notice, take up the cause of angels, but takes up the seed of Abraham. That is why he had to resemble his brothers in every way, to be a sympathizing and trustworthy high priest before God and to cancel the sin that kept them from him. Since he, too, suffered and was tested, he can support those being tested.

Exhortation (3.1–4.2)

For this reason, sanctified brothers, as sharers in a summons from on high, focus your minds on the emissary and high priest we profess, on his fidelity to the one who sent him, like the fidelity of Moses to his house. Yet Jesus earns higher honor than Moses, to the degree that the builder of a house is honored above the house. Every house, you must admit, has a builder; but the builder of everything is God. Now Moses' fidelity as an attendant on his entire household was vindicated by what was later said of him; but Christ's claim on the house is that of a son—and we ourselves share the house he claims, if only we maintain a confident pride in what we hope for.

And so, as the Holy Spirit tells us:

If, today, you should hear his voice,
   keep no hard heart in you,
as when you rebelled
   at being tested in the desert.
Your fathers put me to the test
   by their own standards,
and found out what I could do
   over forty years.
I showed my wrath
   toward that generation,

saying, "They ever stray in heart,
    and do not find the way to me."
So I pledged my wrath
    as to their reaching my peace.

Take care, brothers, not to have a heart so misled by lack of fidelity that you fall off from the living God. Encourage one another, every day that we greet as "today," lest any of you be hardened by the way sin cheats us (for we have our share in Christ if we stay fixed to the end in the venture we began). As the saying is:

If, today, you should hear his voice,
    keep no hard heart in you,
as when you rebelled.

Who was it who, hearing, rebelled, if not all those leaving Egypt with Moses? At whom was he angered over forty years, if not those who strayed, who dropped dead in the desert? Against whom did he swear that they would not reach his peace, if not those who refused to believe? And we find, in fact, that they did not reach it because they lacked fidelity. Let us take care, then, with the promise of reaching peace still available to us, that none of you may prove remiss. We, after all, have heard the revelation, just as they did, though the message they heard did them no good, since they did not keep together in fidelity with those who heeded it.

III. The New Pact Is the Promised New Day (4.3–10)

We, as I said, are reaching peace because of our fidelity, according to the promise—

So I pledged my wrath
    as to their reaching my peace—

though the fulfillment of this was settled from the world's beginning. In one place, after all, it is said of the seventh day, "God was at peace, on the seventh day, from all the things he had fulfilled." Yet, the same text speaks, by contrast, against "their reaching my peace." Thus, since some are allowed to reach peace, the fact that those earlier given the revelation did not reach it (because they disobeyed) makes him set a new day, the "today" he spoke of to David after a lapse of years, in the passage already quoted:

If, today, you should hear his voice,
    keep no hard heart in you.

If, you see, Joshua had given them peace, God would not name another (later) day. So a Sabbath peace is still to come for the people of God. To reach peace, clearly, is to take rest after one's own work, as God rested after the work only he could do.

Exhortation (4.11–16)

Let us press on, then, toward our peace, not following their lead in ignoring what they heard. For God's word lives and gives vitality, sharper than a double-edged knife, to penetrate to the division between impulse and intention, or to the bone's outward articulation and its inner marrow, discriminating what the heart believes and what it follows. Nothing he made escapes his gaze, all is naked and turned about for his inspection. On him rests our diagnosis.

Having, then, a great high priest who has penetrated the heavens, let us stay strong in what we profess, for ours is not a high priest unable to feel our frailty but one tested like us in all our ways, sin apart. With confidence, then, let us approach the throne of favor, to find pity and favor for our rescue in the nick of time.

IV. A Priest with Our Frailties (5.1–10)

Every high priest, you must know, is singled out from other men to act for them in God's affairs, to offer gifts and sacrifices as atonement for their sins. He can sympathize with mistakes and misdeeds, since he, too, has inborn weaknesses, and because of them he must make offerings for his own sins as well as the people's. Nor does one assume this office on his own; he is called to it by God, just as Aaron was. Thus even Christ did not presume to make himself a high priest. That was done by the one who told him

> You are my Son,
>   this day have I brought you forth.

Or as he says elsewhere:

> You are a priest for all time
>   in common with Melchizedek.

While still in the flesh he used pleading and supplication to the one who could rescue him, with a piercing scream and tears, and he was answered for his devotion. Though he was the Son, he learned from suffering what it is to obey and, thus completed, he became the source of everlasting rescue for those who heed him, hailed by God as high priest in common with Melchizedek.

Exhortation (5.11–6.12)

On this point I have much to say, though to reason it out in words is hard, since you are now loath to listen. Actually you should, after so much time, be doing the teaching rather than need teaching in the simplest things God first revealed to you—you have gone back to needing milk, not solid food. It is obvious that anyone drinking milk for lack of true doctrine is a child. Only grown-ups eat solid food; they have a trained faculty for telling good from evil. So let us pass over what you first learned about Christ, and press on to the fullness of teaching. Why lay again the groundwork about renouncing acts that lead to death, or what is fidelity to God, or the proper rites for ablution or the laying on of hands, or how the dead rise and are judged eternally. It is time to go beyond that, God prospering us.

As for those, however, who have once received the light, who have had a taste of heaven's gift and been sharers in the Holy Spirit, who have had a taste of God's

*good word and the miracles still to come—for such people, falling away, to renew
their former resolve is clearly impossible. They again crucify the Son of God, so
far as they are concerned, and hold him up to mockery. See, for instance, how
God blesses land that slakes its thirst from repeated rains and bears a crop
rewarding those who worked it, but if it bears thorns and thistles, it is worthless,
with a curse impending, and fated for the fire. We trust that you, dearly beloved,
though we speak like this, are strong and sure of rescue. God is not unjust, that he
would forget what you have done, or the love you have displayed for his honor, as
you served and are serving his holy ones. We take heart that each of you will
continue this dedication till what you hope for is finally realized, that you will no
longer be loath to hear but eager to be like those who inherit what was promised
by their fidelity and endurance.*

V. In Common with Melchizedek (6.13–7.28)

When, you know, God made a pledge to Abraham, having nothing greater
to swear by, he swore by himself, saying, "Of a surety in blessing I will bless
you, and in prospering you will prosper your line." Thus Abraham, confident of the promise, obtained it. Men, for their part, swear by something
greater than themselves, and put an end to controversy by a binding oath.
But God, to show more firmly that his plan for inheritors of the promise is
irrevocable, pledged himself by the oath. Thus, from a doubly binding bond,
in which there can be no ambiguity from God, we may cling to this strong
commitment as we seek haven, laying hold on the hope held out to us—our
soul's sure anchor, grappling to pull us in through the veil. Jesus blazed this
trail for us, as high priest eternally in common with Melchizedek.

This Melchizedek, you see, was king of Salem, priest of the highest
God, who met Abraham as he came back from slaughtering kings, and
blessed him, and Abraham measured out for him a tenth of all he had won.
The first meaning of his name is King of Justice, the second is King of Salem
(or King of Peace). Fatherless, motherless, tribeless, with no beginning of
his days or ending of his life, he had a commonality with the Son of God,
insofar as he was a priest in perpetuity.

See the scale of this man, to whom the patriarch Abraham gave a tenth of his prize winnings. Descendants of Levi, who obtain priesthood according to the Law, have the prerogative of tithing the people, who (being also sprung from the loins of Abraham) are their brothers. Yet one not descended from the Levites received a tithe from Abraham, and he bestowed his blessing on the receiver of the promises. No one contests that one who is lower down is blessed by one who is higher up. In our case, the men receiving the tithes are mortal, but in the case I speak of, the one who received tithes is still living, according to what is written. So, in a sense, even Levi, the receiver of tithes, also paid them through Abraham, since he was already in the loins of his father when Melchizedek met him.

Now if the priesthood were complete in Levi's line, as was prescribed for the people by the Law, what need was there for a different priesthood in common with Melchizedek, and not in common with Aaron? If the priesthood changes, so of necessity does the Law. Yet the one we speak of was from a different tribe, no member of which officiated at the altar. It is clear that our Lord came from the tribe of Judah, to which Moses assigned no priesthood. And the matter is settled when the new priest appears in commonality with Melchizedek, a priesthood not sanctioned by an authorized lineage but by the miracle of a life never to be taken away. For the text, remember, is

You are a priest for all time
    in common with Melchizedek.

The preceding dispensation was thus set aside as weak and ineffective—for the Law completed nothing—and a new way is opened toward a firmer expectation of companionship with God.

And this priesthood did not lack an oath, as when Levites became priests without an oath, but his was based on the word of him swearing:

The Lord has sworn and will not alter it:
    "You are a priest for all time."

By virtue of that, Jesus is the pledge of a higher Pact. There were many other priests, since death denied them permanence. But, since his is for all time, he holds a priesthood that is indissoluble. That is why he can rescue in every way those rising up to God through him, living always to intervene for them. It was fitting that we have just this kind of high priest—holy, blameless, without taint, not associating with sinners, high above the heavens. He does not need, like those high priests, daily to make offerings first for their own sins and then for those of the people. He, rather, did this once for all when he offered up himself. The Law then appoints high priests having weaknesses; but the Son is faultless forever, by virtue of the oath which supersedes the Law.

Exhortation (8.1–6)

Here is the point of what has been said so far: Our high priest is so great that he sits to the right of Majesty's throne in the heavens, officiating at the Holy Place, in the truest Shrine, not assembled by men but made firm by the Lord. And since every high priest is appointed to offer up gifts and sacrifices, this priest, too, had to have something to offer up. He could not do this on earth, where the Law ordains what and how a priest can sacrifice—making it only a shadow-pattern of what is in heaven, according to the instructions given Moses for making the Shrine, in just these words: "Be careful to make everything just like the pattern laid out for you on the mountain." But our priest presides over higher mysteries, as guarantor of the greater Pact based on greater promises.

VI. The Old Pact Is Canceled (8.7–10.18)

Obviously, if the first Pact had been faultless, there would be no point in waiting for a second. But instead he finds fault in those under it.

> "Look! The days are coming," says the Lord,
>   "when I will conclude, with the house of Jacob
>   and with the house of Judah, a new Pact,

not like the Pact
    I made with their fathers
on the day I took their hand
    to lead them out of Egypt,
since they did not abide by my Covenant,
    so I gave up their care (says the Lord).
Now this is the Pact I will conclude
    for the house of Israel after the former days
    (says the Lord).
While I fix my laws in their minds,
    I shall also write them in their hearts.
And I shall be as their God,
    and they shall be as my people.
And no one must teach his fellow citizen,
    and no one teach his brother,
saying, 'Recognize the Lord,'
    since all will know me,
    from the least to the greatest,
and I will show mercy to their wrongs,
    and will not remember their sins."

By speaking of a new Pact, he made the old one obsolete; and the obsolete, the antiquated, is evanescing.

The first Pact, it is true, had rules for worship, and a sanctuary in the created order. There a Shrine was prepared; in it were the lampstand, and the table, and the place for grain offering—it was called the Holy Place. But beyond a second veil was the Holy of Holies, with the gold incense-altar and the Ark of the Pact cased in gold. Here were the gold jar keeping the manna, the staff of Aaron that blossomed, the tablets of the Pact, and the Cherubim of Splendor hovering above the Purgation Site—things it is now impossible to describe exactly.

Given these arrangements, the priests continually enter the first Shrine to perform the sacred acts, but into the second only the high priest enters, and only once a year, and not without blood to offer for himself and for the people's unrecognized sins. As the Holy Spirit makes clear, the way into the sanctuary cannot be revealed while there is still validity in the first Shrine— which is a symbol for its time, where gifts and sacrifices are offered without the power to restore the inner self of the one performing them, affecting as they do food and drink and ablutions, fleshly requirements imposed before the moment of their being put right.

Christ, however, is now at hand, high priest of blessings that are to come in a greater and final Shrine, one not made by hands, indeed not in this order of Creation. He has made a one-time entry into this Holy Place, pioneering an all-time rescue, not by virtue of goat blood or calf blood, but by his own blood. If, after all, the blood of goats and bulls, and the sprin- kled ashes of a heifer, make holy the unclean, purifying even the flesh, how much more does Christ's blood, unstained, offered in the timeless Spirit, cleanse the inner self of deathly activity to serve the God of life?

This is what makes him the guarantor of a new Pact, so that—a death having taken place for release from offenses committed under the first Pact—those designated might receive the everlasting inheritance that was pledged them. Where inheritance is concerned, it is recognized, the death of the testator must be certified; it has no force so long as the testator is alive. Thus even the first Pact was not initiated without blood. After every requirement of the Law had been promulgated by Moses to the entire people, he took the blood of calves, along with water and scarlet wool and hyssop, and sprinkled the book itself and all the people, saying, "This is the blood of the Pact that God has put into effect for you." And the Shrine and all the instruments of worship he sprinkled in the same way with blood. That is why nearly all purifications under the Law are by blood, since with- out shed blood there is no freeing from sin.

Now if the copy of the heavens must be purified by such sacrifices, heaven itself must be purified by sacrifices that are higher still. Christ, you know, entered no Holy Place of human construction, the mere reflection of what truly is, but into the reality itself, standing face to face with God as our representative—not to offer himself over and over, as the high priest enters the sanctuary annually to offer blood not his own. Doing that would mean, for Jesus, his own repeated dying down through ages. Instead, when the wait of ages ended, he came on the scene a single time, to erase sin by sacrificing himself. And whereas a single death is set for all men, and after that judgment, correspondingly Christ made a single offering to forgive the sins of many, and after that will he appear again, without sin, to rescue those waiting for him.

The Law, remember, is only the reflection cast back upon us of good things still to come, not what those things really are; it can in no way complete its celebrants by the same sacrifices they keep offering endlessly, year after year.

In fact, would not the sacrifices have ceased if those offering them had once for all been purified, so that their inner self no longer had sins to recognize? Indeed, the sacrifices just remind them of the sins they have committed, year after year, since the blood of bulls and goats cannot take sins away.

Therefore he enters Creation with these words:

Sacrifices and offerings you did not want,
    but you fashioned me a body.
Holocausts and sin sacrifices
    you took no pleasure in,
    they pleased you not.
Then I said, "Here am I,
    to do your will, God"
(as it is written in the Scroll of me).

Stating beforehand that "sacrifices and offerings, holocausts and sin-offerings, you did not want and took no pleasure in"—though these be offered in accord with the Law—he goes on to say, "Here am I, to do your will." He removes the former to put in its place the latter. By that decision, we are purified once for all by the sacrifice of the body of Jesus Christ.

Each of the high priests performed his duty day-by-day in a standing position, offering over and over the sacrifices that cannot take away sin. But he, having offered a single sacrifice for sins, is seated eternally to the right of

God, with the expectation that his enemies will be put as a cushion under his feet. For with a single sacrifice he has completed for all time his purified ones. The Holy Spirit itself witnesses this, having said

> "This is the Pact I have sealed with them
>   after past days," says the Lord.
> "Placing my laws in their hearts,
>   I shall also write them in their minds
> And their sins I shall not remember,
>   nor their transgressions."

Since they have been freed from sins, why make offerings for them?

Exhortation (10.19–10.39)

So, brothers, emboldened by the blood of Jesus to enter into the Holy of Holies—where he opened a new and living way for us to pass through the veil (that is, through his flesh)—having now a great priest in the house of God, let us go to him with firm heart and absolute fidelity, our hearts sprinkled clean of all evil intent, and bodies washed with pure water. Let us grip without faltering the hope we profess, since he is true to his promise. Let us keep one another in mind, an inspiration to love and good works, not neglecting the assembly as some do, but strengthening one another, the more since we see what day is coming.

But if we sin again on purpose, after seeing the truth, no sacrifice remains for our sins, only a terrifying judgment to come, and a wild fire voracious of recalcitrants. Anyone rejecting the Law of Moses dies without pity if two or three testify. What worse punishment will he earn who has trampled on the Son of God, disregarding the blood of the Pact in which he was cleansed, and mocking the favors of the Spirit? We know, of course, who says, "Punishment is mine, I shall exact it," and "The Lord will judge his people." Fearful is it to fall into the hands of the living God.

Call to mind former days when, after your enlightenment, you wrestled mightily with persecution, and were either put up for public ridicule and abuse, or sided with those being treated that way. Indeed, you felt as your own what oth-

ers underwent in prison, and submitted contentedly to deprivation of your belongings, conscious that what you own is a greater thing that will last. So do not
give up on your boldness, which has its own prize. You need, you realize, an
endurance that by doing God's will achieves what was promised. Consider:

> Even now, little by little, the one who is coming
>   will arrive, he will not delay.
> By fidelity the just man will live,
> but if he backslides he loses my soul's favor.

We are not ones to backslide, but ones whose fidelity preserves our life.

VII. Fidelity to the Old Pact a Model for Fidelity to the New (11.1–11.40)

Fidelity is the basis of things hoped for, the confirmation of things unseen.
By their fidelity men of old were vindicated. By fidelity we realize how history was put together by the Word of God, how visible things arose from
things invisible.

By fidelity Abel offered God a richer sacrifice than Cain's, and by that
he was vindicated as just, God attesting to his offerings, and therefore he
speaks on after death.

By fidelity Enoch was exempted from seeing death, so he could not
be found, with God exempting him. He was vindicated, that is, because
he pleased God even before his exemption, and without fidelity one cannot
please God, since to approach God one must believe that he is and that he
rewards those seeking him.

By fidelity Noah, divinely warned of dangers not yet visible, complied
and built an ark to rescue his household, and by it he indicted the world,
and became the inheritor of a justice that accords with fidelity.

By fidelity Abraham, when summoned, obeyed and set out for the
land he would inherit—set off not knowing where he was going. By
fidelity he perched on the land promised him as if it were alien property,

lodging in tents with Isaac and Jacob, fellow heirs of what was pledged to both. He was looking ahead, you see, for a city planned and raised by God from its basis. By fidelity, along with Sarah (herself barren), he regained the power to inject seed beyond the normal age, since he trusted God's fidelity to his pledge. Thus from one man, practically moribund, came offspring like to heaven's stars in number and like to sands of the seashore beyond number.

All the foregoing retained their fidelity till death, though not yet in possession of what was pledged them, but seeing it far off and greeting it and presenting themselves as outsiders and transients in the land. People who speak this way are clearly still on a quest for their real home. Were the place they left still on their mind, there was time for them to turn back. But in fact they aspire to a higher place—in fact, to heaven. God therefore takes pride in being called their God, for he has readied a city for them.

By fidelity Abraham took Isaac along and, put to the test, was offering up his only son, though he had received the pledges, which told him, "Your seed shall have title in the name of Isaac." Still he reasoned that God could revive the dead—and, symbolically, that is what happened for him.

By fidelity Isaac blessed what would happen to Jacob and Esau.

By fidelity Jacob, on the point of death, blessed each son of Joseph and saluted his staff at the top.

By fidelity the dying Joseph foresaw the Israelites' wanderings, and identified where his bones would lie.

By fidelity the parents of Moses, at his birth, hid him for three months, since they saw how well favored he was, and they were not intimidated by the king's ban.

By fidelity the grown Moses refused to be known as the son of Pharaoh's daughter, preferring a share in the sufferings of God's people to the momentary pleasures of sin, and holding revilement with Christ greater riches than Egypt's treasures, since he had eyes for nothing but the recompense awaiting him.

By fidelity he forsook Egypt, not intimidated by the wrath of the king, but steadied as he gazed toward the one not yet seen.

By fidelity he enacted the Pasch and the pouring of the blood, so that the slayer of firstborn sons might leave them unaffected.

By fidelity they walked through the Red Sea as on dry land, and when the Egyptians tried to follow they drowned.

By fidelity the walls of Jericho were brought down after being circled for seven days.

By fidelity Rahab the whore did not die with the unbelievers since she did not betray the scouts sent ahead.

What more can I say? Time forbids mention of Gideon, Barak, Samson, Jephtha, David, Samuel, and the prophets, who by fidelity fought down kingdoms, managed the right outcome, realized the pledges, baffled the jaws of lions, quelled the force of fire, eluded the knife's bite, drew strength from frailty, grew strong in war, beat down foreign battalions—women even had their dead revived. Others, however, were torn apart, not accepting release in order to get a higher resurrection. Still others underwent trial by insult and the lash, even by chains and imprisonment. They were stoned, sawn asunder, slain by a knife's blow. They lived homeless in sheepskins and goatskins, deprived, afflicted, ill-treated, these people better than the world deserved; driven into deserts, and mountains, and caves, and earthen tunnels. Yet all of them, vindicated by fidelity, had not received the future things pledged, God holding them in readiness, so that their completion had to come with ours.

Exhortation (12.1–17)

With this in mind, with such a cloud of watchers around us, putting aside every encumbrance and sin that cripples us, let us run with determination the course set before us, keeping our eyes on the source and seal of our fidelity, Jesus—who, in place of available pleasure, submitted himself to the cross, shrugging off its shame, so that now he sits at the right of God's throne. Take the full measure, then, of the one who defied the enmity of sinners ranged against him, lest you flag in weariness of spirit.

You have not yet borne the struggle with sin to the point of bloodshed. Yet you are oblivious to the supporting words that call you sons:

> Do not, my son, neglect the Lord's training,
>   or give up when he rebukes you
> for he trains the one he loves
>   and afflicts every son he accepts.

Bear it as training. God is treating you as sons. What son is not trained by his father? If you lack the training that all sons share, you are bastards, not sons. Moreover, we had fathers in the flesh as our trainers, and we respected them. Should we not far more submit to the Father of our spirits, and thus have life? The first trained us for a brief time, as seemed best to them, but he promotes us to a share in his own holiness. All training seems for a time not easy but hard, though later it reaps as its harvest a life of peace in justice, for those who have endured the training. So stiffen your trembling hands and wobbling knees and pace straight on so as not to become crippled, but healed.

Seek peace with everyone, and that holiness without which no one will see the Lord. Be careful that no one falls short of God's favor, that no "bitter root grow to make trouble," for many the source of contamination—lecherous people, or low-minded as Esau was, who for a single dish gave up his birthright. Remember that he wanted to inherit the blessing but was turned down. He had no way to change his life, though he sought it in tears.

VIII. The New Pact More Majestic (12.18–12.24)

You have not, obviously, arrived this time at a material mountain, with burning fire, darkness, gloom, and whirlwind; no ringing trumpet or spoken words, at whose sound hearers begged to hear no more, so did they cringe from the decree, "Let but a beast touch the mountain, it will be stoned to death." So intimidating was what he saw that Moses said, "I am shaking with fear." No, you have arrived at Mount Zion and the city of a living God, heavenly Jerusalem, with thousands of angels in joyous company, and all of heaven's registered firstborn, and God judging all, and the completed souls of the just, and Jesus, guarantor of the new Pact, and a blood outpoured more eloquent than Abel's.

Exhortation (12.25–13.25)

Be on your guard not to desert God as he speaks. If, after all, those could not escape when they deserted his message delivered on earth, how can we escape, abandoning him while he speaks to us from heaven? He whose voice once caused an earthquake has now declared, "Again, but finally, shall I cause not only earth but heaven to quake." By saying "again, but finally" he indicates the overthrow of all things a quake can affect, meaning that what is not affected will last. Let us be glad, then, that we have received a reign not subject to quake, and celebrate God acceptably, yielding to him with awe, for our God is a fire inextinguishable.

Maintain love for the brothers. Do not be lax in receiving visitors, since some have unknowingly shown hospitality to angels. Keep in mind the imprisoned as if you were in prison, too, and the tortured as if their body were yours. Let marriage be honored by all, and let its bed remain pure, since God condemns the impure and adulterers. Itch not for money, but be content with what you have. For he has said, "I will not let you go, nor will I forsake you," so we can take heart to say,

The Lord is my support, I shall not fear.
How can anyone hurt me?

Heed your leaders, who brought the Word of God to you; observe the result of their conduct, and copy their fidelity. Jesus Christ remains the same, yesterday and today and through the ages. Do not veer off after fancy and unusual teachings—since it is well, you know, for the heart to be steadied by God's favor, not by food codes that did no good for those observing them in the past. We have an altar where officiators at the Shrine are not allowed to eat. The animals, whose blood is brought into the sanctuary by the high priest for sin-offerings, have their carcasses burnt outside the camp—just as Jesus, in order to sanctify the people with his own blood, suffered outside the city gate. Let us go to him outside the camp, to share his humiliation, since we have no lasting city here but are on a quest for that to come. Through him let us always bring an offering of praise to God—the harvest of lips professing his title.

Do not forget good works, and share your good with others, since these are the offerings that please God. Heed your leaders and take guidance from them, since they keep watch over your souls, to render an account of them. Make that responsibility joyful for them, not burdensome to them and no benefit to you. Pray for us, inasmuch as we are relying on an honorable inner self and intending to be honorable in all our acts. I especially urge you to this, so that I may get back to you the sooner.

May the God of peace—who brought out from the dead the great shepherd of the sheep, Jesus our Lord, whose blood sealed the everlasting Pact—may that God fit you in every good way to do his will, fashioning you as a sight pleasing to him through Jesus Christ, to whom be everlasting splendor, amen. I encourage you, brothers, to put up with this supporting address, since I have kept it short for you. Be informed that our brother Timothy has been freed, and if he reaches me soon I shall see you with him. Embrace all your leaders and all the saints. Those in Italy embrace you. The favor of God be with you all.

Index

AVAILABLE FROM PENGUIN

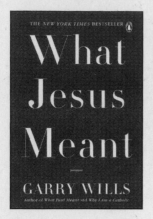

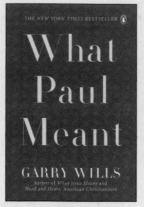

BY GARRY WILLS

Bomb Power
978-0-14-311868-8

The Rosary
978-0-14-303797-2

Explaining America
978-0-14-029839-0

Saint Augustine: A Life
978-0-14-303598-5

Head and Heart
978-0-14-311407-9

Verdi's Shakespeare
978-0-14-312222-7

Martial's Epigrams
978-0-14-311627-1

What Jesus Meant
978-0-14-303880-1

Outside Looking In
978-0-14-311989-0

What Paul Meant
978-0-14-311263-1

Reagan's America
978-0-14-029607-5

What the Gospels Meant
978-0-14-311512-0

PENGUIN BOOKS